ICE CREAM, SHERBET, AND ICES

Enjoy this simple and refreshing summer dessert, Italian Water Ice, made with fresh strawberries.

ICE CREAM, SHERBET, AND ICES

by Linda McDonald

South Brunswick and New York: A. S. Barnes and Company
London: Thomas Yoseloff Ltd

© 1971 by A. S. Barnes and Co., Inc.
Library of Congress Catalogue Card Number: 79-126941

A. S. Barnes and Co., Inc.
Cranbury, New Jersey 08512

Thomas Yoseloff Ltd
108 New Bond Street
London W1Y OQX, England

ISBN 0-498-07786-1
Printed in the United States of America

To my husband,
George,
whose sweet tooth is
responsible for this book

CONTENTS

CONTENTS

LIST OF ILLUSTRATIONS

ACKNOWLEDGMENTS

There are many people to whom full credit is due for the quality of *Ice Cream, Sherbet, and Ices.* First of all, I would like to give credit to Dr. Rufus P. Turner for having been a favorite and inspiring professor with an abundance of patience and critical comment. My sincerest thanks go to Andrea Blensly for untiring help in preparation of the manuscript. I would also like to thank Dr. Joseph A. Marano for his advice and contributions to the book.

There are others to whom I feel a particular gratitude for their generous assistance and contribution. The following have been materially helpful in preparing this book.

Adolph's Ltd.
American Dairy Association
Kay S. Berger
Best Foods
Borden, Inc.
Calavo
California Avocado Advisory Board
California Bush Berry Advisory Board
California Cling Peach Advisory Board
California Honey Advisory Board
California Prune Advisory Board
California Raisin Advisory Board
California Strawberry Advisory Board
Fosselman's Ice Cream
General Foods Kitchens
Gladys E. Maiden
Ethel H. Marano
National Dairy Council
The Nestlé Company, Inc.
Pet Incorporated
The J. E. Porter Company

11

Southern California Gas Company
Squibb-Beech-Nut, Inc.
Sunkist Growers, Inc.
Sunsweet Growers, Inc.
United States Department of Agriculture
Western Research Kitchens

INTRODUCTION

Ice Cream, Sherbet, and Ices has been written for people who do not make frozen desserts as often as they would like. You may have lost the recipe pamphlet that came with your crank-type or electric ice-cream freezer, or perhaps you have lost interest in making frozen desserts because your recipes lack appealing or unique flavors. Or you may be among the many women who, like myself, have searched for a more comprehensive frozen dessert book and have not been able to find one. Whatever the case, this book will bring back the fun of making frozen desserts. Here you will find over 600 recipes for easy-to-make desserts for every occasion and for every taste.

If you do not have time to make your own ice cream, sherbet, and ices, pay particular attention to the second part of the book. It has been designed for you, because these desserts can be made with commercial ice cream and sherbet.

Ice-cream desserts can be easily fashioned to complement any menu. Bombes, mousses, parfaits, and any of the special-occasion desserts can be made ahead of time and stored right in the freezer. The versatility and convenience of these desserts make them year-round favorites. If you have never made an ice-cream pie or a bombe, now is the time to try your hand at it. Why not treat your family to this pleasure? There is nothing to equal a frozen dessert as a "cool" ending to any meal.

MEASURES

	American	English
1 cup of breadcrumbs (fresh)	1½ oz.	3 oz.
1 cup of flour or other powdered grains	4 oz.	5 oz.
1 cup of sugar	7 oz.	8 oz.
1 cup of icing sugar	4½ oz.	5 oz.
1 cup of butter or other fats	8 oz.	8 oz.
1 cup of raisins, etc.	5 oz.	6 oz.
1 cup of grated cheese	4 oz.	4 oz.
1 cup of syrup, etc.	12 oz.	14 oz.

1 English pint	20	fluid ounces
1 American pint	16	fluid ounces
1 American cup	8	fluid ounces
8 American tablespoons	4	fluid ounces
1 American tablespoon	½	fluid ounce
3 American teaspoons	½	fluid ounce
1 English tablespoon	⅔ to 1	fluid ounce (approx.)
1 English tablespoon	4	teaspoons

The American measuring tablespoon holds ¼ oz. flour.

ICE CREAM, SHERBET, AND ICES

1.
ABOUT FROZEN DESSERTS

Frozen desserts are the most popular desserts in the nation. If you have never made ice cream, sherbet, or ices, now is the time to try your hand at these cool and refreshing dishes. The desserts in this book are easy to prepare and can readily be fashioned to complement any menu, especially as a cool ending to your family's meals in the warm spring and summer months.

INGREDIENTS USED

There are certain factors that must be kept in mind when preparing frozen desserts. The most important of these are high-quality dairy and nondairy products. The quality of the ingredients is vital to the flavor, body and texture, color, and melting characteristics of frozen desserts.

What goes into the dessert affects the finished product. There is no substitute for fresh and pure ingredients. Really good ice cream, sherbet, and ices do not contain any filler or other substitutes. Heavy cream, fresh fruit and eggs, granulated sugar, and the finest flavorings available are a must. Only fresh ingredients will produce the full, rich-bodied flavor which frozen desserts should have.

STORING MILK AND CREAM

Fresh dairy products are very perishable. Keep them clean, cold, and tightly covered.

Refrigerate fresh milk, cream, and milk products as soon as

17

possible after purchase or delivery. Letting milk stand in the sunlight causes loss of riboflavin and may affect flavor. Don't mix new milk with old except for immediate use.

Keep unopened cans of evaporated milk at room temperature or in a cool place.

Store unopened nonfat dry milk at a temperature of 75° F. or lower. Keep unused dry milk in the original package or transfer it to a tightly covered container. Close the package immediately after using. If dry milk is exposed to air during storage, it may become lumpy and stale. After dry milk is reconstituted, store it in a refrigerator.

For directions and suggested maximum home-storage periods to maintain good quality, see guide below.

Home Storage Guide

Milk and cream, fresh . . . . Refrigerate, covered. For best flavor, use in 3 to 5 days.

Milk, evaporated:

Unopened . . . . Store at room temperature; use within 6 months.

Opened . . . . Refrigerate, covered. Use in 3 to 5 days.

Milk, sweetened condensed:

Unopened . . . . Store at room temperature. Use within several months.

Opened . . . . Refrigerate, covered. Use in 3 to 5 days.

Milk, dry:

Unopened . . . . Store nonfat dry milk at room temperature. Use within a few months. Store dry whole milk in refrigerator. Use within a few weeks.

Reconstituted . . . . Refrigerate, covered. Use in 3 to 5 days.

Cream, pressurized whipped . . . . . . Refrigerate. Use within a few weeks.

Frozen Desserts . . . . Store in freezing compartment of refrigerator; use in 2 or 3 days. Or store in airtight wrap in home freezer at 0° F.; use within 1 month.

COOKING WITH MILK AND CREAM

In recipes in this book, "milk" refers to fresh whole milk. Evaporated milk and reconstituted nonfat dry milk may be used in place of whole milk in some recipes.

Milk should be heated or cooked at a low temperature. Heat it slowly; do not let it boil. With care, milk can be heated satisfactorily over direct heat. A double boiler also works well for heating milk.

At high temperatures, the protein in milk coagulates into a film on top and a coating on the sides of the pan. Prolonged high temperatures also cause off-flavors and—sometimes—scorching.

Milk mixtures thickened with flour or cornstarch need constant stirring during cooking to prevent lumping.

Evaporated milk may be diluted with an equal volume of water and used like fresh milk for cooking and baking. Full-strength evaporated milk adds extra nutritive value.

WHIPPING CREAM

Cream is easiest to whip when it is chilled to between 35° and 40° F. For best results, chill bowl and beater as well as cream. With a rotary beater or electric mixer, whip the cream rapidly—just until it mounds and holds its shape. Be careful not to over-whip.

To sweeten whipped cream: For each cup of unwhipped cream, add 2 to 4 tablespoons of sugar after whipping is completed. If sugar is added too soon, whipping time increases and the volume decreases. Sweetened whipped cream is less stiff and less stable than unsweetened whipped cream.

One cup (½ pint) whipping cream yields about 2 cups of cream after whipping.

UNDILUTED EVAPORATED MILK

Undiluted evaporated whole milk can be whipped and substituted for cream.

To use in a recipe calling for whipped cream: Chill evaporated milk in a bowl in the freezing compartment of a refrigerator until ice crystals form around edges. Chill beater, too. Use ⅔ cup unwhipped evaporated milk instead of 1 cup of unwhipped whipping cream. Whip chilled milk with rotary beater or electric mixer until stiff. This makes about 2 cups of whipped milk.

To whip evaporated milk for a dessert topping: Chill ½ cup evaporated milk, bowl, and beater as above. Whip chilled milk until it is stiff. Add 1 tablespoon lemon juice and continue beating until milk is very stiff. Blend in ½ cup granulated or confectioner's sugar and ½ teaspoon vanilla. This makes about 1½ cups whipped topping. The foam is stable for 45 minutes to 1 hour if refrigerated.

PRESSURIZED WHIPPED CREAM

Pressurized whipped cream whips when released from a can. Serve immediately.

STORING EGGS

Put eggs in the refrigerator promptly after purchase—they cannot be expected to maintain their quality if held in a hot car or kitchen.

For best flavor and cooking quality, use eggs within a week, if possible. Eggs held in the refrigerator for a long time may develop off-flavors and lose some thickening and leavening power.

Cover leftover yolks with cold water and store in the refrigerator in a tightly closed container. Extra egg whites should also be refrigerated in a tightly covered container. Use leftover yolks and whites within a day or two.

USING EGGS FOR THICKENING

Careful temperature control is needed when eggs are used to thicken a liquid mixture, such as a custard.

To guard against curdling when combining egg with a hot liquid or mixture of ingredients, stir the liquid into the egg a little at a time, or dilute the egg with a small amount of hot mixture and stir it into the remaining hot mixture.

To prevent overheating during surface cooking, use a double boiler and keep the water just below boiling. For oven cooking, set the baking dish in a pan of hot water in a moderate oven. Remove egg mixtures from the heat promptly when done. In ice-cream mixes and sauces, a starchy thickening agent—flour, cornstarch, or gelatin—is often used in combination with egg. Because starch needs longer cooking than egg, combine it with the liquid first and cook thoroughly before adding the egg.

USING EGG WHITES FOR LEAVENING

How much leavening power egg whites provide depends on the amount of air beaten in and retained when you are preparing the food.

Egg whites whip more easily and give greater volume at room temperature than when first taken from the refrigerator. For best results, beat whites until they are stiff, but not dry. With the right amount of beating, they will be moist and glossy; just stiff enough to stand in peaks. Overbeating whites often results in a product with less volume or one that divides into layers, with heavier ingredients settling to the bottom.

Combine beaten egg whites and other ingredients with a folding, not a stirring, motion. Mix thoroughly, but only enough to blend the ingredients well.

Cooking temperature also affects the leavening power of egg whites. With too high a temperature, the protein coagulates before the air bubbles have expanded fully, and a heavy product results. The product also may be overdone on the outside before the interior is set.

CAUTION ON USE OF CRACKED OR SOILED EGGS

Cracked or soiled eggs may contain bacteria that can produce food poisoning. For your protection, use cracked or soiled eggs only when they are thoroughly cooked or when the foods in which they are an ingredient are thoroughly cooked.

USING FROZEN EGGS

Thaw only the amount of frozen eggs needed at one time. A half-pint container will thaw overnight in the refrigerator. Because eggs spoil easily when they become warm, it is best to thaw frozen-egg products in the refrigerator. If thawed eggs are not used immediately, keep them in the refrigerator and use within 24 hours.

Frozen-egg products, like dried-egg solids, require thorough cooking to be safe. Use them only in baked foods or in mixtures that are cooked for a long time on top of the range.

In recipes, you can use 3 tablespoons of frozen whole eggs for one shell egg; 1⅓ tablespoons of frozen yolk for one fresh yolk; and 2 tablespoons of frozen white for one fresh white.

STORING DRIED-EGG SOLIDS

Store dried-egg solids in a dry, cool place where temperature is not more than 50° F., preferably in the refrigerator. Dried-egg solids will stay sweet and mild in flavor for about a year if properly stored.

After a package of dried-egg solids is opened, refrigerate any unused portion in a container with a close-fitting lid. If not covered tightly, dried-egg solids absorb moisture and odors from the air, become lumpy and will not mix readily with liquid. Dried-egg solids that develop a slight off-flavor can be used in baked products where the flavor probably will not be noticed.

USING DRIED-EGG SOLIDS

Dried-egg products, prepared from high-quality eggs under controlled sanitary conditions, can replace shell eggs in many recipes.

Dried-egg products should be used only in dishes that are thoroughly cooked. Some processors, however, maintain rigid bacteriological control to insure against contamination and specify on the label that the product is safe to use in uncooked or slightly heated preparations. Unless the label confirms this control, do not use dried-egg products in egg-milk drinks, ice creams, soft custards cooked on top of the range, or in other slightly cooked mixtures.

Baking affords the most thorough cooking of foods containing dried-egg solids, but some foods can be safely cooked on top of the range if heated long enough.

RECONSTITUTING DRIED-EGG SOLIDS

Dried-egg solids are reconstituted by blending with water. Reconstitute only the quantity needed at one time. To reconstitute, sift dried-egg solids. Place lightly in a measuring spoon or cup and level the top with a spatula or straight edge of a knife. Put lukewarm water in a bowl, sprinkle the dried-egg solids over the water, and stir to moisten the egg. Then beat until smooth, scraping the egg mixture from the sides of the bowl as you beat.

Use reconstituted egg immediately, or cover tightly, refrigerate, and use within an hour.

*Amounts of dried-egg product and water to replace specified
numbers of whole eggs, egg yolks, or egg whites*

	You may use:	
If a recipe calls for—	Dried-egg product, sifted	Lukewarm water
Whole eggs:		
1	2½ tablespoons	2½ tablespoons
6	1 cup	1 cup
Egg Yolks:		
1	2 tablespoons	2 teaspoons
6	¾ cup	¼ cup
Egg Whites:		
1	2 teaspoons	2 tablespoons
6	¼ cup	¾ cup

COOKING WITH DRIED-EGG SOLIDS

Reconstituted dried-egg solids can be used in the same way as
shell eggs in any recipe that requires thorough cooking. It is often
quicker and easier, however, to combine the dried-egg powder
with the other dry ingredients and then increase the liquid in the
recipe by adding the amount of water needed to reconstitute the
egg.

FLAVORING

Fruit flavors should be made with fresh fruit only; vanilla-
flavored desserts should be made with pure extract or the vanilla
bean itself; nut flavors require fresh nuts; coffee should be flavored with pure coffee; and for chocolate, use the highest grade
chocolate available. Fine flavors are produced by fresh fruits and
nuts, and pure extracts. The natural, delicate flavor produced by
fresh and pure ingredients can be easily distinguished from the
artificial flavors of low quality products.

FLAVOR DEFECTS

Many factors contribute to flavor defects. The more common
defects in quality are caused by: dairy products of low quality;
tainted dairy products; unclean containers; overheating the mix;
failure to cool the mix before freezing; inferior flavoring sub-

stances; too much flavoring; not enough flavoring; copper contamination; old ingredients; unpleasant odors absorbed from the air; cream whipped too stiff; folding whipped cream into a warm mixture; slow freezing; failure to store frozen desserts 0° F. or below; uneven distribution of fruits and nuts through the ice cream; and excess sugar and syrup.

QUANTITIES

The quantities produced may vary slightly according to the freshness of the eggs and whether hand or electric beaters are used.

STORAGE OF FROZEN DESSERTS

Ice cream, sherbet, and ices should be stored in containers that are as air-tight as possible. Unpleasant odors absorbed from the air will damage the flavor. Frozen desserts should not be pressed or packed into containers. When storing, the temperature should be maintained uniformly between − 10° and 0° F.

SERVING FROZEN DESSERTS

Before serving, all desserts should "ripen" for a few hours, if not over night. Ice cream, sherbets, and ices should not be eaten when they are frozen solid. If you cannot cut or scoop the dessert easily and freely, it is too hard to eat. A temperature averaging 15° F. improves the flavor and makes serving easier. Remove the dessert from the freezer to the refrigerator to soften. Allow about 20 minutes for a half gallon, 10 minutes for a pint, and 5 minutes if you are going to slice the dessert.

FROZEN DESSERTS MADE IN THE REFRIGERATOR OR DEEP FREEZE

Place the mix in ice-cube trays or a cake pan. Allow it to freeze until about a half inch of ice cream is frozen to the sides and bottom of the container. Turn the mixture out in a cold mixing bowl and whip thoroughly. Repeat this procedure 2 or 3 times at half hour intervals and return to the container for complete freezing. The temperature control should be set at the coldest point.

If you would like to modify crank-type or electric freezer recipes for refrigerator freezing, the sugar proportion must be lower. One part sugar to 4 parts mix is about right—or you may substitute one third of the sugar for corn syrup. If you want to make a light ice cream, use beaten egg whites. A smoother quality ice cream can be achieved if 1 teaspoon of gelatin is used for each cup of liquid mix.

FROZEN DESSERTS MADE IN A CRANK-TYPE OR ELECTRIC ICE-CREAM FREEZER

OPERATING INSTRUCTIONS

The manufacturer of your crank-type or electric ice cream freezer will usually include a manual of instructions with his product. Long experience with customers' needs and perhaps frustrations gives the freezer manual a real expert quality; and you should follow it to the letter for best results. In case, though, your original instructions are no longer available the following general rules may help you.

1. Don't tighten the screws holding the scrapers to the iron dasher. These screws are set at the factory and should remain loose to function properly.
2. The can revolves around the dasher. The dasher does not move.
3. The hole in the side of the tub is for drainage of excess brine. This hole must be left open at all times.
4. Electric models are commonly equipped with a 110-120 volt, 50-60 cycle alternating current motor which, when run for a short time, becomes quite warm. This is normal with motors of this type and need cause no concern.

Before using an electric machine put three drops of medium oil in the hole marked "oil" on top of the motor cover. When not in use keep this motor in a dry place and keep all parts of the freezer clean and dry. Wipe all surplus brine solution off before storing.

How to Make Frozen Desserts with Your Freezer

1. PREPARE YOUR MIX. Chill before using. (See tested recipes on the following pages.)
2. PREPARE YOUR ICE. Prepare a separate container of finely chipped or shaved ice. The ice may be chipped by placing it

in a cloth bag and breaking it into small pieces with a mallet or hammer.

3. INSERT DASHER IN CAN. Pour mix into can up to ⅔ full, but no more. Place the cover on the can.

4. PLACE ASSEMBLED CAN IN TUB. Be sure the can rests in proper position in the receptacle at the bottom of the tub.

5. PLACE POWER UNIT IN POSITION. Grasp the motor housing (electric models) or the main frame (hand models) and engage the driving gear socket with the hub on the can cover. On electric models, twist the frame into the locked position. On hand models, tighten the locking screws.

6. START CAN REVOLVING (ELECTRIC MODELS ONLY). Insert the plug into the proper electrical outlet used in your area. Do not put ice or salt in the tub until the can has been revolving for approximately 2 minutes.

7. INSERTING ICE AND SALT. In using your freezer, the proportion of rock salt to ice by weight is most important. If "powdery" or fine salt crystals are present, one cup may weigh almost double the same amount of coarse rock salt. Too much of this finer rock salt will stall the unit before the ice cream is completed.

FOR FOUR QUARTS:

Measure out two cups of rock salt and divide it into three equal parts. Use two of these parts when loading the freezer with ice and salt. Distribute about 3 inches of ice in the bottom of the tub, then distribute a portion of the salt, then more ice, alternating the distribution until the mixture is level with the top of the can. After 15 minutes add the remaining salt. If you are using a slow-freezing mix, add still more salt after ½ hour, as necessary.

FOR SIX QUARTS:

Measure out 3 cups of salt and continue as above.

If too much salt is used, the ice-cream mix will freeze too rapidly and produce a coarse-textured ice cream. An excessive amount of salt will reduce the freezing time to the extent that a crust of frozen cream will form on the inside of the can. This will stop the scrapers (and possibly stall the motor on the electric model), resulting in a "mushy" mix in the center.

8. DISCONNECT MOTOR (ELECTRIC MODELS ONLY). When the ice cream mix has been agitated and arrives at the consistency of heavy whipped cream, it is ready for packing. This time can best be determined when you hear the motor "labor." THEN UNPLUG THE MOTOR (the motor will not shut itself off automatically on most machines). Further churning will stall the motor, causing serious damage and will not improve the quality of the dessert.

DISCONTINUE CHURNING (HAND MODELS ONLY). When the ice cream mix has reached the proper packing consistency it becomes difficult to turn the handle. Further churning may cause serious damage, and will not improve the quality of the dessert.

9. PREPARE FOR HARDENING. Remove the power unit from the freezer. Remove the top of the can. Take out the dasher gradually and scrape any excess ice cream back into the can. Place a sheet of waxed paper across the top of the can, press down the cover over the waxed paper, and plug the hole in the can cover.

10. PACK FOR HARDENING: *Remember—running the motor (or, on hand models, turning the crank) does not "freeze" or harden ice cream.* Drain off the brine through the drainage holes on the side by tipping the tub. The actual hardening process begins when you pack the tub with an additional two cups or so of salt, and more ice, until the entire can and cover are covered with this ice-salt mixture. Cover the tub with a burlap bag or other suitable insulating material, and let it stand until frozen hard.

2.

ICE CREAM

Ice cream is a taste-tempting food that is rich in energy-giving vitamins and other food essentials. Health and growth-promoting proteins, calcium, and riboflavin are its main nutrients. Dairy products, as well as fruit, nuts, eggs and sugar enhance its nutritive value. There is no other food product that contributes so much nutritive value in such an appealing form, and is so universally liked as ice cream.

Ice cream can be made with or without eggs, fruits, nuts, etc. There are many variations in its composition, but the basic ingredients are cream, milk, sugar, flavoring, and stabilizer. Stabilizer gives ice cream its body and keeps it creamy and smooth-textured. Eggs, gelatin, junket, flour, and cornstarch are the most commonly used stabilizers.

The ingredients added to ice cream must always be of the highest quality. Dairy products of low quality, overripe fruit, and rancid nuts will spoil the flavor of a whole freezer of ice cream. These factors must be kept in mind when preparing the mix. It is poor economy to use low-quality products.

DIRECTIONS FOR FREEZING ICE CREAM

The first thing to do is to prepare your mix. The mixture of your choice should be thoroughly chilled before it is poured into the freezing container. In selecting your recipe remember that the larger the amount of sugar or sweetening in a mixture, the slower it will freeze. Do not use more sugar than the recipe indicates. The mix may not freeze at all if too much sugar is present! Measure your ingredients carefully. The ideal ice cream should have a uniform natural color, and desirable melting properties. What goes into ice cream affects the finished product so be sure to use fresh and pure ingredients. Fresh fruit, when available, is the best source of flavor. Frozen and canned fruits can be substituted for fresh, but do not expect the rich-bodied flavor which only fresh ingredients will produce. It is best to use pureed fruit since the flavor is more evenly distributed. Large bits of fruit freeze to icy particles. If bits of fruit are used, they should be heated with the sugar and then cooled before being added to the mixture. Do not use whole or large slices of fruit as they create a coarse-textured ice cream.

If a recipe calls for whipped cream, beat it only to soft peaks. If the cream is whipped too stiff, it will taste buttery and the dessert will not have a good volume. Never fold whipped cream or evaporated milk into a warm mixture. The cream as well as other ingredients should be thoroughly chilled before freezing. If possible, chill overnight and freeze the following day. Or, prepare your mixture in the morning and freeze later the same day.

Add nuts, marshmallows, wine, liqueurs, and other special ingredients when the mixture is partially frozen. Continue to freeze until firm and store in containers. (See Chapter 1 for freezing instructions.)

If a refrigerator or deep freeze is used to make ice cream adjust it to the lowest temperature. Rapid freezing, by preventing large ice crystals from forming, improves the texture of the dessert; so be sure that the freezing unit is not heavily frosted or frequently opened. To insure a smooth texture the mix should be whipped 2 or 3 times during the freezing process, at 30-minute intervals. Then allow freezing until firm.

The recipes that follow offer a number of ice-cream types, which may be even further varied and embellished to produce an infinite variety of flavor, texture and richness. Please note, however, that fruit pulp, crushed peppermint candy, nut meats, liqueurs, etc., should be added only after the mix has been partly frozen. True quality in ice cream depends more on weight than volume. Commercial ice cream is usually 50 percent air. If instructions are followed, the ice cream produced in your freezer will have no more than 33⅓ percent air and will thus be of much finer quality than the commercial variety. All recipe yields are approximate.

ALMOND ICE CREAM

4 eggs, stiffly beaten
2 cups sugar
1 quart cream, whipped
1 teaspoon pure vanilla extract

> ½ teaspoon pure almond extract
> 2 cups milk
> 1¼ cups toasted blanched almonds

Combine sugar and eggs. Beat until thick and yellow. Stir in lightly whipped cream, vanilla extract, almond extract, and milk. Freeze. When partly set, blend in almonds. Store in containers and freeze until firm. *Makes 2 quarts.*

ALMOND CRUNCH FLAVORING

> 1 cup butter, melted
> 1½ cups sugar
> 2 teaspoons light corn syrup
> 4 tablespoons water
> dash of salt
> 1 cup chopped toasted almonds.

Combine the butter, sugar, corn syrup, water and salt. Cook until the candy thermometer reaches 305°. Add nuts and blend well. Pour immediately onto a buttered cookie sheet. When hardened crush into small pieces. Add 1½ cups to 2 quarts of vanilla ice cream.

ALMOND PRALINE FLAVORING

> ¾ cup almonds
> 1½ cups sugar
> ½ teaspoon cream of tartar

Combine almonds, sugar, and cream of tartar in a heavy skillet. Cook until the mixture looks like a dark caramel. Pour the praline into a buttered cookie sheet. When set, pulverize. Add ¾ cup of praline powder to 2 quarts of vanilla ice cream.

ANISE FLAVORING

> 1 teaspoon anise flavoring

Combine 1 quart of softened vanilla ice cream with anise flavoring. Blend well and freeze until firm.

APPLESAUCE ICE CREAM refrigerator

2 tablespoons sugar
2 egg whites, stiffly beaten
1½ cups unsweetened applesauce
⅓ cup milk
½ teaspoon cinnamon
¼ cup honey
⅛ teaspoon salt
2 egg yolks, slightly beaten
1 cup whipping cream

Beat sugar in egg whites. Blend applesauce, milk, cinnamon, honey, salt, and egg yolks together. Whip cream until thick. Fold into applesauce mixture. Add egg whites. Stir once. Freeze in refrigerator tray. *Makes 1 quart.*

APRICOT ICE CREAM refrigerator

1 cup dried apricots
1 cup water
½ cup sugar
⅓ cup water
2 egg whites, stiffly beaten
1 cup cream, whipped
⅛ teaspoon almond extract

Cook apricots in 1 cup of water until tender. Puree. Boil sugar and water until syrup threads. Beat the syrup into the egg whites. Combine egg whites and puree. Add cream and flavoring. Freeze. *Makes 1 quart.*

APRICOT ICE CREAM

4 egg yolks, beaten
4 egg whites, stiffly beaten
2¼ cups sugar
juice of 1 lemon
rind of 1 lemon
3 cups cream
2 cups apricot puree

Combine egg yolks, sugar, and lemon juice. Beat until thick and creamy. Add lemon rind and cream. Fold in egg whites. Freeze. When partly set add puree, store in containers, and freeze until firm. *Makes 2 quarts.*

APRICOT 'N CREAM RIPPLE

1½ cups apricot puree
    rind of 1 lemon
  2 teaspoons lemon juice
  ¾ cup sugar
  ⅔ cup cream, whipped
  ¼ teaspoon pure almond extract

Combine puree, lemon juice, lemon rind, and sugar. Chill for 1 hour. Blend almond extract into whipped cream. Fold whipped cream into the apricot puree. Ripple this mixture into 1 quart softened vanilla ice cream. Note: A puree made from dried apricots gives a stronger flavor.

AVOCADO ICE CREAM refrigerator

1½ cups mashed ripe avocado
  3 tablespoons lemon juice
  1 tablespoon orange juice
    rind of 1 lemon
  ½ cup sugar
  ½ teaspoon salt
1½ cups cream, lightly whipped
  2 egg whites, beaten until frothy

Combine avocado, lemon juice, orange juice, lemon rind, sugar, and salt. Blend thoroughly until the sugar is dissolved. Add cream. A few drops of green food coloring will enhance the color of the ice cream. Freeze until partly set. Stir in egg whites and refreeze. *Makes 1 quart.*

AVOCADO ICE CREAM

¾ cup sugar
  1 tablespoon cornstarch
    dash of salt

1 quart extra rich milk
2 eggs beaten
3 tablespoons lemon juice
rind of 1 lemon
½ cup sugar
2 avocados, mashed
1 cup cream

Combine ¾ cup sugar, cornstarch, and salt in the top of a double boiler. Stir in the milk and cook, stirring constantly. When mixture coats a spoon add the eggs and blend thoroughly. Cool. Combine lemon juice, lemon rind, ½ cup sugar and avocado. Whip or blenderize until smooth. If desired, add a few drops of green food coloring. Combine the remaining ingredients and freeze. *Makes 2 quarts.*

BANANA ICE CREAM No. 1

⅓ cup corn syrup
2 tablespoons cornstarch
¾ cup sugar
½ teaspoon salt
3 cups milk
2 eggs, beaten slightly
2 teaspoons vanilla
1 cup light cream
1½ cups mashed bananas
1 tablespoon lemon juice

Combine corn syrup, cornstarch, sugar, salt, and milk in top of double boiler. Mix in eggs, and cook over boiling water. Stir the mixture constantly until it is slightly thickened, about 5 minutes. Chill. Add vanilla and cream. Mix mashed bananas and lemon juice; add to chilled custard mixture just before freezing. *Makes 2 quarts.*

BANANA ICE CREAM No. 2

2 eggs
1 cup sugar
¼ teaspoon salt
4 cups evaporated milk
1½ tablespoons vanilla
2 cups mashed bananas

Beat eggs in a 2½-quart bowl. Slowly add the sugar and salt and beat until well blended. Gradually stir in evaporated milk and vanilla. Beat the bananas in with a rotary beater. Freeze. *Makes about 1 gallon.*

BANANA ICE CREAM refrigerator

½ cup sugar plus 2 tablespoons
1 tablespoon flour
dash of salt
1 cup milk
1 cup half and half
¾ cup cream
4 large well-ripened bananas, mashed
1 tablespoon lemon juice
rind of 1 lemon

Combine sugar, flour, salt, and milk. Cook in a double boiler until thickened. Cool. Add half and half, cream, bananas, lemon juice, and rind. Blend well. Freeze. *Makes 1 quart.*

BANANA FLAVORING No. 1

3 ripe bananas, crushed
1 tablespoon sugar
1 teaspoon lemon juice

Combine bananas, sugar, and lemon juice. Blend until smooth. Stir into 1 pint of vanilla ice cream that has been softened.

BANANA FLAVORING No. 2

4 bananas
1⅓ tablespoons lemon juice
dash of salt

Skin bananas, scrape and force through sieve. Stir in lemon juice and salt. Add to 1 quart of any vanilla ice-cream mixture. Freeze.

BANANA ICE CREAM FRENCH STYLE refrigerator

2 cups half and half
1 cup sugar
¼ teaspoon salt
6 egg yolks, beaten
2 cups heavy cream, lightly whipped
3 cups mashed bananas
2 tablespoons lemon juice
¼ cup sugar

Scald half and half. Gradually stir in 1 cup sugar and salt. Mix until the sugar is completely dissolved and add the well-beaten egg yolks. Beat with an egg beater for 2 minutes. Cook over low heat and stir constantly until mixture comes to a boil, but do not boil. Cool. Pour into refrigerator trays or a large cake pan. Freeze until partly set. Turn the mixture into a chilled bowl and whip until smooth. Fold in whipped cream. Combine bananas, lemon juice, and ¼ cup sugar, blending well. Stir into the ice-cream mixture and freeze. If desired, serve with warm fudge sauce. *Makes 2½ quarts.*

BANANA ORANGE ICE CREAM refrigerator

¾ cup evaporated milk
½ cup mashed banana
2 tablespoons lemon juice
½ cup orange juice
⅔ cup sugar
    dash of salt
2 tablespoons lemon juice

Put the evaporated milk into ice tray of refrigerator. Chill until ice crystals begin to form around edges. Mix together banana, lemon juice, orange juice, sugar, and salt. Continue blending until sugar is dissolved. Let stand. Put ice cold milk into a cold quart bowl. Whip with cold rotary beater by hand, or with electric beater at high speed, until fluffy. Add lemon juice and continue whipping until stiff. Add the banana mixture gradually, beating at low speed until blended. Put into a 1-quart ice tray and freeze, without stirring, at coldest temperature until firm. *Makes 1 quart.*

BANANA RHUBARB ICE CREAM refrigerator

1 pound red rhubarb
1 cup sugar
½ cup water
1½ cups cream, whipped
1 egg, beaten
2 bananas, mashed
2 tablespoons lemon juice

Combine rhubarb, sugar, and water. Cook covered for 25 minutes over medium heat. Cool. Stir in whipped cream, beaten egg, mashed bananas, and lemon juice. Freeze. *Makes 1 quart.*

BERRY ICE CREAM

2 teaspoons gelatin
½ cup water
1¾ cups evaporated milk, warmed
½ cup sugar
1 teaspoon vanilla
1½ cups cream, whipped
1 pint crushed berries,
    sweeten to taste
    rind of 1 lemon

Soften gelatin in water and dissolve in warmed milk. Add sugar and vanilla. Continue stirring until dissolved. Cool. Add cream. Combine berries and lemon rind. Set aside. Freeze ice-cream mixture until thick. Add berries. Freeze until firm. *Makes 1½ quarts.*

BISQUE FLAVORING

1 cup finely chopped almonds or hazelnuts

Stir chopped almonds or hazelnuts into 1 quart of vanilla ice cream that has been softened.

BLACKBERRY ICE CREAM

2 cups blackberries
1 cup sugar

2 cups heavy cream
2 tablespoons lemon juice

Crush the blackberries and force the pulp through a fine sieve to remove the seeds. Add the sugar to the heavy cream and stir until the sugar is dissolved. Stir in the berry puree and lemon juice. Freeze and harden. *Makes 1½ quarts.*

BLUEBERRY ICE CREAM

1¼ cups granulated sugar
¼ teaspoon cream of tartar
¾ cup water
5 egg yolks, beaten
3 cups cream, lightly whipped
1 vanilla bean (scrape out the seeds)
3 cups ripe blueberries, mashed
rind of 1 lemon

Combine the sugar, cream of tartar, and water. Boil until the syrup spins a thread. Pour the hot syrup over the beaten egg yolks. Beat until the mixture is cool. Add the cream and the vanilla seeds. Mix thoroughly and freeze until thick. Stir in the blueberries and lemon rind. Mix well before storing in containers. *Makes 2 quarts.*

BLUEBERRY FLAVORING

1 quart blueberries
1 cup sugar

Cook the blueberries in a small amount of water until soft. Stir in the sugar and blend until dissolved. Strain and cool. Add to 1 quart of vanilla ice cream.

BURNT ALMOND FLAVORING

1 cup finely chopped toasted almonds

Caramelize half the sugar in any vanilla ice cream recipe. To do this, melt the sugar until dark brown in a heavy buttered skillet. Add to the ice-cream mix and freeze until partly set. Stir in toasted almonds. Freeze until firm.

BUTTER PECAN ICE CREAM

½ cup sugar
1 tablespoon flour
dash of salt
1 cup milk
1 cup half and half
1 cup cream
2 teaspoons pure vanilla extract
¾ cup chopped pecans
2½ tablespoons butter

Blend sugar, flour and salt. Slowly stir in the milk and cook in a double boiler until the mixture coats a spoon. Lightly brown the pecans in the butter. Drain the nuts on a piece of paper toweling to drain off the excess butter. Combine all ingredients and freeze. *Makes 1 quart.*

BUTTER PECAN ICE CREAM refrigerator

2 eggs
⅓ cup light brown sugar, packed
⅔ cup corn syrup
1 cup milk
1 cup heavy cream
½ cup chopped pecans
2 tablespoons butter
⅛ teaspoon salt
1 teaspoon vanilla

Beat eggs in large bowl until foamy. Gradually add sugar, then syrup, beating until mixture is thick. Stir in cream, milk, and vanilla. Turn into freezing tray. Freeze until almost firm, about 1 hour. Turn into a chilled bowl; cut apart and beat until smooth. Combine pecans, butter, and salt. Toast in moderate oven about 10 minutes, stirring once or twice. Fold into ice-cream mixture. Return to tray and freeze until firm. *Makes 1 quart.*

BUTTERSCOTCH ICE CREAM

1¼ cups brown sugar, packed
⅓ cup butter
1 cup water

4 egg yolks
3 cups cream
¼ teaspoon salt
1½ teaspoons vanilla

Melt butter and sugar in a heavy skillet, stirring constantly. Be sure to melt over low heat. Add water and simmer for 5 minutes. Add the sugar mixture to the egg yolks and beat for 3 minutes. Cool. Add remaining ingredients and freeze. *Makes 2 quarts.*

BUTTERSCOTCH FLAVORING

brown sugar
2 tablespoons butter

Substitute brown sugar for granulated sugar in any vanilla ice cream mix. Cook the sugar with 2 tablespoons butter until melted. Boil 1 minute and add to hot milk. Cool mixture. Freeze.

BUTTERSCOTCH REVEL

½ cup butterscotch sauce

Revel 1 pint of vanilla ice cream with butterscotch sauce.

CANDY 'N CREAM REVEL

1 cup cream, whipped
6 small candy bars, chopped

Fold chopped candy bars into whipped cream. Chill in refrigerator for 1½ hours. Fold or revel this mixture into 1 quart of softened vanilla ice cream.

CANDIED ORANGE ICE CREAM

2 cups sugar
1 cup water
2 cups orange juice
2 cups half and half

2 egg yolks, beaten
2 cups cream, beaten
¼ cup candied slivered orange peel
rind of 1 orange

Boil sugar and water for 5 minutes. Cool. Stir in orange juice. Cook half and half and egg yolks in a double boiler until thick. Cool. Stir in cream, orange peel, and orange rind. Freeze. If desired, stir in candied orange peel when the ice cream mixture is partly frozen. *Makes 2 quarts.*

CARAMEL FLAVORING

1 vanilla ice cream mix, your choice

Caramelize half the sugar and add it slowly to the warmed milk. Cool, and freeze until firm.

CHERRY ICE CREAM

2 cups sugar
4 cups fresh sour cherries, pitted and chopped
1 quart half and half
rind of 1 lemon

Combine the cherries and sugar. Heat in a double boiler until warm. Let stand for 1 hour. Stir in half and half and lemon rind. Freeze. This cherry ice cream is exceptionally tasty when frozen in a crank-type ice-cream freezer. *Makes 2 quarts.*

CHOCOLATE ICE CREAM No. 1

2 cups milk
2 squares unsweetened chocolate
1 cup sugar
2 tablespoons flour
dash of salt
2 eggs, beaten
1½ teaspoons pure vanilla extract
2 cups cream

Combine sugar, flour, and salt. Add the eggs and beat for 2 minutes. Slowly add the milk, stirring constantly. Break the unsweetened chocolate and add to the milk mixture. Cook in a double boiler until the chocolate melts and the mixture coats a spoon. Cool. Beat thoroughly and add the remaining ingredients. Freeze. *Makes 1½ quarts.*

CHOCOLATE ICE CREAM No. 2

> 2 eggs
> ¾ cup sugar
> ¼ teaspoon salt
> 6 cups evaporated milk
> 2 cups chocolate syrup
> 1 tablespoon vanilla

Beat the eggs. Add the sugar and salt and continue beating until well blended. Gradually stir in evaporated milk, chocolate syrup, and vanilla. Freeze. *Makes about 1 gallon.*

CHOCOLATE ICE CREAM No. 3

> ⅓ cup corn syrup
> 2 tablespoons cornstarch
> ¾ cup sugar
> ½ teaspoon salt
> 3 cups milk
> 4 ounces unsweetened chocolate
> 2 eggs, beaten slightly
> 2 teaspoons vanilla
> 1 cup light cream

Combine corn syrup, cornstarch, sugar, salt, and milk in top of double boiler. Mix in eggs, and add chocolate. Cook over boiling water, stirring constantly until mixture is slightly thickened, about 5 minutes. Chill. Add vanilla and light cream. Beat until smooth and freeze. *Makes 2 quarts.*

CHOCOLATE ICE CREAM No. 4

> 1 cup sugar
> ½ cup water
> 6 beaten egg yolks

6 ounces dark sweet chocolate
½ ounce bitter chocolate
6 cups thick cream
2 cups half and half

Combine sugar and water. Cook until the syrup forms a thread. Pour over beaten yolks and beat until very stiff. Dissolve chocolate over a slow fire. Combine all ingredients. Freeze. *Makes 2 quarts.*

CHOCOLATE ICE CREAM No. 5

4 teaspoons gelatin
1 cup ice water
3½ cups evaporated milk, warmed
1½ cups sugar
4 squares unsweetened chocolate
2 teaspoons vanilla
3 cups cream, whipped

Combine gelatin and cold water. Combine milk, sugar, chocolate, and vanilla. Cook in a double boiler until smooth. Cool. Stir in cream and freeze. *Makes 2 quarts.*

CHOCOLATE ICE CREAM refrigerator No. 1

⅔ cup sweetened condensed milk
1 square unsweetened chocolate
½ cup water
½ teaspoon vanilla extract
1 cup heavy cream

Turn refrigerator temperature control to coldest setting. In top of double boiler put sweetened condensed milk and chocolate. Cook over rapidly boiling water, stirring often, until thick. Remove from heat. Stir in water gradually. Stir in vanilla extract, and chill in refrigerator. Whip cream to soft custard consistency. Fold into chilled mixture. Turn into ice cube tray and freeze until firm, about 1 hour. Turn into chilled, medium size bowl; break into pieces. Whip until fluffy but not melted. Quickly return to tray, cover tray and return to freezing unit. Freeze until firm. *Makes 1½ pints.*

CHOCOLATE ICE CREAM refrigerator No. 2

2 eggs
⅓ cup sugar
⅔ cup corn syrup
⅓ cup cocoa
1½ cups milk
1 cup heavy cream
1 teaspoon vanilla

Beat eggs in large bowl until foamy, gradually add sugar. Combine syrup, cocoa, and ½ cup of the milk in a saucepan. Bring to boil over medium heat, stirring constantly. Cool slightly; add to egg-sugar mixture. Stir in remaining milk, cream, and vanilla. Turn into freezing tray. Freeze until almost firm, about 1 hour. Turn into a chilled bowl; cut apart and beat until smooth. Return to tray and freeze until firm. *Makes 1 quart.*

CHOCOLATE CHIP ICE CREAM

2 cups half and half
½ cup sugar
⅛ teaspoon salt
3 egg yolks, beaten
1 cup heavy cream
1 teaspoon vanilla
4 squares semisweet chocolate, grated

Combine half and half, sugar, salt, and egg yolks. Cook in a double boiler until the mixture coats a spoon. Cool. Add cream and vanilla and beat until smooth. Freeze. When partly set, stir in grated chocolate. Freeze until firm. *Makes 1½ quarts.*

CHOCOLATE ICE CREAM FRENCH STYLE refrigerator

⅓ cup sugar
⅓ cup water
1 6-ounce package semisweet chocolate chips
3 egg yolks, beaten
1½ cups cream, whipped

Combine sugar, water, and chocolate. Cook in a double boiler until dissolved. Beat the chocolate mixture into egg yolks. Continue beating until thick and cool. Fold in whipped cream and freeze. Stir once during freezing. *Makes 1 quart.*

CHOCOLATE ICE CREAM FRENCH STYLE No. 1

½ cup sugar
⅔ cup water
2 6-ounce packages semisweet chocolate pieces
6 egg yolks
3 cups cream

Boil sugar and water rapidly for 3 minutes. Reduce heat and add chocolate. Stir until smooth. Or put into a blender container and blend on high speed until chocolate sauce is smooth. Add egg yolks and blend. Fold chocolate into cream and freeze. *Makes 1½ quarts.*

CHOCOLATE ICE CREAM FRENCH STYLE No. 2

½ cup sugar
¼ cup water
¼ teaspoon cream of tartar
4 eggs
6 ounces semisweet chocolate
4 tablespoons strong black coffee
3½ cups heavy cream

Combine sugar, water, and cream of tartar, and cook the syrup until it spins a thread, or a candy thermometer registers 230° F. Beat the eggs until they are thick and light colored. Pour the syrup into them gradually, beating the mixture until it is very stiff. Melt the semisweet chocolate with the coffee. Stir this well into eggs and syrup with 3½ cups heavy cream. Freeze. *Makes 2 quarts.*

CHOCOLATE REVEL

½ cup chocolate syrup

Stir the chocolate syrup into 1 pint of vanilla ice cream. Freeze until firm.

CHOCOLATE SUPREME ICE CREAM refrigerator

2 cups whipping cream
⅔ cup sweetened condensed milk
⅔ cup chocolate syrup
½ teaspoon vanilla

Combine cream, condensed milk, chocolate syrup, and vanilla. Refrigerate until cold. Whip about 2 minutes or until thick. Pour into refrigerator tray and freeze until firm. When ready to serve, garnish with slivered almonds or chocolate sauce. *Makes 1 quart.*

COCONUT ICE CREAM

½ cup sugar
⅛ teaspoon salt
4 egg yolks, beaten
2 cups extra rich milk
1 cup cream
2 teaspoons pure vanilla extract
1 cup freshly grated coconut

Combine sugar, salt, and egg yolks in milk. Cook for 4 minutes in a double boiler. Cool. Whip until smooth. Stir in cream and vanilla. When partly set, stir in the coconut. Freeze until firm. *Makes 1 quart.*

COCONUT PINEAPPLE ICE CREAM refrigerator

4 eggs, beaten
rind of 2 lemons
½ teaspoon salt
1 vanilla bean, or
2 teaspoons vanilla extract
1½ cups orange blossom honey
3 cups heavy cream
3 cups half and half
1 3½ ounce can coconut
1 8½ ounce can pineapple

Combine eggs, lemon rind, salt, vanilla, honey, cream, and half and half. Blend thoroughly and freeze until partly set. When ice cream is thick, stir in coconut and pineapple. Freeze in refrigerator or deep freeze until firm. This ice cream is slow in freezing. *Makes 2 quarts.*

COFFEE ICE CREAM

1 cup sugar
½ cup water
6 beaten egg yolks
½ teaspoon vanilla
3 to 4 tablespoons instant coffee
4 cups thick cream
3 cups half and half

Combine sugar and water. Cook until the syrup spins a thread. Pour over the beaten egg yolks and continue beating until very stiff. Add vanilla, coffee, and cream. Freeze. *Makes 2 quarts.*

COFFEE ICE CREAM refrigerator No. 1

⅔ cup sweetened condensed milk
½ cup water
2 teaspoons instant coffee
1½ teaspoons vanilla extract
1 cup heavy cream

Turn refrigerator temperature control to coldest setting. Combine sweetened condensed milk, water, coffee, and vanilla extract. Chill in refrigerator. Whip cream to soft custard consistency. Fold into chilled mixture. Turn into ice cube tray and freeze to firm mush, about 1 hour. Turn into chilled bowl; break into pieces. Whip until fluffy but not melted. Quickly return to tray, cover tray and return to freezing unit. Freeze until firm. *Makes 1½ pints.*

COFFEE ICE CREAM refrigerator No. 2

2 cups half and half
¼ cup strong coffee
1½ teaspoons gelatin
¼ cup water

dash of salt
¾ cup sugar
2 teaspoons vanilla
2 cups cream, whipped

Heat cream and coffee. Soften gelatin in water, and stir into the warm cream and coffee mixture. Stir in salt, sugar, and vanilla. Continue blending until the sugar is dissolved. Freeze until the ice cream is thick. Add whipped cream and freeze until firm. *Makes 1½ quarts.*

COFFEE 'N CREAM REVEL

1 cup cream, whipped
2 tablespoons extra strong coffee, chilled
1 teaspoon rum extract
¼ cup sugar

Combine whipped cream with coffee, rum extract, and sugar. Blend thoroughly and revel into 1 quart of softened vanilla ice cream.

COFFEE PECAN ICE CREAM

2 eggs
1½ cups sugar
¼ teaspoon salt
3 tablespoons instant coffee
6 cups evaporated milk
1 tablespoon vanilla
1 cup finely cut pecans, unsalted

Beat eggs until thick. Slowly add sugar, salt, and instant coffee. Beat until well blended. Gradually stir in evaporated milk, vanilla, and pecans. Freeze. *Makes about 1 gallon.*

CRUNCHY LEMON ICE CREAM refrigerator

¾ cup evaporated milk
1 tablespoon melted butter
¼ cup crushed corn flakes
¼ cup finely cut nuts

    2 tablespoons brown sugar
    6 tablespoons frozen lemonade
      concentrate
 ¼ cup sugar
      dash of salt

Put evaporated milk into ice tray of refrigerator. Chill until crystals begin to form around edges. Meanwhile, mix melted butter, corn flakes, cut nuts and brown sugar. Put ice-cold milk into a cold 1 or 2-quart bowl. Whip with cold rotary beater by hand, or with electric beater at high speed, until fluffy. Gradually add frozen lemonade concentrate, sugar and salt. Whip until stiff. Pour into a 1 quart ice tray. Sprinkle crumb mixture over top. Freeze, without stirring, at coldest temperature until firm. *Makes 1 quart.*

EGGNOG ICE CREAM refrigerator

    1 pint milk
    1 2-inch stick of cinnamon
    6 whole cloves
    6 whole allspice
    1 cup sugar
    3 egg yolks, well beaten
 ¼ teaspoon salt
 ¼ teaspoon nutmeg
    1 tablespoon gelatin
 ¼ cup cold water
    1 pint whipping cream
    3 egg whites, stiffly beaten
 ½ cup rum or brandy or
    1 tablespoon rum extract

Scald milk with spices over a low flame. Strain. Add sugar to beaten egg yolks, beat thoroughly. Add salt, nutmeg and milk. Cook over low flame until mixture coats the spoon, stirring constantly. Remove from stove. Add gelatin which has been soaked in water for 5 minutes. Cool. Fold in whipped cream and egg whites. Freeze in refrigerator trays until mushy. Then slowly add brandy, rum, or extract and finish freezing. *Makes 1 quart.*

EGGNOG ICE CREAM

    3 egg yolks, beaten
 ¾ cup sugar

dash of salt
1 quart half and half
1 tablespoon sherry extract
3 egg whites, stiffly beaten
nutmeg

Combine the yolks, sugar, salt, and one cup of half and half. Cook in a double boiler until mixture coats a spoon. Cool. Combine remaining ingredients. Blend well and freeze. *Makes 2 quarts.*

FRUIT ICE CREAM No. 1

2 cups sugar
¼ cup cornstarch
¼ teaspoon salt
4 cups milk
4 eggs, beaten
2 tablespoons vanilla
4 cups table cream
2 cups crushed or pureed sweetened fruit

Mix sugar, cornstarch, and salt in the top of a double boiler. Blend in milk gradually. Cook over hot water, stirring occasionally until thickened, 12 to 15 minutes. Stir a small amount of the hot cornstarch mixture into the beaten eggs; then stir the eggs into the remaining cornstarch mixture. Cook over hot water, stirring constantly 4 to 5 minutes longer, or until the mixture is about the consistency of pudding. Chill thoroughly. This step is essential for a smooth ice cream. Stir in vanilla and cream. Freeze until the ice cream is thick. Stir in the sweetened fruit, and allow to ripen. *Makes about 1 gallon.*

FRUIT ICE CREAM No. 2

2 cups half and half
2 cups fruit puree
¼ teaspoon salt
¾ to 1 cup sugar or sweeten to taste

Combine all ingredients and freeze until firm. *Makes 1½ quarts.*

FRUIT ICE MILK

2 cups sugar
¼ cup cornstarch
¼ teaspoon salt
2 quarts skim milk
3 eggs beaten
1 tablespoon unflavored gelatin
1½ tablespoons vanilla
2 cups crushed or pureed
    sweetened fruit

Mix sugar, cornstarch, and salt in the top of a double boiler. Blend
in 4 cups skim milk gradually. Cook over hot water, stirring occasionally until thickened, 12 to 15 minutes. Stir a little of the hot
cornstarch mixture into the beaten eggs; then stir the eggs into
the remaining cornstarch mixture. Cook over hot water, stirring
constantly 4 to 5 minutes longer, or until the mixture is about the
consistency of soft custard. Soften gelatin in 1 cup skim milk. Stir
into hot mixture. Chill thoroughly. This step is essential for a
smooth ice milk. Stir in vanilla and remaining 3 cups skim milk.
Freeze. When the ice milk is thick, stir in the crushed or pureed
fruit. Freeze until firm. *Makes about 1 gallon.*

FRUIT 'N CREAM RIPPLE

1½ cups fruit puree
    rind of 1 lemon
2 teaspoons lemon juice
¾ cup sugar
1 cup cream, whipped
½ teaspoon pure vanilla extract

Combine fruit puree, lemon rind, lemon juice, and sugar. Chill for
1 hour. Blend vanilla extract into whipped cream and stir into the
fruit mixture. Ripple into 1 quart of softened vanilla ice cream.

GINGER ICE CREAM

2 cups milk
1¼ cups sugar
    dash of salt

    2 teaspoons ground ginger
    2 cups cream
    1 tablespoon vanilla extract

Combine milk, sugar, salt, ginger, and vanilla extract. Cook in a
double boiler until dissolved. Cool. Stir in cream and freeze. *Makes
1½ quarts.*

GINGER FLAVORING

⅓ cup slivered crystallized ginger

Fold the crystallized ginger into 1 quart of softened vanilla ice
cream. Refreeze until firm.

GINGER 'N SHERRY FLAVORING

    ½ cup chopped preserved ginger
    3½ tablespoons ginger syrup
    2 tablespoons sherry

Combine preserved ginger, ginger syrup, and sherry. Stir into
1 quart of vanilla ice cream.

GUAVA ICE CREAM No. 1

    1 cup sugar
      dash of salt
    3 egg yolks, beaten
    1 cup milk
    1½ cups guava puree
    1 tablespoon lemon juice
      rind of 1 lemon
    1 cup half and half
    1 cup cream, whipped

Combine sugar, salt, and eggs. Slowly add milk and cook in a
double boiler until the mixture coats a spoon. Cool. Stir in the
guava puree, lemon juice, lemon rind, half and half, and whipped
cream. Freeze. *Makes 1½ quarts.*

GUAVA ICE CREAM No. 2

2½ cups guava puree
2 cups sugar
2 tablespoons lemon juice
rind of 1 lemon
2 cups half and half

Combine guava puree, sugar, lemon juice, lemon rind, and half and half. Stir until the sugar is dissolved. Freeze. *Makes 1½ quarts.*

HONEY ICE CREAM

1 quart milk
1 quart heavy cream
1¾ cups honey
1 tablespoon pure vanilla extract
6 eggs

In saucepan, combine milk, cream, and honey. Heat to lukewarm; add vanilla. Chill. Beat egg whites until stiff. Using same beater, beat egg yolks until thick. Fold into chilled mixture. Freeze. *Makes 1 gallon.*

HONEY CHOCOLATE ICE CREAM

1 quart milk
1 quart heavy cream
1¾ cups honey
1 tablespoon pure vanilla extract
6 eggs
2 cups chocolate pieces

In saucepan, combine milk, cream, honey, and chocolate pieces. Heat and mix thoroughly. Continue cooking until the chocolate is dissolved. Stir in vanilla and chill. Beat egg whites until stiff. Using same beater, beat egg yolks until thick. Fold into chilled mixture. Freeze. *Makes 1 gallon.*

KUMQUAT ICE CREAM refrigerator

1 quart cream
2 cups sugar
4 egg yolks

4 egg whites, stiffly beaten
1 cup minced kumquats
rind of 1 lemon
1 tablespoon Cointreau
(Curaçao or orange liqueur may be
substituted)

Heat cream in the top of a double boiler. Combine egg yolks and
sugar, beating thoroughly. Slowly stir into warm cream and cook
until thickened. Stir occasionally. Cool. Add kumquats, lemon rind,
and Cointreau. Fold in stiffly beaten egg whites and freeze until
firm. *Makes about 1½ quarts.*

LEMON ICE CREAM No. 1

4 eggs, beaten
2½ cups sugar
1 quart half and half
1½ quarts milk
1 tablespoon lemon extract
¼ teaspoon salt
rind of 3 lemons

Combine eggs and sugar, beat until thick. Stir in half and half,
milk, lemon extract, salt, and lemon rind. Blend thoroughly.
Freeze. *Makes 2 quarts.*

LEMON ICE CREAM No. 2

4 lemons
2 cups sugar
4 cups half and half
(cream may be substituted)
2 tablespoons grated lemon rind

Dissolve sugar in half and half. Squeeze the juice from lemons.
Slowly stir in lemon rind and juice into the half-and-half mixture.
Freeze immediately. *Makes 1½ quarts.*

LEMON ICE CREAM refrigerator

2 eggs
½ cup sugar
⅔ cup corn syrup

½ cup lemon juice
1 cup milk
1 cup cream
1 teaspoon grated lemon rind

Beat eggs in large bowl until foamy. Gradually add sugar, then corn syrup, beating until mixture is thick. Stir in lemon juice, milk, cream, and lemon rind. Turn into freezing tray. Freeze until almost firm, about 1 hour. Turn into a chilled bowl; cut apart and beat until smooth. Return to tray and freeze until firm. *Makes 1 quart.*

LEMON CUSTARD ICE CREAM

1¼ cups sugar
1 tablespoon flour
dash of salt
1 cup milk
1 cup half and half
1 cup cream
rind of 4 lemons
¼ cup lemon juice

Combine sugar, flour, and salt. Slowly stir in milk and cook in a double boiler until mixture coats a spoon. Cool. Add half and half, cream, lemon rind, and lemon juice. Freeze. *Makes 1 quart.*

LEMON CUSTARD ICE CREAM refrigerator

½ cup evaporated milk
1 egg yolk
⅓ cup sugar
¼ teaspoon grated lemon rind
1 tablespoon lemon juice
dash of salt
1 egg white
1½ tablespoons lemon juice
¼ cup graham cracker crumbs

Put evaporated milk into ice tray of refrigerator. Chill until ice crystals begin to form around edges. In a large bowl, mix egg yolk, sugar, grated lemon rind, lemon juice, and salt. Put ice-cold milk into cold quart bowl and add egg white. Whip with a cold rotary beater by hand, or with electric beater at high speed, until fluffy. Add the lemon juice and beat until stiff. Add the sugar mixture gradually, beating at low speed until well blended. Put into a 1-quart ice tray. Sprinkle top with graham cracker crumbs. Freeze, without stirring, at coldest temperature until firm. *Makes 1 quart.*

LEMON HONEY ICE CREAM refrigerator

                2 eggs, beaten
                ½ cup sugar
                ½ cup orange honey
                   rind of 1 lemon
                3 tablespoons lemon juice
                2 cups cream, whipped
                ¼ cup chopped toasted almonds

Combine eggs, sugar, and honey. Beat until fluffy. Add lemon rind, and lemon juice. Beat until thoroughly blended. Stir in cream and freeze until partly set. Remove from refrigerator and turn into a chilled bowl. Beat until fluffy. Stir in almonds and freeze until firm. *Makes 1 quart.*

LEMON PRUNE ICE CREAM

                1 cup chopped cooked prunes
                1 teaspoon grated lemon rind
                ¼ cup lemon juice
                2 eggs, well beaten
                   dash of salt
                1 cup light corn syrup
                ½ cup table cream
                1½ cups milk

To chopped prunes add lemon rind and juice. Beat eggs light; beat in salt, corn syrup, cream and milk. Add prune mixture and blend well. If you like a stronger lemon flavor, add 1 or 2 tablespoons more lemon juice. Pour into freezing tray of refrigerator. Freeze until mushy, then beat with fork; continue freezing until firm. *Makes 1 quart.*

LIME ICE CREAM

                2 eggs, beaten well
                ½ cup sugar
                ½ cup light corn syrup

1½ cups milk
¼ cup lime juice
1 teaspoon grated lime rind
green food coloring
1 cup heavy cream

Beat the eggs well and gradually beat in ½ cup sugar. Stir in corn syrup, milk, lime juice, lime rind, and a few drops of green food coloring. Whip 1 cup heavy cream and fold into the ice cream mixture. Freeze. *Makes 1½ quarts.*

MACAROON FLAVORING

1 cup macaroon crumbs
2 tablespoons sherry

Stir the sherry into 1 quart of softened vanilla ice cream. Blend in macaroon crumbs and refreeze.

MANGO ICE CREAM

1¼ cups granulated sugar
¼ teaspoon cream of tartar
¾ cup water
5 egg yolks, beaten
3 cups cream, whipped
1 vanilla bean
(scrape out the seeds)
3 cups ripe mango puree

Combine sugar, cream of tartar, and water. Boil in a saucepan until the syrup spins a thread. Pour the hot syrup over the beaten egg yolks. Beat until the mixture is cool. Add the cream and vanilla seeds. Mix thoroughly and freeze. When the ice-cream mixture is thick, stir in the mango puree. Refreeze. *Makes 1½ quarts.*

MAPLE ICE CREAM

2 eggs
1⅔ cups brown sugar
¼ teaspoon salt
7 cups evaporated milk

1 tablespoon vanilla
1 teaspoon maple flavoring

Beat the eggs into the brown sugar and salt. Gradually stir in evaporated milk, vanilla, and maple flavoring. Freeze. *Makes about 1 gallon.*

MAPLE ICE CREAM refrigerator

2 eggs
⅓ cup light brown sugar, packed
⅔ cup 100 percent pure maple syrup
1 cup milk
1 cup heavy cream
1 teaspoon vanilla

Beat eggs in large bowl until foamy. Gradually add sugar, then maple syrup, beating until mixture is thick. Stir in milk, cream, and vanilla. Turn into freezing tray. Freeze until almost firm, about 1 hour. Turn into a chilled bowl; cut apart and beat until smooth. Return to tray and freeze until firm. *Makes 1 quart.*

MAPLE NUT FLAVORING

1 cup nut meats, chopped
100 percent pure maple syrup
(maple sugar or maple flavoring
may be substituted)

Use maple syrup or maple sugar in any vanilla ice cream omitting sugar. Or substitute maple flavoring in place of vanilla. When the mixture is partly frozen stir in the nut meats. If desired, omit the nut meats.

MAPLE NUT ICE CREAM refrigerator

⅔ cup sweetened condensed milk
½ cup water
2 teaspoons maple flavoring
1 cup heavy cream
¼ cup coarsely chopped walnut meats

Turn refrigerator temperature control to coldest setting. Combine sweetened condensed milk, water, and maple flavoring. Chill in refrigerator. Whip cream to soft custard consistency. Fold into chilled mixture. Turn into ice cube tray and freeze to firm mush, about 1 hour. Turn into chilled bowl; break into pieces. Whip until fluffy but not melted. Fold in coarsely chopped walnut meats. Quickly return to tray, cover tray and return to freezing unit. Freeze until firm. *Makes 1½ pints.*

MARASCHINO CHERRY ICE CREAM

 1¼ cups sugar
 1½ teaspoons gelatin
 1 quart cream
 1 egg, beaten
 1 teaspoon vanilla
 dash of salt
 1 teaspoon grated lemon rind
 ½ cup chopped maraschino cherries
 1 tablespoon cherry juice

Combine sugar and gelatin, mix thoroughly. Add 2 cups of cream and heat until gelatin is dissolved. Slowly add egg, mixing well. Cook until the mixture thickens slightly. Cool. Stir in vanilla, salt, lemon rind, cherries, and juice. Freeze. *Makes 1½ quarts.*

MEXICAN CHOCOLATE FLAVORING

 ½ cup semisweet chocolate, grated
 1 teaspoon cinnamon

Stir the grated chocolate and cinnamon into 1 quart of softened vanilla ice cream. Refreeze until firm.

MINCEMEAT ICE CREAM refrigerator

 ½ cup half and half
 ¼ cup water
 ⅓ cup sugar
 dash of salt
 2 egg yolks, beaten
 juice of 1 lemon

rind of 1 lemon
½ teaspoon vanilla
1 cup cooked mincemeat
1 cup cream

Combine sugar, salt, and eggs. Beat until thick and creamy. Slowly add half and half and water. Cook in a double boiler until slightly thickened, about 5 minutes. Remove from heat. Stir in lemon juice, lemon rind, vanilla, mincemeat, and cream. Freeze. *Makes 1 quart.*

MINT CHIP ICE CREAM

2 eggs
1½ cups sugar
¼ teaspoon salt
6 cups evaporated milk
2 teaspoons mint extract
few drops green food coloring
1⅓ cups coarsely grated milk chocolate
(one 4½-ounce plain
milk chocolate bar)

Beat eggs in a 2½-quart bowl. Add sugar and salt and beat until well blended. Gradually beat in evaporated milk. Stir in until well blended mint extract and green food coloring. Add the coarsely grated milk chocolate. Freeze. *Makes about 1 gallon.*

MINT PILLOW 'N CREAM RIPPLE

1 cup cream, whipped
1 cup after-dinner mint pillows

Fold mint pillows into whipped cream. Chill in the refrigerator for 1½ hours to bring out the flavor and to soften the mints. Fold or revel this mixture into 1 quart of softened vanilla ice cream. Refreeze until firm.

MOCHA ICE CREAM refrigerator

1 square unsweetened chocolate
1 cup sweetened condensed milk

1 cup strong coffee
¼ teaspoon vanilla
½ cup all purpose cream

Melt chocolate. Add condensed milk. Stir for 5 minutes or until mixture thickens. Add coffee. Chill. Add vanilla. Whip cream to the consistency of thick custard. Fold into chilled mixture. Freeze in refrigerator tray, stirring once or twice during freezing process. *Makes 1½ pints.*

NESSELRODE ICE CREAM

1½ teaspoons gelatin
¼ cup water
1½ cups half and half
⅓ cup sugar
¼ cup seedless raisins
2 egg yolks, beaten
   dash of salt
½ cup Nesselrode fruit mix,
   finely chopped
½ teaspoon vanilla
   rind of 1 lemon
1 cup cream

Soften gelatin in water. Combine half and half, sugar, raisins, egg yolks, and salt. Cook in a double boiler until mixture coats a spoon. Stir in gelatin and blend until dissolved. Cool. Stir in Nesselrode fruit mix, vanilla, lemon rind, and cream. Freeze. *Makes 1½ quarts.*

NUTMEG COCONUT FLAVORING

½ cup angel flake coconut
½ teaspoon freshly
   grated nutmeg

Blend coconut and grated nutmeg into 1 quart of softened vanilla ice cream. Refreeze until firm.

ORANGE ICE CREAM

1 cup milk
½ cup sugar

dash of salt
3 egg yolks
¾ cup half and half
1 cup cream
1 cup fresh orange juice
rind of 3 oranges
1 tablespoon lemon juice
rind of 1 lemon
¼ teaspoon orange extract

Combine milk, sugar, salt, and egg yolks. Cook until the mixture coats a spoon. Cool. Stir in half and half and cream. Add orange juice, orange rind, lemon juice, lemon rind, and orange extract. Freeze. *Makes 1 quart.*

PAPAYA ICE CREAM

3 cups papaya puree
5 tablespoons lemon juice
rind of 1 lemon
1 cup orange juice
3 cups cream
2 cups sugar

Combine papaya puree, lemon juice, lemon rind, orange juice, and sugar. Whip until fluffy. Stir in cream and freeze. *Makes 1½ quarts.*

PEACH ICE CREAM No. 1

½ cup sugar
1½ teaspoons gelatin
1 quart half and half
1 egg, beaten
½ teaspoon vanilla
¼ teaspoon pure almond extract
dash of salt
3 cups mashed peaches (use fresh peaches only)
¾ cup sugar

Combine ½ cup sugar and gelatin, mix thoroughly. Add 2 cups half and half and heat until gelatin is dissolved. Slowly add egg, mix well. Cook until the custard mixture thickens slightly. Cool. Stir ¾ cup sugar into the peaches. Let stand 20 minutes. Combine remaining ingredients and freeze. *Makes 2 quarts.*

PEACH ICE CREAM No. 2

2 eggs
1½ cups sugar
¼ teaspoon salt
¼ cup lemon juice
4 cups evaporated milk
2 10-ounce packages frozen peaches
few drops yellow food coloring,
if desired

Beat eggs in 2½-quart bowl. Add sugar, salt, and lemon juice and beat until well blended. Gradually beat in evaporated milk. Add and beat until well blended frozen peaches and yellow food coloring. Freeze. *Makes about 1 gallon.*

PEACH ICE CREAM No. 3

4 egg yolks, beaten
2 cups milk
1 cup sugar
dash of salt
2 cups heavy cream
2 cups crushed peaches,
sweetened to taste
1 teaspoon pure almond extract

Combine egg yolks, milk, sugar, and salt. Beat well and cook in a double boiler until mixture coats a spoon. Cool. Add almond extract and cream and freeze until partly set. Stir in peaches and freeze until firm. *Makes 2 quarts.*

PEACH ICE CREAM No. 4

2 cups fresh peaches
1 cup sugar
1 tablespoon lemon juice
1 quart heavy cream

Mash thoroughly 2 cups fresh peaches, peeled and sliced, with sugar and lemon juice. Let peaches stand for 30 minutes. Stir into heavy cream. Freeze. *Makes 2 quarts.*

PEACH ICE CREAM refrigerator

1½ cups fresh peach puree
1½ cups cream, whipped
1 tablespoon lemon juice
   dash of salt
1 cup sugar
¼ teaspoon almond extract

Dissolve the sugar in the puree. Add lemon juice and salt. Let stand 15 minutes. Stir in whipped cream and almond extract. Place in refrigerator trays and freeze. Stir frequently during the freezing process. *Makes 1½ pints.*

PEACH BUTTERMILK ICE CREAM

1 tablespoon gelatin
1 cup sugar
2 cups buttermilk
2 egg yolks, beaten
¼ teaspoon salt
2 pints whipping cream
1 tablespoon vanilla
2 cups diced freestone peaches
   (1-pound 4-ounce can, or
   fresh peaches)

Mix gelatin and sugar in saucepan; stir in buttermilk. Simmer over low heat, stirring slowly until gelatin is dissolved. Gradually add hot buttermilk mixture to eggs, stirring constantly. Blend in salt, whipping cream and vanilla. Chill thoroughly. Add peaches after the freezing process and before hardening, mixing just enough to blend well. *Makes 2 quarts.*

PEACH RUM FLAVORING

2 cups freshly chopped peaches
½ cup sugar
3 tablespoons rum

Combine peaches, sugar, and rum. Chill for three hours. Add to 1 quart of softened vanilla ice cream.

PEANUT BRITTLE FLAVORING

2 cups sugar
1 cup light corn syrup
½ cup water
1 teaspoon salt
2 cups skinless peanuts
1 teaspoon butter
1 teaspoon vanilla
1½ teaspoons baking soda

Combine sugar, syrup, water, and salt. Bring to a boil and add the peanuts. When the syrup turns a golden brown add the butter and vanilla. When the candy thermometer reads 300° F. remove from heat. Stir in baking soda. Spread the mixture on a buttered cookie sheet. As it cools, stretch thinner. When hard, pulverize or break into tiny pieces. Stir in ½ to ⅔ cup of peanut brittle into each quart of vanilla ice cream.

PEANUT BRITTLE ICE CREAM

1½ teaspoons gelatin
¼ cup cold milk
1 quart cream
½ cup sugar
¼ teaspoon salt
½ pound crushed peanut brittle

Soften gelatin in cold milk. Heat two cups of cream. Add sugar, salt, and gelatin, stirring until dissolved. Cool. Combine the remaining cream with the sugar and gelatin mixture. Freeze. Add peanut brittle after the freezing process and before hardening, mixing just enough to blend well. *Makes 1½ quarts.*

PECAN BRITTLE FLAVORING

1 cup sugar
½ cup light corn syrup
dash of salt
2 tablespoons water
2 tablespoons butter
½ teaspoon vanilla
1 cup pecans

Avocado Ice Cream

Lemon Ice Cream

Peach Ice Cream

Pineapple Ice Cream

Strawberry Ice Cream

Vanilla Ice Cream

Lemon Sherbet

Orange Sherbet

Peach Sherbet

Cranberry Ice

Nectar Ice

Cook the sugar, corn syrup, salt, and water until it reaches 305° F. on a candy thermometer. Add butter, vanilla, and pecans. Stir quickly and pour immediately into a buttered cookie sheet. When hardened crush into a powder or into small pieces. Add ¾ cup to 2 quarts of vanilla ice cream. Add the pecan brittle after the freezing process and before hardening, mixing just enough to blend well.

PEANUT BUTTER FUDGE FLAVORING

2 cups sugar
2 tablespoons light corn syrup
¼ cup peanut butter
¼ cup milk
1 teaspoon white cider vinegar

Combine sugar, milk, syrup, and vinegar. Cook to the soft ball stage. Cool. Add the peanut butter and beat constantly until thick and creamy. Pour into a buttered pan and chill overnight. When set, chop into small pieces. Add ⅔ cup of chopped peanut-butter fudge to 1 quart of vanilla ice cream. Add the fudge after the freezing process and before hardening, mixing just enough to blend well.

PEANUT BUTTER AND JELLY REVEL

½ cup peanut butter
½ cup strawberry jelly

Blend the peanut butter with the jelly. Use this mixture to revel 1 quart of vanilla ice cream. Add the peanut butter and jelly revel after the freezing process and before hardening, mixing just enough to blend slightly.

PEANUT BUTTER RIPPLE

⅓ cup peanut butter, crunch style
6 tablespoons honey

Blend honey and peanut butter until thoroughly mixed. Add to 1 quart of vanilla ice cream after the freezing process and before hardening, mixing just enough to ripple slightly.

PECAN BUTTER CRUNCH FLAVORING

1 cup crisp rice cereal
3 tablespoons brown sugar
½ cup chopped pecans
3 tablespoons butter

Combine these ingredients and cook until crisp. Cool. Add to one quart of vanilla ice cream after the freezing process and before hardening, mixing just enough to blend well.

PECAN PRALINE FLAVORING

2 cups sugar
1 cup light brown sugar
1 cup hot water
2 cups small pecans

Combine sugars and hot water. Cook in a heavy skillet until the mixture looks like a dark caramel. Stir in the pecans. Cook until the candy thermometer reaches 236° F. Remove from heat and beat until the praline appears slightly granular. Pour into a buttered cookie sheet and let harden. Crush into a powder or into small pieces. Add ¾ cup to 2 quarts of vanilla ice cream.

PEPPERMINT ICE CREAM

1½ teaspoons gelatin
¼ cup cold water
1 quart cream
½ cup half and half, warmed
dash of salt
1 cup crushed peppermint candy

Add the crushed candy to the cream. Let stand in the refrigerator until the candy dissolves. Soften the gelatin in cold water and add to the warmed half and half. Stir until dissolved. Cool. Combine all ingredients. Freeze. *Makes 1½ quarts.*

PEPPERMINT ICE CREAM refrigerator

½ envelope unflavored gelatin
¼ cup cold milk

1½ cups half and half, scalded
⅛ teaspoon salt
1 cup crushed peppermint stick candy
3 beaten egg yolks
2 cups heavy cream, whipped
   red food coloring

Soften gelatin in cold milk. Combine half and half, salt, peppermint candy, and egg yolks. Cook over low heat. Stir constantly until mixture comes to a boil. Cool. Beat until smooth. Pour into refrigerator tray and freeze until firm. Scoop the mixture into a chilled bowl and beat until smooth. Stir in food coloring to tint pink and fold in whipped cream. Freeze. Stir occasionally during the freezing process. If desired, serve with additional crushed peppermint candy. *Makes 1¼ quarts.*

PEPPERMINT CANDY ICE CREAM refrigerator

⅔ cup sweetened condensed milk
½ cup water
1 cup heavy cream
1 cup crushed peppermint stick candy

Turn refrigerator temperature control to coldest setting. In quart measure or pitcher combine sweetened condensed milk and water. Chill in refrigerator. Whip cream to soft custard consistency. Fold into chilled mixture. Turn into ice-cube tray. Cover tray top with waxed paper, or foil. Freeze to firm mush, about 1 hour. Turn into chilled, medium sized bowl; break into pieces. Whip until fluffy but not melted. Fold in candy. Quickly return to tray, cover tray and return to freezing unit. Freeze until firm. *Makes 1½ pints.*

PEPPERMINT CHIP ICE CREAM refrigerator

2 cups cream, whipped
1 cup milk
   dash of salt
½ pound peppermint stick candy, crushed

Combine whipped cream, milk, salt, and peppermint stick candy. Freeze. Stir occasionally until frozen firm. *Makes 1 quart.*

PEPPERMINT CHIP ICE CREAM

2 cups milk
¾ cup sugar
⅛ teaspoon salt
2 eggs, beaten
¼ pound peppermint candy, crushed
1 cup cream, whipped

Combine sugar, salt, and eggs. Beat thoroughly and slowly add milk, beating constantly. Cook in the top of a double boiler until the mixture coats a spoon. Cool and then stir in the crushed candy. Combine the remaining ingredients and freeze. *Makes 1 quart.*

PERSIMMON ICE CREAM

1½ teaspoons gelatin
¼ cup water
    dash of salt
¼ cup sugar
1½ cups half and half
4 egg yolks, beaten
    rind of 2 lemons
2 tablespoons lemon juice
1 cup cream
2 cups persimmon puree

Soften gelatin in water. Combine sugar, salt, eggs, and half and half. Blend thoroughly and cook in a double boiler until mixture coats a spoon. Stir in gelatin. Cook until dissolved. Cool. Stir in remaining ingredients. Blend well and freeze. *Makes 1½ quarts.*

PINEAPPLE ICE CREAM

4 egg yolks, beaten
2 cups milk
1 cup sugar
    dash of salt
2 cups heavy cream
2 cups sweetened chopped fresh pineapple

Combine egg yolks, milk, sugar, and salt. Beat well and cook in a double boiler until mixture coats a spoon. Cool. Add the cream and freeze until thick. Pineapple should be stirred in after the freezing process and before hardening, mixing just enough to blend well. *Makes 1½ quarts.*

PINEAPPLE 'N CREAM ICE CREAM

1 cup shredded fresh pineapple
1 teaspoon lemon juice
¾ cup sugar
1 quart heavy cream

Place shredded fresh pineapple in a large bowl with lemon juice and sugar. Mix thoroughly, crushing the pineapple against the side of the bowl with a wooden spoon. Let this mixture stand for 30 minutes and then stir it into 1 quart heavy cream. Freeze. *Makes 1½ quarts.*

PINEAPPLE CRUSH ICE CREAM

3 pints thin cream
½ cup sugar
2 cups canned pineapple crushed

Add pineapple to cream, let stand 30 minutes. Stir in the sugar. Blend until dissolved. Freeze. *Makes 2½ quarts.*

PINEAPPLE ORANGE ICE CREAM

2 eggs
1½ cups sugar
¼ teaspoon salt
4 cups evaporated milk
2 cups crushed pineapple (a 1-pound can)
2 tablespoons grated orange rind
1 cup orange juice
⅓ cup lemon juice

Beat the eggs in a 2½-quart bowl. Add the sugar and salt and beat until well blended. Gradually stir in evaporated milk, crushed pineapple, grated orange rind, orange juice, and lemon juice. Freeze. *Makes about 1 gallon.*

PISTACHIO 'N CREAM ICE CREAM

3/4 cup pistachio nuts
1½ cups sugar
8 egg yolks
3 cups heavy cream
3 cups milk
1 teaspoon rose water
green food coloring

Chop pistachio nuts finely. Mix with sugar. Beat egg yolks until light and foamy. Blend in cream, milk, and flavoring. Cook over low heat for about 10 minutes or until mixture comes to a boil. Cool. Beat briskly and add food coloring. Freeze. *Makes 2 quarts.*

PRUNE ICE CREAM refrigerator No. 1

2 cups uncooked "tenderized" prunes
1 cup milk
½ cup granulated sugar
1 teaspoon granulated gelatin
1 tablespoon cold water
4 eggs, beaten
1 tablespoon vanilla
¼ teaspoon salt
½ pint whipping cream

Wash prunes in hot water, cut from pits and put through food chopper, using a fine knife. Combine milk and sugar and heat to boiling. Moisten gelatin in cold water, add to milk and stir until dissolved. Pour hot mixture over well beaten eggs, stirring to prevent curdling; add vanilla, salt, cream, prunes, and beat until well blended. Freeze in freezing tray of automatic refrigerator with temperature control at coldest setting until firm enough to serve, or pack in rock salt and finely crushed ice. *Makes about 1 quart.*

PRUNE ICE CREAM refrigerator No. 2

2 egg whites, stiffly beaten
1 cup sugar
1½ cups strained cooked prunes
1 cup fresh orange juice

2 tablespoons lime juice
2 tablespoons lemon juice
grated rind of 1 orange
2 cups heavy cream, slightly whipped

Slowly add the sugar to the stiffly beaten egg whites, beating until thick. Add prunes and mix well. Add all the juices and orange peel. Stir in cream and freeze. *Makes 1½ quarts.*

PRUNE CARAMEL ICE CREAM refrigerator

1 cup cooked prunes
½ cup granulated sugar
¼ cup water
1½ cups milk
2 eggs
⅛ teaspoon salt
1 teaspoon vanilla extract
⅛ teaspoon mace
1 cup whipping cream

Cut prunes from pits into small pieces and chill. Combine ¼ cup sugar and water and cook until a golden brown in color. Add milk and cook and stir until sugar is dissolved. Pour over beaten eggs, stirring briskly to prevent curdling. Add remaining sugar, salt, flavoring and spice; cool. Fold in whipped cream. Turn into refrigerator tray and place in freezing compartment with control set at lowest temperature. Freeze until firm. Turn out into chilled bowl and beat with rotary beater until smooth and fluffy. Fold in prunes. Return to freezing compartment and freeze to desired consistency. When firm, reset temperature control to normal. *Makes about 1 quart.*

PUMPKIN ICE CREAM refrigerator

2 cups half and half
1½ tablespoons cornstarch
1 teaspoon cinnamon
½ teaspoon ginger
½ teaspoon mace
½ teaspoon salt
1½ cups sugar
1½ cups pumpkin

rind of 1 orange
4 egg yolks, beaten
2 teaspoons gelatin
¼ cup cold water
1 cup diced walnuts
1 cup cream, whipped

Soften gelatin in cold water. Combine half and half, cornstarch, cinnamon, ginger, mace, salt, and sugar. Cook over low heat until thickened. Add pumpkin, orange rind, egg yolks, and dissolved gelatin, stirring until well blended. Pour into refrigerator tray and chill until slightly thickened. Remove from freezer and add walnuts and whipped cream, mixing thoroughly. Freeze until firm. *Makes 1½ quarts.*

PUMPKIN PECAN ICE CREAM refrigerator

1 tablespoon cornstarch
¾ cup sugar
½ teaspoon cinnamon
¼ teaspoon ginger
1 cup milk
2 egg yolks, slightly beaten
¾ cup sieved canned pumpkin
¼ teaspoon salt
½ cup whipping cream
⅓ cup broken pecans
2 egg whites, stiffly beaten

Mix cornstarch, sugar, cinnamon and ginger. Add milk and beaten egg yolks. Cook over low heat until thick, stirring constantly. Add pumpkin and salt. Cool. Fold in whipped cream, nuts, and egg whites. Freeze in refrigerator tray. *Makes 1 quart.*

RAISIN ALMOND FLAVORING

½ cup raisins, chopped
⅓ cup toasted almonds, chopped
2 tablespoons cocoa

Make your favorite vanilla ice cream and add the cocoa with the sugar. After the freezing process and before hardening, fold in raisins, and almonds. Makes flavoring for 1 quart of vanilla ice cream.

RASPBERRY ICE CREAM No. 1

2 cups sugar
1½ envelopes gelatin
6 eggs, well beaten
3 cups half and half
1 quart cream
1 tablespoon vanilla
3 cups crushed raspberries,
    sweetened to taste

Combine sugar and gelatin. Stir in eggs and half and half. Cook in a double boiler until mixture thickens slightly. Cool. Stir in cream and vanilla; freeze. Add raspberries after the freezing process and before hardening, mixing just enough to blend well. *Makes 3 quarts.*

RASPBERRY ICE CREAM No. 2

2 eggs
1½ cups sugar
¼ teaspoon salt
¼ cup lemon juice
4 cups evaporated milk
2 10-ounce packages frozen raspberries
    few drops red food coloring,
    if desired

Beat eggs in a 2½-quart bowl. Add sugar, salt, and lemon juice and beat until well blended. Gradually beat in evaporated milk. Stir in raspberries and food coloring and beat until well blended. Freeze. *Makes about 1 gallon.*

RASPBERRY ICE CREAM No. 3

2 pints fresh raspberries
1 cup sugar
2 pints thin cream
    dash of salt

Wash and hull berries, chop, sprinkle with sugar, cover, and let stand 2 hours in warm place. Mash and strain. Stir in cream and salt. Freeze. *Makes 2 quarts.*

RASPBERRY FLAVORING

1 quart raspberries
½ cup sugar

Wash and hull berries, chop, sprinkle with sugar, cover, and let stand 30 minutes. Mash and strain. Add to 1 quart of vanilla ice cream after the freezing process and before hardening, mixing just enough to blend well.

RASPBERRY MALLOW ICE CREAM refrigerator

¼ pound marshmallows
2 cups fresh raspberries
⅓ cup sugar
⅛ teaspoon salt
1 cup cream, whipped
1 tablespoon lemon juice
rind of 1 lemon

Combine marshmallows, raspberries, sugar, and salt. Cook in a double boiler until the mixture is smooth and fluffy. Stir occasionally. Cool. Add lemon juice and lemon rind to the cooled mixture and fold in cream. Freeze. Stir occasionally until firm. *Makes 1½ quarts.*

RHUBARB ICE CREAM refrigerator

3 cups sliced rhubarb
¾ cup sugar
1 cup water
rind of 1 lemon
2 tablespoons lemon juice
⅛ teaspoon salt
2 egg whites
⅓ cup sugar
1¼ cups cream, whipped

Combine rhubarb, sugar, and water. Cook until tender; cool. Stir in lemon rind and lemon juice. Freeze until thickened. Whip egg whites until fluffy, add salt and sugar. Continue beating until thick. Blend into chilled rhubarb mixture, add cream, and freeze until firm. *Makes 2 quarts.*

ROCKY ROAD FLAVORING

2½ cups miniature marshmallows
1½ cups toasted almonds, chopped

Add marshmallows and almonds to 2 quarts of chocolate ice cream. Add after the freezing process and before hardening, mixing just enough to blend well.

RUM DATE FLAVORING

1 cup quartered pitted dates
½ cup coarsely chopped walnuts
8 candied red cherries, chopped
2 tablespoons dark rum

Combine dates, walnuts, cherries, and rum; let stand 1 hour. Add 1 quart of vanilla ice cream. Add the flavoring after the freezing process and before hardening, mixing just enough to blend well.

SNOW ICE CREAM

Fresh, clean snow
Lightly whipped cream, sweetened to taste
Fruit puree, sweetened
Vanilla (other flavoring may be substituted)

Set out a cookie sheet or bread board to collect freshly fallen snow. Be sure the snow is clean. (The first snow is not as clean as snow that has fallen for a day or overnight.) Arrange the snow in a chilled bowl. Do not compact it. Combine the flavoring or ingredients of your choice and pour over the snow. Serve immediately.

SPICED PRUNE ICE CREAM refrigerator

1 can evaporated milk
 (14½ ounces)
1 teaspoon granulated gelatin
1 tablespoon cold water
¼ teaspoon cinnamon
⅛ teaspoon nutmeg

> 1/8 teaspoon cloves
> dash of salt
> 2 cups cooked prunes
> 2 tablespoons brown sugar
> 1 teaspoon vanilla

Scald milk. Soften gelatin in cold water and dissolve in hot milk. Add spices, salt, mix well and chill. Remove pits from prunes and cut into pieces. Whip milk until stiff, add sugar, vanilla, and prunes, and mix thoroughly. Pour into tray of refrigerating unit and freeze until set. *Makes 1 quart.*

SPICY PRUNE ICE CREAM refrigerator

> 2 cups cooked prunes
> 2 cups milk
> 2/3 cup granulated sugar
> 1/4 teaspoon salt
> 1/4 teaspoon cloves
> 3 eggs
> 2 cups whipping cream
> 2 teaspoons vanilla extract

Cut prunes from pits into small pieces. Scald milk with sugar, salt and cloves. Beat eggs lightly and pour hot milk slowly into them, stirring to blend. Place over hot water and cook and stir until mixture coats spoon. Cool. Fold in whipped cream, prunes, and vanilla. Turn into refrigerator trays and place in freezing compartment with control set at lowest temperature. Freeze until barely firm. Reset temperature control to normal. *Makes about 1½ quarts.*

SPUMONI ICE CREAM refrigerator

> 1/2 cup marsala
> 12 egg yolks
> 3/4 cup sugar
> 2 tablespoons water
> 1 teaspoon almond extract
> 3 cups heavy cream

Combine all ingredients, except cream, in a double boiler. Cook beating constantly until the mixture is warm and begins to thicken.

Do not let water boil in the double boiler. Pour custard into a bowl and whip until thick and smooth. Stir in cream and freeze. When mushy, whip and refreeze. Serve with toasted almonds that have been chopped. *Makes 2 quarts.*

STRAWBERRY ICE CREAM No. 1

2 eggs
1½ cups sugar
¼ teaspoon salt
¼ cup lemon juice
4 cups evaporated milk
2 10-ounce packages frozen strawberries
few drops red food coloring,
if desired

Beat eggs in a 2½-quart bowl. Add sugar, salt, and lemon juice and beat until well blended. Gradually beat in evaporated milk. Stir in strawberries and food coloring and beat until well blended. Freeze. *Makes about 1 gallon.*

STRAWBERRY ICE CREAM No. 2

4 egg yolks, beaten
2 cups milk
1 cup sugar
dash of salt
2 cups heavy cream
2 cups sweetened crushed strawberries

Combine egg yolks, milk, sugar, and salt. Beat until creamy and cook in a double boiler until mixture coats a spoon. Cool. Add the cream and freeze. Stir in strawberries after the freezing process and before hardening, mixing just enough to blend well. *Makes 2 quarts.*

STRAWBERRY ICE CREAM No. 3

1 quart fresh strawberries, pureed
1 cup sugar
1 tablespoon lemon juice

rind of 1 lemon
dash of salt
1 tablespoon gelatin
2 tablespoons cold water
1 cup half and half
3 cups cream

Add sugar, lemon juice, lemon rind, and salt to the strawberries. Let stand at room temperature for 1 hour. Soften the gelatin in cold water. Heat half and half and dissolve the gelatin in it. Cool. Combine all ingredients and freeze. *Makes 2 quarts.*

STRAWBERRY ICE CREAM refrigerator No. 1

⅔ cup evaporated milk
1 10-ounce package frozen strawberries, thawed
¼ cup sugar
dash of salt
1 tablespoon lemon juice

Put the evaporated milk into ice tray of refrigerator. Chill until crystals begin to form around the edges. Meanwhile, mix strawberries, sugar and salt together. Let stand. Put ice cold milk into a cold quart bowl. Whip with cold rotary beater by hand, or with electric beater at high speed, until fluffy. Add lemon juice and beat until stiff. Add the strawberry mixture gradually, beating at low speed until well blended. Put into a 1-quart ice tray and freeze until firm without stirring. *Makes 1 quart.*

STRAWBERRY ICE CREAM refrigerator No. 2

⅔ cup sweetened condensed milk
½ cup water
1 cup crushed fresh strawberries
¼ cup sugar
1 cup heavy cream

Turn refrigerator temperature control to coldest setting. Combine sweetened condensed milk and water. Sweeten berries to taste. Stir into milk mixture. Chill in refrigerator. Whip cream to soft custard consistency. Fold into chilled mixture, and turn into ice cube tray. Freeze to firm mush, about 1 hour. Turn into chilled, medium sized bowl; break into pieces. Whip until fluffy but not melted. Quickly return to tray, cover tray and return to freezing unit. Freeze until firm. *Makes 1½ pints.*

STRAWBERRY ICE CREAM refrigerator No. 3

1 cup sugar
½ cup water
2 pints fresh strawberries
⅓ cup orange juice
2 tablespoons lemon juice
1 cup heavy cream, whipped

In saucepan, combine sugar and water; boil 5 minutes; cool. Puree strawberries in electric blender or force through sieve. Combine puree, orange and lemon juices with sugar syrup; fold in whipped cream and pour into refrigerator trays; freeze until firm. *Makes 1 quart.*

STRAWBERRY ICE CREAM FRENCH STYLE

8 egg yolks, beaten
8 egg whites, stiffly beaten
¼ teaspoon salt
1 quart half and half
1 teaspoon vanilla
rind of 1 lemon
1 tablespoon lemon juice
3 cups strawberries, crushed
and sweetened to taste
(about 1½ cups sugar)

Combine yolks, whites, salt, and half and half. Beat until well blended. Stir in vanilla, lemon rind, and lemon juice. Mix until thoroughly blended and stir in strawberries. Freeze. *Makes 1½ quarts.*

STRAWBERRY FLAVORING

1 quart strawberries
½ cup sugar

Mash strawberries and stir in sugar. Let stand 1 hour and strain. Add to 1 quart of vanilla ice cream after the freezing process and before hardening, mixing just enough to blend well.

STRAWBERRY GELATO ICE CREAM refrigerator

> 2 envelopes unflavored gelatin
> ½ cup cold water
> 2 cups instant nonfat dry milk crystals
> 1 quart whole milk
> 2 cups sugar
> 1 pint fresh strawberries
>   if desired, few drops red food coloring

Sprinkle gelatin over water to soften. Stir instant crystals into whole milk; blend in softened gelatin and sugar. Stir over low heat until gelatin dissolves. Cool. Meanwhile, blend strawberries in electric blender or force through food mill. Sieve the strawberry puree, then stir into gelatin mixture along with food coloring. Turn into refrigerator trays and freeze until firm, then beat until smooth. Serve with additional strawberries, if desired. *Makes 1 quart.*

TOASTED ALMOND FLAVORING

> ½ cup toasted slivered almonds

Roast the almonds in an oven at 350° F. Stir frequently until golden brown. Stir the almonds into 1 pint of vanilla ice cream. Add almonds after the freezing process and before hardening, mixing just enough to blend well.

TOFFEE FLAVORING

> ¾ cup butter, melted
> 1½ cups firmly packed brown sugar
>   dash of salt
> 1 teaspoon cider vinegar
> 2 tablespoons water
> ½ pound milk chocolate, melted
> 1 cup pecans, chopped

Combine the butter, sugar, salt, vinegar, and water. Cook in a heavy skillet until candy thermometer reaches 300° F. Pour into a buttered cookie sheet. Spread the melted chocolate on the hot toffee and cover with pecans. When firm, turn the toffee over and add remaining melted chocolate and pecans. Chill until hard. When hardened, crush into small pieces. Add 1½ cups of toffee to 2 quarts of vanilla ice cream.

TOFFEE BUTTERSCOTCH ICE CREAM refrigerator

    1 package butterscotch pudding mix,
      (not instant)
 1½ cups half and half
 1½ cups strong coffee
    ½ cup light corn syrup
    1 teaspoon vanilla
    1 cup cream, whipped
    ¾ cup chopped nuts

Combine pudding mix, half and half, and coffee. Cook until thickened. Add corn syrup and vanilla. Cool. Freeze until partly set and whip until smooth. Fold in cream and nuts. Freeze until firm. *Makes 1 quart.*

TOFFEE 'N CREAM FLAVORING

    1 cup cream, whipped
    1 cup toffee, crushed

Fold crushed toffee into whipped cream. Chill in refrigerator for 1½ hours. Fold or revel this mixture into 1 quart of softened vanilla ice cream. Add after the freezing process and before hardening, mixing just enough to blend well.

TOM AND JERRY FLAVORING

    2 tablespoons rum
    1 tablespoon brandy

Add rum and brandy to 1 quart of vanilla ice cream after the freezing process and before hardening, mixing just enough to blend well.

TORTONI FLAVORING

½ cup angel flake coconut, toasted
½ cup candied fruit, chopped
1 teaspoon pure almond extract

Stir coconut, candied fruit, and almond extract into 1 quart of softened vanilla ice cream. Add after the freezing process and before hardening, mixing just enough to blend well.

VANILLA BEAN ICE CREAM

1¼ cups granulated sugar
¼ teaspoon cream of tartar
¾ cup water
5 egg yolks, beaten
3 cups cream, whipped
1 vanilla bean
(scrape out the seeds)

Combine sugar, cream of tartar, and water. Let boil until the syrup will spin a thread. Pour the hot syrup over the beaten egg yolks. Beat until the mixture is cool. Stir in the cream and vanilla seeds. Mix thoroughly and freeze. *Makes 2 quarts.*

VANILLA ICE CREAM No. 1

2 cups sugar
¼ cup cornstarch
¼ teaspoon salt
4 cups milk
4 eggs, beaten
2 tablespoons vanilla
4 cups cream

Mix sugar, cornstarch, and salt in the top of a double boiler. Blend in milk gradually. Cook over hot water, stirring occasionally until thickened, 12 to 15 minutes. Stir a small amount of the hot cornstarch mixture into the beaten eggs; then stir the eggs into the remaining cornstarch mixture. Cook over hot water, stirring constantly 4 to 5 minutes longer, or until the mixture is about the consistency of pudding. Chill thoroughly. This step is essential for a smooth ice cream. Stir in vanilla and cream. Freeze. *Makes about 1 gallon.*

VANILLA ICE CREAM No. 2

⅓ cup corn syrup
2 tablespoons cornstarch
¾ cup sugar
½ teaspoon salt
3 cups milk
2 eggs, beaten slightly
2 teaspoons vanilla
1 cup light cream

Combine corn syrup, cornstarch, sugar, salt and milk in top of double boiler. Mix in eggs. Cook over boiling water, stirring constantly until mixture is slightly thickened, about 5 minutes. Chill. Add vanilla and light cream. With electric freezer, or crank freezer, freeze until thick. Pack in containers and freeze until firm. *Makes 2 quarts.*

VANILLA ICE CREAM No. 3

1 quart milk
1 cup heavy cream
1 cup sugar
1 to 2 teaspoons vanilla
dash of salt
2 junket tablets
2 tablespoons cold water

Dissolve junket tablets in cold water, mix milk, cream, sugar, salt, and vanilla. Heat to lukewarm. Add junket tablets, mix well and pour immediately into can which has dasher in place. Let stand at least 10 minutes to set and then freeze. *Makes 2 quarts.*

VANILLA ICE CREAM No. 4

1½ quarts milk
4 eggs
2⅓ cups sugar

       1 quart cream
       1½ tablespoons pure vanilla extract
       ½ teaspoon salt

Combine the sugar, salt, and eggs. Add the milk and beat thoroughly. Cook in a double boiler until the mixture coats a spoon. Cool. Stir in the remaining ingredients and freeze. *Makes 1 gallon.*

VANILLA ICE CREAM No. 5

       1 cup milk
       1 tablespoon cornstarch
       ½ cup sugar
       dash of salt
       2 eggs
       2 cups cream
       2 teaspoons pure vanilla extract

Combine the cornstarch, sugar, and salt. Mix thoroughly. Beat in the eggs and then add the milk. Cook in a double boiler until the mixture is smooth. Cool. Stir in remaining ingredients and freeze. *Makes 1 quart.*

VANILLA ICE CREAM No. 6

       2 tablespoons gelatin
       ¼ cup water
       3 cups sugar
       1 quart milk
       4 egg yolks, beaten
       4 egg whites, stiffly beaten
       1 quart cream
       2 teaspoons vanilla

Soften gelatin in water. Heat milk, add sugar and egg yolks. Cook in a double boiler until the custard is thickened. Fold in cream, egg whites and vanilla. Freeze. *Makes 3 quarts.*

VANILLA ICE CREAM No. 7

       3 cups sugar
       1 tablespoon flour

5 eggs
1 quart milk
1 quart cream
1 large can evaporated milk
1 tablespoon pure vanilla extract

Combine sugar and flour, mix thoroughly. Add eggs one at a time and beat until thick and creamy. Continue beating and add cream, milk, and vanilla extract. Freeze. *Makes 3 quarts.*

VANILLA ICE CREAM No. 8

9 eggs
3 cups sugar
¼ teaspoon salt
1½ quarts cream
1½ quarts milk
8 teaspoons pure vanilla extract

Beat eggs until creamy. Add sugar, and salt. Beat until thick. Stir in cream, milk, and vanilla extract. Freeze. *Makes 1 gallon.*

VANILLA ICE CREAM No. 9

3 cups thin cream
1 tablespoon gelatin
¼ cup cold water
1 cup hot milk
¾ cup sugar
dash of salt
1 to 2 teaspoons vanilla

Soften gelatin in cold water. Dissolve gelatin in hot milk and combine remaining ingredients. Freeze. *Makes 1½ quarts.*

VANILLA ICE CREAM refrigerator No. 1

⅔ cup sweetened condensed milk
½ cup water
1½ teaspoons vanilla extract
1 cup heavy cream

Turn refrigerator temperature control to coldest setting. Combine sweetened condensed milk, water, and vanilla extract. Chill in refrigerator. Whip cream to soft custard consistency. Fold into chilled mixture. Turn into ice cube tray and freeze to firm mush, about 1 hour. Turn into chilled bowl; break into pieces. Whip until fluffy but not melted. Quickly return to tray, cover tray and return to freezing unit. Freeze until firm. *Makes 1½ pints.*

VANILLA ICE CREAM refrigerator No. 2

2 eggs
⅓ cup sugar
⅔ cup corn syrup
1 cup heavy cream
1½ cups milk
1½ teaspoons vanilla

Beat eggs in large bowl until foamy. Gradually add sugar, then corn syrup, beating until mixture is thick. Stir in cream, milk and vanilla. Turn into freezing tray. Freeze until almost firm, about 1 hour. Turn into a chilled bowl; cut apart and beat until smooth. Return to tray and freeze until firm. *Makes 1 quart.*

VANILLA ICE CREAM COUNTRY STYLE

6 eggs, well beaten
1¼ cups sugar
¼ teaspoon salt
2 cups heavy cream
2 cups extra rich milk
2 tablespoons pure vanilla extract

Beat eggs, sugar, and salt until thick. Slowly stir in cream, milk, and vanilla. Blend well. Freeze. *Makes 2 quarts.*

VANILLA ICE CREAM FRENCH STYLE No. 1

1 cup sugar
½ cup water
6 beaten egg yolks
1 vanilla bean

(scrape out seeds)
7 cups thick cream

Combine sugar and water. Cook until the syrup spins a thread. Slowly pour over the beaten yolks and continue beating until very stiff. Add the vanilla seeds, and cream. Freeze. *Makes 2 quarts.*

VANILLA ICE CREAM FRENCH STYLE No. 2

2 cups milk
3 egg yolks, slightly beaten
½ cup sugar
⅛ teaspoon salt
1 cup cream
2 teaspoons vanilla

Mix sugar, salt, and egg yolks. Pour in milk. Cook in double boiler until mixture coats spoon. Cool, strain, add cream and vanilla, and freeze. *Makes 1¼ quarts.*

VANILLA ICE CREAM PHILADELPHIA STYLE

1 quart half and half
¾ cup sugar
¼ teaspoon salt
2 teaspoons pure vanilla extract

Heat 1½ cups half and half. Stir in sugar and salt and stir until completely dissolved. When cool, stir in vanilla extract and remaining half and half. Freeze. *Makes 1½ quarts.*

VANILLA CUSTARD ICE CREAM No. 1

4 eggs, beaten
2½ cups sugar
3 cups milk
1 quart heavy cream
1 quart half and half
1 vanilla bean or
2 tablespoons pure vanilla extract
¼ teaspoon salt
rind of ½ lemon

Combine eggs, sugar, and milk. Cook over low heat until thick, stirring constantly. Cool. Add remaining ingredients and blend thoroughly. Freeze. *Makes 1 gallon.*

VANILLA CUSTARD ICE CREAM No. 2

2 cups milk
1 tablespoon flour
1 cup sugar
1 egg or 2 egg yolks, slightly beaten
⅛ teaspoon salt
1 to 2 teaspoons vanilla
2 cups half and half

Mix flour, sugar and salt, add egg slightly beaten, and milk gradually; cook over hot water 10 minutes, stirring constantly. If custard should have a curdled appearance, it will disappear in freezing. When cool, add cream and flavoring. Freeze. *Makes 1½ quarts.*

VANILLA ICE MILK

2 cups sugar
¼ cup cornstarch
¼ teaspoon salt
2 quarts skim milk
3 eggs, beaten
1 tablespoon gelatin
1½ tablespoons vanilla

Mix sugar, cornstarch, and salt in the top of a double boiler. Blend in 4 cups skim milk gradually. Cook over hot water, stirring occasionally until thickened, 12 to 15 minutes. Stir a little of the hot cornstarch mixture into the beaten eggs; then stir the eggs into the remaining cornstarch mixture. Cook over hot water, stirring constantly 4 to 5 minutes longer, or until the mixture is about the consistency of soft custard. Soften gelatin in 1 cup skim milk. Stir in hot mixture. Chill thoroughly. This step is essential for a smooth ice milk. Stir in vanilla and remaining 3 cups skim milk. Pour into ice-cream freezer. Freeze. *Makes 1 gallon.*

VANILLA MALLOW ICE CREAM

1 cup half and half
24 large marshmallows
2 teaspoons pure vanilla extract
1 cup cream, whipped

Combine half and half and marshmallows in a double boiler. Cook until the marshmallows are almost melted. Remove from heat and stir in vanilla. Cool. Fold in whipped cream. Blend thoroughly. Freeze. *Makes 1 quart.*

WALNUT BUTTER CRUNCH FLAVORING

½ cup crisp rice cereal
¼ cup walnuts
1½ tablespoons brown sugar
2 tablespoons butter

Melt butter in a skillet. Add remaining ingredients. Cool. Add to 1 pint of vanilla ice cream. Add after the freezing process and before hardening, mixing just enough to blend well.

3.

SHERBET

Sherbet is a frozen dessert made with cream or milk that has been added to sweetened fruit juice or puree. These desserts can be frozen in a crank-type or electric freezer, or in a refrigerator tray.

Gelatin and egg whites are used as a stabilizer in making sherbets. The egg whites are usually beaten into the mixture after it is partly frozen. The sugar content of sherbet is almost double that of ice cream. In making good sherbet avoid using too much sugar. An excess of sugar results in a soft dessert, and not enough sugar results in a hard, crumbly product. If sherbets are too sweet they will not freeze at all. One part sugar to four parts of liquid is about right. Liqueurs and wines should be stirred in after the dessert is frozen.

If a sherbet refuses to harden, there may be too much acid fruit or sugar in the mixture. To stiffen a mushy dessert, stir in beaten egg whites and continue freezing. Sherbets freeze well in refrigerator trays or deep freezers. Or you may use your crank-type or electric freezer. When the mixture is partly frozen in a refrigerator tray, spoon it into a chilled bowl and beat until blended. This procedure may be repeated two or three times more, at half-hour intervals, before you freeze until firm. For further information see Chapter 1.

Sherbets may be served plain or in a bombe or mold surrounded by fruit. Orange sections, fresh pineapple, and other acid fruits are delicious with sherbet. Or garnish individual servings with chopped nuts, rum, liqueurs, preserved or candied fruit, or a sauce or topping of your preference. If you decorate with whipped cream do not use too much—a dab will do.

Remove sherbet from the freezer to refrigerator about 20 minutes before serving. Do not serve when it is frozen hard. Remember, sherbet may be appropriately served with the meat course, as well as for dessert.

APPLESAUCE SHERBET

2 cups buttermilk
2 cups applesauce
1 cup sugar
  juice of 1 large lemon
  rind of 1 large lemon

Combine all ingredients and freeze until firm. It is not necessary to stir this sherbet during the freezing process. *Makes 1 quart.*

AVOCADO SHERBET

¾ cup lemon juice
¾ cup orange juice
2 cups sugar
  rind of 2 lemons
1½ cups mashed avocado
3 cups heavy cream, lightly whipped

Combine all ingredients, except cream, blending until sugar is completely dissolved. Pour into small cake pan or ice cube trays and freeze until mushy but not firm. Remove from freezer and turn out into a chilled bowl. Whip for about 1 minute. Fold in the lightly whipped cream and whip again for 1 minute. Refreeze until firm. *Makes 1½ quarts.*

AVOCADO CRANBERRY SHERBET

4 cups fresh cranberries
¾ cup water for cranberries
1 cup sugar
½ tablespoon plain gelatin
1 cup water
2 tablespoons fresh lime or lemon juice
1½ cups finely diced avocado

Cook cranberries in ¾ cup of water; add sugar when berries are soft and stir until it is dissolved. Strain berries through a coarse sieve. Soften gelatin in ¼ cup cold water and dissolve in hot cranberry puree. Add lime juice and remaining 1 cup water. Pour into refrigerator tray. Place in freezing compartment with control set at lowest temperature and freeze. Cut avocado into halves lengthwise and remove seed and skin. Dice fruit fine. Stir sherbet twice during freezing process, adding avocado when sherbet is almost firm. *Makes 1 quart.*

AVOCADO 'N JUICE SHERBET

1½ cups mashed ripe avocado
½ cup lemon juice
⅔ cup orange juice
½ cup pineapple juice
rind of 2 lemons
1¼ cups sugar
1 cup half and half
¼ teaspoon salt
⅛ teaspoon almond extract

Mix fruit juices and mashed avocado. Add remaining ingredients and beat until thoroughly blended. A few drops of green food coloring will enhance the color. Freeze. *Makes 1½ quarts.*

BANANA SHERBET

1 teaspoon gelatin
1 cup water
1 cup sugar
2 tablespoons lemon juice
½ cup orange juice
3 medium sized bananas, mashed
2 egg whites, stiffly beaten

Soften gelatin in ¼ cup water. Boil remaining water and sugar until dissolved. Stir in gelatin. Cool. Add fruit juice and bananas. Freeze until mushy. Blend in egg whites. Freeze until firm and beat until fluffy. Refreeze. *Makes 1 quart.*

BANANA CRANBERRY SHERBET

       1 pound cranberries
     2¾ cups water
     2½ cups sugar
       ½ teaspoon salt
       2 ripe bananas, mashed
         juice of 2 lemons
         juice of 3 oranges
         rind of lemon

Boil cranberries in water until soft. Strain and add sugar. Cool.
Add remaining ingredients and freeze. *Makes 1½ quarts.*

BANANA PINEAPPLE SHERBET

       ¾ cup sugar
     1½ cups crushed pineapple
       3 large bananas, crushed
       ½ cup orange juice plus 2 tablespoons
       ¼ cup lemon juice
       2 egg whites, stiffly beaten

Combine sugar and crushed pineapple. Stir until dissolved. Stir in
bananas, orange juice, lemon juice, and blend thoroughly. Freeze
until mushy. Beat sherbet and egg whites until light and fluffy.
Refreeze. *Makes 1 quart.*

BERRY SHERBET

     1½ cups fresh strawberries or
         raspberries
       ⅓ cup sifted confectioner's sugar
       ⅔ cup sweetened condensed milk
       2 tablespoons lemon juice
       2 egg whites (at room temperature)

Turn refrigerator temperature control to coldest setting. Mash
berries and force through a sieve. Stir in sugar. In a medium sized
bowl, combine sweetened condensed milk and lemon juice. Fold in

berry puree. Chill in refrigerator. Whip egg whites until stiff but not dry. Fold into chilled mixture. Turn mixture into ice cube tray. Freeze to a firm mush, about 1 hour. Turn into chilled, medium sized bowl; break into pieces. Whip until fluffy but not melted. Quickly return to tray, cover tray and return to freezing unit. Freeze until firm. *Makes about 1½ pints.*

BLACK CHERRY SHERBET

1 3-ounce package black cherry
  dessert gelatin
⅛ teaspoon salt
½ cup sugar
1 cup boiling water
2 cups half and half

Dissolve dessert gelatin, salt, and sugar in boiling water. Chill until slightly thickened. Add half and half and beat until fluffy. Freeze. *Makes 1½ pints.*

BUTTERMILK SHERBET

1 cup sugar
2 cups fresh buttermilk
1 cup canned crushed pineapple
2 tablespoons lemon juice
1 tablespoon gelatin
¼ cup cold water
¾ cup hot water
  dash of salt

Combine sugar, salt and buttermilk. Soften gelatin in ¼ cup cold water, then dissolve in ¾ cup hot water. Add to buttermilk mixture. Stir until thoroughly dissolved. Add pineapple and lemon juice to mixture, mixing well. Pour into freezer. Freeze until firm. *Makes 1½ quarts.*

BUTTERMILK LEMON SHERBET

2 eggs
½ cup sugar

¾ cup light corn syrup
2 cups buttermilk
½ cup lemon juice
1 tablespoon grated lemon rind

Beat eggs until foamy; gradually beat in sugar, then corn syrup. Continue beating until mixture is thick. Fold in remaining ingredients. Turn mixture into refrigerator tray. Freeze with cold control set for fast freezing until mixture is almost firm. Turn into chilled bowl and beat with rotary beater or electric mixer until smooth. Return to tray and freeze until firm, about three hours. *Makes 1 quart.*

CHAMPAGNE SHERBET

1¼ cups sugar
1 cup water
1¾ cups champagne
3 tablespoons lemon juice
¼ teaspoon cream of tartar
2 egg whites, stiffly beaten
3 tablespoons sugar
½ teaspoon vanilla

Boil sugar and water for 5 minutes. Cool. Stir in champagne and lemon juice. Freeze until mushy. Add cream of tartar, sugar, and vanilla to eggs. Stir the sherbet into the egg whites and beat until fluffy. Freeze. Additional champagne may be added over each serving. *Makes 1½ pints.*

CIDER SHERBET

1 tablespoon gelatin
2 tablespoons cold water
1¼ cups cider
¼ cup sugar
¼ cup lemon juice
1 egg white

Soften gelatin in cold water. Heat cider and sugar to boiling point and stir in the gelatin. Add lemon juice. Pour into freezing tray. Cool. Place tray in freezing unit until mixture is chilled and thickened. Remove to a chilled bowl and whip until frothy. Fold in stiffly beaten egg white. Return to refrigerator tray and freeze. Stir 3 or 4 times during first hour of freezing. *Makes 1½ pints.*

COCONUT MILK SHERBET

        1 teaspoon gelatin
     2½ cups coconut milk
        ½ cup light corn syrup
        2 egg whites, stiffly beaten
        ½ cup sugar
        ¼ teaspoon vanilla

Soften gelatin in ¾ cup coconut milk. Stir in sugar and cook in a double boiler until dissolved. Cool. Add remaining milk and freeze until mushy. Stir the syrup into the egg whites and beat until stiff. Fold in coconut mixture and vanilla and freeze. *Makes 1 quart.*

CONCORD GRAPE SHERBET

        2 cups sour cream
        2 cups milk
        3 cups sugar
        2 eggs beaten
        2 cups 100% pure concord grape juice
           juice of 1 lemon
           rind of 1 lemon

Combine all ingredients and blend until the sugar has dissolved. Pour into a large cake pan or individual freezer trays and place in freezer. Stir periodically during the freezing process. This sherbet is very smooth and creamy. Men are particularly fond of this flavor. *Makes ½ gallon.*

CRANBERRY SHERBET

     1¾ cups sugar
        1 cup water
        1 quart fresh cranberries
     1¾ cups water

2 teaspoons gelatin
¼ cup water
  rind of 1 lemon
2 egg whites, stiffly beaten

Combine sugar and water and boil for 5 minutes. Cool. Boil cranberries in 1¾ cups water until soft. In the meantime, soften gelatin in ¼ cup water and add to the warm cranberry juice. Stir in lemon rind. When cool combine all ingredients and freeze until mushy. Stir in beaten egg whites, beat until fluffy. Refreeze. *Makes 1 quart.*

CRANBERRY APPLE SHERBET

2 cups cranberries
1 cup water
1 cup apple sauce
1 cup sugar
2 tablespoons lemon juice
2 tablespoons orange juice
⅔ cup cream, whipped

Combine cranberries, water and sugar. Cook until tender. Puree the cranberries. Cool. Stir in the remaining ingredients and freeze until firm. *Makes 1 quart.*

CRANAPPLE SHERBET

2 cups cranberries
2 cups diced apples
2½ cups water
2½ cups sugar
¼ cup cold water
1 tablespoon gelatin
5 tablespoons lemon juice
  rind of 1 lemon

Combine cranberries, apples, water and sugar. Cook until tender. Strain and puree. Reserve the juice. Soften gelatin in cold water. Dissolve over hot water. Combine all ingredients. Cool. Freeze until firm. *Makes 1 quart.*

CREAMY LEMON SHERBET

1 envelope unflavored gelatin
2 cups milk
1 cup sugar
2 teaspoons grated lemon peel
⅔ cup freshly squeezed lemon juice
⅛ teaspoon salt
2 egg whites

Soften gelatin in ½ cup cold milk. In saucepan, scald remaining milk and sugar; add gelatin, stirring until dissolved. Chill until cool; slowly stir in lemon peel and juice and salt. Pour into ice cube trays or shallow pan; freeze until crystals form and mixture is very thick. Stir occasionally. Combine with egg whites in chilled large mixer bowl; beat at high speed until very light and foamy. Scrape beaters to remove any bits of clinging peel. Return to trays; freeze until firm. *Makes 1 quart.*

CREME de MENTHE SHERBET

1½ cups sugar
¾ cup lemon juice
¼ teaspoon salt
3 cups milk
4 teaspoons gelatin
2 tablespoons cold water
1 cup creme de menthe
2 egg whites, stiffly beaten

Combine sugar, lemon juice, and salt. Stir until well blended. Warm the milk and add to the sugar mixture. Soften gelatin in cold water and add to warm milk mixture. Stir until dissolved. Add creme de menthe and freeze for 1 hour. Pour mixture into bowl and beat until fluffy. Fold in egg whites and freeze until firm, stirring occasionally. Milk may curdle when mixed with lemon juice. This will not affect the flavor or consistency of the sherbet. *Makes 1½ quarts.*

FRUIT SHERBET

1 cup water
¼ cup sugar
1 tablespoon gelatin

2 cups fruit puree
dash of salt
½ to ¾ cup sugar
2 tablespoons lemon juice
rind of 1 lemon

Combine water, sugar, and gelatin. Cook over low heat until the gelatin dissolves. Combine remaining ingredients and freeze in refrigerator trays. *Makes 1 quart.*

FRUIT JUICE SHERBET

1 envelope gelatin
1 cup sugar
⅛ teaspoon salt
1¾ cups boiling water
1 cup fruit juice, any flavor
except pineapple
¼ cup lemon juice

Combine gelatin, sugar and salt. Stir in boiling water and blend until dissolved. Add juices. Freeze until mushy. Beat well and freeze again. *Makes 1½ pints.*

GINGER LEMON SHERBET

1½ cups sugar
1½ quarts extra rich milk
6 tablespoons finely chopped
candied ginger
2½ tablespoons lime juice
½ cup lemon juice
rind of 5 lemons

Combine sugar, ginger, lime juice, lemon juice, and rind. Mix thoroughly and slowly stir in milk. The milk may curdle but it will have no affect on the final texture of the dessert. Freeze. *Makes 1½ pints.*

GRAPEFRUIT SHERBET

1 cup sugar
1 cup water
2 teaspoons gelatin

½ cup water
4 tablespoons lemon juice
1¾ cups fresh grapefruit juice
½ cup orange juice
⅛ teaspoon salt
rind of 1 lemon
2 egg whites, stiffly beaten

Boil sugar and water for 8 minutes. Soften gelatin in water. Add to the hot syrup. Cool. Freeze until mushy. Add juices, salt, and lemon rind. Fold in egg whites. Blend thoroughly and freeze. *Makes 1 quart.*

GUAVA SHERBET

1 teaspoon gelatin
1 cup guava juice, unsweetened
½ cup sugar
1½ cups guava puree
dash of salt
½ cup light syrup
2 egg whites, stiffly beaten

Soften gelatin in ¼ cup guava juice. Add remaining guava juice and sugar. Cook in a double boiler and stir until dissolved. Cool. Add puree and salt. A few drops of red food coloring will enhance the color. Freeze until mushy. Beat the syrup into the egg whites. Combine this with the guava mixture. Freeze. *Makes 1 quart.*

LEMON SHERBET No. 1

2 eggs
½ cup sugar
¾ cup corn syrup
2 cups buttermilk
½ cup lemon juice
1 tablespoon grated lemon rind

Beat eggs in large bowl until foamy. Gradually beat in sugar, then syrup, beating until mixture is thick. Stir in buttermilk, lemon juice and grated lemon peel. Turn into freezing tray. Freeze until almost firm, about 1 hour. Turn into a chilled bowl; cut apart and beat until smooth. Return to tray and freeze until firm, about 3 hours. *Makes 1 quart.*

LEMON SHERBET No. 2

2 cups sour cream
4 cups milk
3 cups sugar
2 eggs beaten
¾ cup fresh lemon juice
   unstrained
   rind of 4 lemons

Combine all ingredients and blend until the sugar has dissolved. Pour into a cake pan or refrigerator trays. Freeze until firm. Stir periodically during the freezing process. *Makes ½ gallon.*

LEMON SHERBET No. 3

1½ cups sugar
2 cups water
⅓ cup lemon juice
   rind of 4 lemons
   dash of salt
1 egg white, stiffly beaten

Combine sugar and water. Boil 5 minutes. Cool. Stir in lemon juice, rind, and salt. Freeze until partly set. Beat well and fold in egg white. Refreeze. *Makes 1 quart.*

LEMON SHERBET No. 4

1½ cups frozen lemonade concentrate
    (2 6-ounce cans)
1¾ cups sugar
¼ teaspoon salt
2 tablespoons grated lemon rind
6 cups evaporated milk

Beat together lemonade, sugar, salt, and lemon rind. Slowly stir in evaporated milk. Freeze. *Makes about 1 gallon.*

LEMON MILK SHERBET

2 teaspoons gelatin
2⅔ cups rich milk or top milk

> or half milk and cream
> ⅔ cup sugar
> ½ cup light corn syrup
> ½ cup lemon juice
> ⅛ teaspoon salt

Soften gelatin in ½ cup of the milk. Place dish over hot water and stir until the gelatin is dissolved. Add the remaining milk and cool. Combine the sugar, corn syrup, lemon juice, and salt. Add the mixture gradually to the milk, stirring constantly. Pour the mixture into refrigerator tray and place it in freezer unit. Set at coldest point. Wet the bottom of the tray to hasten freezing. When the frozen mixture is firm, after about 20 minutes, remove it to a chilled bowl and break it up with a fork. Beat it with a rotary beater until light and fluffy and return it to the tray. Again wet the bottom of the tray and return it to the freezer unit. When the sherbet is of serving thickness, after about ½ hour, turn the control to normal refrigerator temperature and hold the sherbet until time to serve, from one to three hours. *Makes 1 quart.*

LIME SHERBET

> ⅔ cup sugar
> 1¾ cups water
> ¼ cup water
> 1½ teaspoons gelatin
> ½ cup fresh lime juice
> rind of 1 lemon
> 2 egg whites, stiffly beaten

Boil sugar and 1¾ cups of water for 8 minutes. Soften gelatin in ¼ cup water. Add to the hot sugar and water mixture. Cool. Freeze until mushy. Add lime juice and lemon rind. A few drops of green food coloring will enhance the color of the sherbet. Stir in the egg whites. Freeze. *Makes 1 quart.*

LYCHEE SHERBET

> 1 tablespoon gelatin
> ¼ cup cold water
> 1 cup extra rich milk
> ⅔ cup half and half
> 1 teaspoon lemon juice

1 cup lychee juice
1½ cups sugar

Soften gelatin in cold water. Heat milk and stir in gelatin, and sugar. Mix until dissolved. Cool. Combine remaining ingredients and freeze. *Makes 1 quart.*

MANGO SHERBET

3 cups sliced mango
¾ cup water
2½ cups sugar
¾ cup water
½ cup lemon juice
3 cups milk
1 egg white

Cook mangos in water until soft. Puree and cool. Combine sugar and ¾ cup water and heat. Stir until dissolved. Cool syrup, combine remaining ingredients and freeze. *Makes 2 quarts.*

MIXED FRUIT SHERBET

1 fresh pineapple, cut in chunks
½ cup orange juice concentrate
2 ripe bananas, crushed
rind of 1 lemon
½ cup sugar
½ cup cream

Combine all ingredients. Blend in an electric blender until smooth. Freeze. *Makes 1 quart.*

MULBERRY SHERBET

1 cup mulberry juice
24 marshmallows
¼ cup orange juice
2 tablespoons lemon juice
2 egg whites, stiffly beaten
2 tablespoons sugar

Cook mulberry juice and marshmallows in a double boiler until dissolved. Cool. Add juices and freeze until mushy. Beat sugar into egg whites. Beat in mulberry mixture. Freeze. *Makes 1 quart.*

ORANGE SHERBET No. 1

1 cup evaporated milk
1 tablespoon grated orange rind
⅓ cup orange juice
1 tablespoon lemon juice
½ cup sugar
⅛ teaspoon salt

Put evaporated milk into refrigerator tray. Chill until ice crystals begin to form around edges. Put ice cold milk into a cold 1 or 2-quart bowl. Whip with cold rotary beater by hand, or with electric beater at high speed, until fluffy. Gradually add orange rind, orange juice, lemon juice, sugar, and salt. Whip until stiff. Put into a 1-quart ice tray and freeze, without stirring, at coldest temperature until firm. *Makes 1 quart.*

ORANGE SHERBET No. 2

2 cups sour cream
1 quart milk
3 cups sugar
2 eggs, beaten
1 large can orange concentrate
rind of 4 oranges

Combine all ingredients and blend until the sugar has dissolved. Pour into a container and place in freezer. Stir periodically during the freezing process. *Makes ½ gallon.*

ORANGE GINGER SHERBET

1 3-ounce package orange
    gelatin dessert
    dash of salt
½ cup sugar
1 cup warm ginger ale

1 cup cold orange juice
1 cup cold ginger ale

Dissolve gelatin dessert, salt and sugar in warm ginger ale. Chill. Add cold orange juice, and ginger ale. Freeze until partly set. Beat until fluffy and refreeze until firm. *Makes 1 quart.*

ORANGE PINEAPPLE SHERBET

1 3-ounce package orange-
    pineapple gelatin dessert
    dash of salt
½ cup sugar
1 cup boiling water
2 cups pineapple juice

Dissolve gelatin dessert, salt, and sugar in boiling water. Chill until slightly thickened. Add pineapple juice and blend thoroughly. Freeze until partly set. Beat until fluffy and refreeze until firm. *Makes 1 quart.*

PACIFIC DOUBLE DIP SHERBET

1½ cups sugar
¼ cup freshly squeezed lemon juice,
    unstrained
¼ cup freshly squeezed orange juice,
    unstrained
1 can (1 pound, 1 ounce) peeled
    apricots, drained
1 can (13-ounce) evaporated milk,
    very cold
⅛ teaspoon salt

Heat mixture of sugar and citrus juices in saucepan, stirring constantly, until sugar dissolves; do not boil. Press apricots through a fine sieve or whirl in a covered electric blender to yield 1 cup apricot puree. Combine puree with hot mixture; chill until cool. Beat chilled evaporated milk in small mixer bowl until slightly fluffy and it begins to hold its shape. Stir in salt, then carefully fold into cooled apricot mixture. Pour into ice cube trays or shallow pan; freeze until firm. *Makes 2 quarts.*

PAPAYA SHERBET

  1½ cups papaya puree
  3 tablespoons lemon juice
  ½ cup orange juice
  rind of 1 lemon
  1½ cups milk
  1 cup sugar

Combine all ingredients and blend until sugar is dissolved. Freeze. *Makes 1 quart.*

PASSION FRUIT SHERBET No. 1

  1 teaspoon gelatin
  2 cups water
  ½ cup sugar
  dash of salt
  1 cup passion-fruit juice
  ⅓ cup light corn syrup
  2 egg whites, stiffly beaten

Soften gelatin in ½ cup water. Combine remaining water, sugar, and salt. Heat until dissolved. Cool. Add passion fruit juice and gelatin that has been dissolved over hot water. Freeze until mushy. Whip syrup into egg whites and blend into the passion-fruit mixture. Freeze until firm. *Makes 1 quart.*

PASSION FRUIT SHERBET No. 2

  4 egg yolks
  1 cup sugar
  2 cups half and half
  dash of salt
  1½ cups passion-fruit juice
  2 tablespoons lemon juice
  ¼ cup sugar
  4 egg whites, stiffly beaten

Cook egg yolks, sugar, cream, and salt in a double boiler until the mixture coats a spoon. Cool. Add fruit juice and freeze until mushy. Beat sugar into egg whites and fold into the passion-fruit mixture. Beat once during freezing process. *Makes 1½ quarts.*

PEACH SHERBET

4 cups diced fresh peeled peaches
1 cup sifted confectioner's sugar
1⅓ cups sweetened condensed milk
¼ cup lemon juice
4 eggs separated

Combine diced peaches and sugar. With fork, toss lightly to thoroughly coat peaches. In large bowl, combine sweetened condensed milk, lemon juice and egg yolks. Blend thoroughly. Stir in peaches. Beat egg whites until stiff but not dry. Fold into peach mixture. Freeze 1½ to 2 hours, or until mixture has firm mush consistency throughout. Spoon into chilled large bowl. Break up mixture with fork. Beat until fluffy. Return to freezing tray. Cover with foil. Freeze until firm, about 2 hours. *Makes 2 quarts.*

PEACH VELVET SHERBET

8 to 10 canned cling peach halves
¼ cup lemon juice
¼ cup orange juice
1 teaspoon grated lemon rind
1 cup granulated sugar
⅛ teaspoon salt
½ teaspoon plain gelatin
1 tablespoon cold water

Press peaches through sieve and measure 2 cups pulp. Blend in juices, lemon rind, sugar and salt. Soften gelatin in cold water and dissolve over hot water. Add peach mixture to gelatin slowly, stirring constantly until well mixed. Pour into refrigerator tray and place in freezing compartment with control set at lowest temperature. Freeze until firm without stirring. Place in chilled bowl and beat with rotary beater until light and fluffy. Return to freezing compartment and freeze. When firm, reset temperature control to normal. Garnish with sliced peaches if desired. *Makes 1 quart.*

PINEAPPLE BUTTERMILK SHERBET

2 cups buttermilk
½ cup sugar
1 cup canned crushed pineapple

    1 teaspoon lemon juice
    2 egg whites, stiffly beaten
    2 tablespoons sugar
      rind of 1 lemon
    1 teaspoon vanilla extract

Combine buttermilk, sugar, lemon juice, and pineapple. Freeze until mushy. Add 2 tablespoons sugar, lemon rind and vanilla to egg whites. Stir all ingredients together and beat until fluffy. Freeze. *Makes 1 quart.*

PINEAPPLE YOGURT SHERBET

    2 cups plain yogurt
    2 cups crushed pineapple and juice

Freeze yogurt until mushy. Stir in pineapple and juice. Whip until thoroughly blended. Freeze until firm. *Makes 1 quart.*

RASPBERRY CREAM SHERBET

    1 quart cream, whipped
    1 egg white, stiffly beaten
    1 cup sugar
    1½ cups raspberry juice

Combine cream that has been whipped with sugar and raspberry juice. Stir until dissolved. Freeze until thick. Add egg whites and beat until smooth. Freeze. *Makes 1½ quarts.*

ROMAN SHERBET

    1 cup sugar
    1 cup water
      rind of 1 orange
      rind of 1 lemon
      juice of 2 oranges
      juice of 3 lemons
    1 quart dry white wine
    1 egg white, stiffly beaten

½ cup plus 2 tablespoons sugar
¼ cup water
¼ teaspoon pure vanilla extract

Boil 1 cup sugar and water for 5 minutes. Cool. Stir in orange
rind, lemon rind, orange juice, lemon juice, wine, and whip until
well blended. Freeze until mushy. Cook remaining sugar, water,
and vanilla until it reaches the soft ball stage. Pour syrup over
the egg white, beating constantly. Add this to the sherbet which
has been partly frozen. Whip until fluffy. Refreeze. *Makes 2 quarts.*

STRAWBERRY SHERBET

4 quarts strawberries, sliced
4 cups sugar
3 cups milk
½ cup fresh orange juice
rind of ½ lemon
pinch cinnamon

Mix strawberries and sugar. Place in refrigerator for 1½ hours.
Blend strawberries in an electric blender. Strain. Add remaining
ingredients. Pour into a large cake pan, or refrigerator trays. Place
in freezer. Stir periodically during the freezing process. When
very thick pack in containers and store in freezer until serving
time. *Makes ½ gallon.*

STRAWBERRY SPICE SHERBET

4 quarts strawberries
4 cups sugar
3 cups half and half
½ cup orange juice
rind of 1 orange
½ teaspoon cinnamon

Mix strawberries and sugar. Place in refrigerator for 1½ hours.
Blend strawberries in an electric blender. Strain. Add remaining
ingredients. Pour into a large cake pan, or refrigerator trays.
Place in freezer. Stir periodically during the freezing process.
When very thick pack in containers and store in freezer until serv-
ing time. *Makes ½ gallon.*

TROPICAL LEMON SHERBET

¾ cup sieved avocado
¼ cup lemon juice
1½ cups milk
½ cup sugar
¼ teaspoon salt

To prepare avocado, cut into halves lengthwise and remove seed and skin. Force fruit through sieve. Combine with lemon juice, milk, sugar, and salt, mixing well. Pour into refrigerator tray and place in freezing compartment with control set at lowest temperature. Freeze until firm stirring occasionally with a fork. When firm, reset temperature control to normal. *Makes 1½ pints.*

4.

ICES

Ices are frozen desserts made of sweetened fruit juices or puree usually diluted with water. Ices do not contain stabilizers, although egg white is sometimes used as a binder. These desserts must be stirred at intervals during the freezing process. See the instructions for frozen desserts and for making sherbet.

Ices are not difficult to make and can even be made days before you want to serve them. Like ice cream, they can be molded after freezing into a variety of shapes. Ices can be attractively served in fancy-cut fruit shells. You may use hollowed-out lemons, oranges, grapefruit and melons, and garnish them with leaves.

Any of the recipes for water ices, by adding egg white or gelatin, may be used for sherbets. When the water-ice mixture is half frozen, stir in from 1 to 4 stiffly beaten egg whites and continue freezing. Instead of egg white use 2 tablespoons gelatin, soaked in 6 tablespoons of cold water for 5 to 10 minutes and then dissolve in the hot syrup. If syrup is not made, use ¼ cup hot water. Add before freezing.

You can made frappés by whipping a partly frozen ice. A frappé is the same as an ice except that it is served in the mushy stage.

APRICOT ICE

3½ cups dried apricots
2⅓ cups orange juice
6 tablespoons lemon juice
1 cup sugar

Cook the dried apricots according to package directions. Cool and puree. Add juices and sugar. Stir until dissolved. Freeze. *Makes 1 quart.*

111

AVOCADO ICE No. 1

1 cup sieved avocado
2 cups orange juice
1 cup water
¾ cup sugar
dash of salt

To prepare avocado, cut into halves, remove seed and skin and force fruit through sieve. Combine with all remaining ingredients and beat until well blended. Turn into refrigerator tray, place in freezing compartment with control set at lowest temperature and freeze until firm. Turn out into chilled bowl and beat with rotary beater until smooth. Return to freezing compartment and freeze to desired consistency. Reset temperature control to normal. *Makes about 1 quart.*

AVOCADO ICE No. 2

1 avocado
2 cups grapefruit juice
½ cup sugar
¼ teaspoon salt
crystallized ginger

Cut avocado lengthwise into halves; remove seed and skin. Mash or sieve fruit. Stir in grapefruit juice, sugar and salt. Freeze until firm. Turn into chilled bowl; beat with rotary beater until smooth and fluffy. Freeze to desired consistency. Serve with ginger garnish. *Makes 1½ pints.*

AVOCADO ORANGE ICE

1 cup sieved avocado
2 cups orange juice
1 cup water
¾ cup sugar
salt to taste

To prepare avocado, cut into halves and remove seed and skin. Force fruit through a sieve. Combine all ingredients and beat until well blended. Pour into refrigerator tray. Place in freezing compartment with control set at lowest temperature and freeze until firm. Stir 2 or 3 times while freezing. When firm, reset temperature control to normal. *Makes about 1 quart.*

AVOCADO PINEAPPLE ICE

      2 cups pineapple juice
    ½ cup sugar
        dash of salt
      1 medium sized avocado

Stir pineapple juice, sugar, and salt until sugar and salt are dissolved. To prepare avocado, cut fruit into halves and remove seed and skin. Force through a sieve and blend into first mixture. Turn into refrigerator tray, place in freezing compartment with control set at lowest temperature, and freeze until firm. Turn out into chilled bowl and beat with rotary beater until smooth. Return to freezing compartment and freeze until firm. *Makes about 1½ pints.*

BLACK RASPBERRY ICE

      2 teaspoons gelatin
    ½ cup cold water
    ½ cup hot water
    ¾ cup sugar
      2 cups black raspberry concentrate
    ¼ cup lemon juice
        rind of one lemon
        dash of salt
      2 egg whites, stiffly beaten

Dissolve the gelatin in cold water. Combine the gelatin with hot water and stir until dissolved. Add the sugar. Let stand 5 minutes, stirring occasionally. Stir in remaining ingredients except the egg whites. Freeze until mushy. Turn out into a chilled bowl and whip until fluffy. Fold in the beaten egg whites and freeze until firm. *Makes 1½ quarts.*

COFFEE ICE

    ¾ cup sugar
      1 cup boiling water

3 cups ice water
4 teaspoons instant coffee
whipped cream

Dissolve the sugar in boiling water. Add instant coffee and cool. Stir in ice water and freeze to a mush. Whip thoroughly and re-freeze. Garnish with whipped cream if desired. *Makes 1 quart.*

CONCORD GRAPE ICE

2 teaspoons plain gelatin
½ cup ice water
3 cups concord grape juice
½ cup lemon juice
¾ cup sugar
rind of 1 lemon
dash of salt

Soften the gelatin in cold water. Heat one cup of the grape juice. Add gelatin to warm grape juice and stir until dissolved. Cool. Combine all of the remaining ingredients and freeze until firm. *Makes 1 quart.*

CRANBERRY ICE

1 quart cranberries
2 cups water
juice of 2 lemons
2 cups sugar

Cook the cranberries and water for 8 minutes. Press through a sieve, and then add sugar and lemon juice. Cool and freeze. *Makes 1½ pints.*

FRUIT ICE

1 1-pound 14-ounce can apricots, plums
or peaches
½ cup water
¾ cup syrup
⅔ cup sugar

⅓ cup lemon juice
2 egg whites

Empty fruit and syrup into strainer placed over a bowl; press fruit through strainer; reserve. Combine water, syrup, and sugar in a saucepan. Bring to boil over medium heat, stirring until sugar dissolves. Boil 5 minutes. Cool. Add lemon juice and fruit puree. Turn into freezing tray or trays. Freeze until mixture is almost firm. While mixture is in freezer, beat egg whites until stiff but not dry. Turn almost frozen mixture into a chilled bowl. Cut apart and beat until smooth. Fold in beaten egg whites. Return to tray and continue freezing until firm. Note: 2 12-ounce cans nectar may be substituted for the pureed canned fruit. *Makes about 1 quart.*

GRAPE ICE

½ cup light corn syrup
½ cup sugar
1 cup hot water
2 teaspoons gelatin
¼ cup cold water
1 6-ounce can frozen grape concentrate
¾ cup ice water
½ cup orange juice
  rind of 1 lemon
  dash of salt
2 egg whites, stiffly beaten

Soften the gelatin in cold water. Combine the syrup, sugar and hot water. Add the gelatin to the hot mixture and stir until dissolved. Add the remaining ingredients, except the egg whites. Freeze until mushy. Turn into a chilled bowl and whip until fluffy. Beat in the egg whites, blending thoroughly. Freeze until firm. *Makes 1 quart.*

ITALIAN WATER ICE

2 cups sugar
1 cup water
4 pints fresh strawberries
¼ cup lemon juice

⅓ cup orange juice
pink champagne, optional

Combine sugar and water in medium saucepan. Heat and stir until sugar dissolves; then boil 5 minutes. Cool. Force strawberries through food mill or blend in electric blender; strain to remove seeds. Blend strawberry puree, lemon and orange juices into cool syrup. Pour into ice cube trays. Wrap trays in aluminum foil. Freeze until firm. Twenty minutes before serving, remove from freezer and let soften slightly. Serve in sherbet glasses with champagne, if desired. *Makes 1 quart.*

LEMON ICE

2 cups sugar
4 cups orange and spice tea
⅛ teaspoon salt
¾ cup lemon juice
rind of 2 lemons

Combine sugar, tea, and salt. Boil for 5 minutes. Add lemon rind. Chill until mushy. Add lemon juice and whip until thoroughly blended. Freeze until firm. *Makes 1 quart.*

LEMON ORANGE ICE

4 cups water
⅛ teaspoon salt
2 cups sugar
rind of 2 oranges
2 cups frozen orange juice
4 teaspoons lemon juice

Combine water, salt, and sugar. Boil for 5 minutes. Chill. Add orange rind, orange juice, and lemon juice. Freeze until firm. *Makes 1½ quarts.*

LEMON ORANGE YOGURT ICE

1 cup orange yogurt
1 cup lemon sherbet

½ cup fresh orange juice
1 teaspoon orange rind

Combine yogurt and lemon sherbet. Blend thoroughly. Stir in orange juice and orange rind. Mix until smooth by hand or in a blender. Serve immediately or freeze until firm. *Makes 1½ pints.*

LIME ICE

1½ teaspoons gelatin
¼ cup cold water
3 cups water
1½ cups sugar
    dash of salt
    juice of 8 limes
    rind of 2 limes
2 egg whites, stiffly beaten
    green food coloring

Soften the gelatin in ¼ cup cold water. Add 1½ more cups of water with the sugar and salt. Pour into a saucepan and boil for 5 minutes. Stir in the gelatin and cool. Stir in lime juice, and lime rind. Green food coloring will enhance the color of the dessert. Freeze until mushy. Turn into a chilled bowl and whip until fluffy. Fold in the egg whites and freeze until firm. *Makes 1½ quarts.*

NECTAR ICE

3 cups fruit nectar
½ cup water
¾ cup corn syrup
⅔ cup sugar
⅓ cup lemon juice
2 egg whites

Combine syrup, sugar, and water in a saucepan. Bring to boil over medium heat, stirring until sugar dissolves. Boil 5 minutes. Cool. Add lemon juice and fruit nectar. Turn into freezing tray. Freeze until mixture is almost firm. While mixture is in freezer, beat egg whites until stiff but not dry. Turn almost frozen mixture into a chilled bowl. Cut apart and beat until smooth. Fold in beaten egg whites. Return to tray and continue freezing until firm. *Makes about 1 quart.*

ORANGE ICE No. 1

2 teaspoons gelatin
¼ cup cold water
1½ cups sugar
1 cup water
2 cups orange juice
½ cup lemon juice
1½ tablespoons orange rind
2 egg whites, stiffly beaten

Soften gelatin in cold water. Combine the sugar and 1 cup of water. Boil for 3 minutes. Add gelatin, stir until dissolved. Cool. Add orange juice, lemon juice, and orange rind. Freeze until mushy. Turn out into a chilled bowl and whip until fluffy. Fold in the egg whites and freeze until firm. *Makes 1½ quarts.*

ORANGE ICE No. 2

12 oranges, freshly squeezed
2 lemons, freshly squeezed
6 cups water
1½ cups sugar
(or sweeten to taste)
rind of 4 oranges, if desired

Strain the orange and lemon juice. Combine with the water and sugar. Stir until dissolved. Freeze. *Makes 1½ quarts.*

ORANGE ICE No. 3

4 cups water
rind of 2 oranges
2 cups sugar
2 cups orange juice
¼ cup lemon juice

Boil sugar and water for 5 minutes. Add fruit juice and rind. Cool, strain and freeze. *Makes 1½ quarts.*

ORANGE YOGURT ICE

1 cup orange yogurt
1 cup orange sherbet
½ cup fresh orange juice
1 teaspoon orange rind

Combine yogurt and orange sherbet. Stir until thoroughly blended. Add orange juice and rind. Serve immediately or freeze until firm. *Makes 1½ pints.*

PEACH ICE

2 cups fresh peaches, pureed
¼ cup lemon juice
¾ cup plus 2 tablespoons orange juice
1 cup sugar
2¾ cups water

Boil sugar and water for 5 minutes. Freeze until mushy. Add the peach puree and juices. Freeze until firm. *Makes 1½ quarts.*

PINEAPPLE ICE

1 large pineapple
juice of 1 lemon
rind of 1 lemon
1½ cups sugar
(or sweeten to taste)
2 quarts water

Peel and grate the pineapple. The pineapple should be grated very fine. Add the juice of one lemon, the lemon rind, sugar, and water. Freeze. *Makes 2 quarts.*

PINEAPPLE JUICE ICE

3¼ cups fresh pineapple juice
½ cup sugar
more sugar if desired

Combine the pineapple and sugar. Stir until dissolved. Freeze. *Makes 1 quart.*

CRUSHED PINEAPPLE ICE

1 cup sugar
4 cups water
1 cup crushed pineapple and juice
¼ cup lemon juice
2 tablespoons orange juice

Boil sugar and water for 5 minutes. Chill in refrigerator tray until mushy. Add pineapple and fruit juice. Blend thoroughly. Freeze. *Makes 1½ quarts.*

POMEGRANATE ICE

1 tablespoon gelatin
¼ cup water
1 cup hot water
4 cups pomegranate juice
juice of 2 limes
¾ cup lemon juice
rind of 1 lemon
2 cups sugar
3 cups ice water

Soften the gelatin in ¼ cup water. Dissolve in hot water. Cool. Combine remaining ingredients and freeze. Red food coloring will enhance the color of the ice. *Makes 2½ quarts.*

RASPBERRY ICE

4 cups water
1½ cups sugar
2 cups raspberry juice
2 tablespoons lemon juice

Boil sugar and water 5 minutes, cool. Add raspberry juice and lemon juice. Strain and freeze. *Makes 1½ quarts.*

RASPBERRY FLUFF ICE

1½ quarts raspberry juice,
sweetened to taste

> 2 cups water
> ½ cup sugar
> 3 egg whites, stiffly beaten

Freeze raspberry juice and water until mushy. Beat the egg whites into the raspberry mixture. Slowly add the sugar. Continue whipping until fluffy. Freeze. *Makes 2 quarts.*

SNOW ICE

> Fresh, clean snow
> Sweetened fruit juice
> Sugar
> Vanilla
> (other flavoring may be substituted)

Set out a cookie sheet or bread board to collect freshly fallen snow. Be sure the snow is clean. (The first snow is not as clean as snow that has fallen for a day or overnight.) Arrange the snow in a chilled bowl. Do not compact it. Combine the flavoring or ingredients of your choice and pour over the snow. Serve immediately.

STRAWBERRY ICE

> 2 cups sugar
> 2 cups water
> 1 quart fresh strawberries, mashed
> 1 tablespoon lemon juice
> ¼ teaspoon salt
> rind of 1 lemon

Boil sugar and water for 8 minutes. Cool. Stir in strawberries, lemon juice, and salt. Freeze until mushy. Stir in lemon rind. Whip until smooth. Freeze. *Makes 1 quart.*

STRAWBERRY YOGURT ICE

> 1 cup strawberry yogurt
> 1 cup strawberry sherbet
> 1 teaspoon fresh lemon juice
> 2 tablespoons sugar
> ½ cup crushed strawberries

Combine the yogurt and strawberry sherbet. Mix until well blended. Stir in lemon juice, strawberries, and sugar. Beat by hand until smooth. Serve immediately or freeze until firm. *Makes 1½ pints.*

WATERMELON ICE No. 1

1 ripe watermelon,
    sweeten to taste
3 egg whites, stiffly beaten

Scrape the pulp and water from the melon. Sweeten to taste. Freeze until mushy. Whip until smooth and beat in the egg whites. Stir frequently during the freezing process. Freeze until firm. *Makes 1½ quarts.*

WATERMELON ICE No. 2

3 cups watermelon juice
½ cup sugar
    dash of salt
1 tablespoon lemon juice
    rind of 1 lemon
1 tablespoon gelatin

Soften gelatin in ½ cup watermelon juice. Heat until dissolved. Combine remaining ingredients and freeze. *Makes 1 quart.*

WINE ICE

1½ cups sugar
½ cup water
1 quart ginger ale
1 cup red wine
    juice of 1 lemon
    rind of 1 lemon, if desired

Boil sugar and water until dissolved. Strain through cheesecloth. Cool. Add ginger ale, wine, lemon juice, and freeze until firm. White wine may be used along with a few drops of food coloring. *Makes 1½ quarts.*

5.

SAUCES AND TOPPINGS

Ice cream, sherbet, and ices are delicious just as they are, but for a more elaborate dessert, serve them with a sauce. The sauce may be served over the frozen dessert or in a separate bowl. Or arrange ice cream and other frozen desserts in layers in tall parfait glasses, and garnish with a dab of whipped cream, chopped nuts, toasted coconut, or a cherry.

The art of garnishing desserts is based upon a knowledge of how flavors can be combined for both appearance and taste. Almost any dessert, and particularly the simple ones, gain quick glamour by garnishing with a sauce or topping just before serving.

If a sauce cannot complement the dessert, omit it. If the dessert is tart, use a bland sauce; if it is bland, use a tart sauce to which liqueur or wine has been added as a finishing touch.

When preparing a sauce that has been thickened with flour or cornstarch, be sure that it is free from lumps; and cook the sauce thoroughly to avoid a raw taste. Whether you need a sauce that is bland or tart, hot or cold, thick or thin, smooth or crunchy, you will find an appropriate choice among the recipes that follow. Experiment with these easy-to-make toppings. There are many ways to serve them and you will surely have many ideas of your own for creating new ones.

AMBER SAUCE

2 tablespoons cornstarch
½ teaspoon salt
½ cup honey
1¼ cups water

      2 tablespoons butter
      ¼ cup tart fruit juice
        sherry wine or brandy

Mix cornstarch, salt and honey. Gradually add water. Cook over low heat until thick and clear. Add butter and fruit juice, blend thoroughly. Serve warm.

APPLESAUCE TOPPING

   1¼ cups boiling water
    1 3-ounce package orange dessert gelatin
   1¾ cups applesauce
    1 tablespoon lemon juice
      rind of 1 lemon
    2 egg whites, stiffly beaten
    2 tablespoons sugar

Combine gelatin and hot water, stir until dissolved. Add applesauce, lemon juice, and lemon rind. Chill until thickened. Add sugar to egg whites and beat well. Combine all ingredients and store in refrigerator until ready for use. This topping is excellent for applesauce parfaits. Layer with vanilla ice cream.

APRICOT ALMOND TOPPING

   ½ cup diced dried apricots
   ½ cup water
   ¼ cup sliced, toasted, unsalted almonds

Cook the diced apricots in ½ cup water for 5 minutes. Cool. Add toasted almonds. Layer between scoops of ice cream.

APRICOT SAUCE

   12 ripe apricots, pureed
    3 cups sugar
    2 cups water
    1 tablespoon kirsch

Bring sugar and water to a boil. Skim off any scum that gathers on the syrup. Add puree. When the sauce coats a spoon remove from heat. Add kirsch. This sauce may be served hot or cold. If served hot add ½ tablespoon butter.

APRICOT WINE TOPPING

        1 cup apricot puree
        3 tablespoons wine
          rind of 1 orange

Combine all ingredients and serve over ice cream. This topping may be served hot or cold.

BERRY AND CHEESE TOPPING

        1 cup cream, whipped
        1 egg white, stiffly beaten
     1¼ cups cottage cheese
      ¼ teaspoon salt
      ½ teaspoon vanilla
        2 tablespoons sugar
        2 cups fresh raspberries
          (other berries may be substituted)

Combine egg white and cream. Stir in cottage cheese, salt, vanilla, and sugar. Beat until fluffy. Alternate layers of cheese mixture, berries, and vanilla ice cream. The cheese mixture, and berries should be thoroughly chilled before serving.

BITTERSWEET MOCHA SAUCE

      ¼ cup butter
        2 squares bitter chocolate
     1½ cups sugar
      ⅛ teaspoon salt
      ¾ cup table cream
      ½ teaspoon vanilla
        1 tablespoon instant coffee

Melt butter and chocolate over very low heat. Add sugar gradually, blending well. Mixture will be thick and dry. Add salt; stir in cream, gradually. Cook 5 to 6 minutes to dissolve sugar. Remove from heat; add vanilla. Stir in instant coffee. Serve hot or cold.

BLUEBERRY PORT SAUCE

1 cup port wine
¼ cup brown sugar
rind of 1 lemon
½ cup blueberries

Combine port, sugar, and lemon rind. Stir until sugar dissolves and mixture comes to a boil. Add blueberries and bring to a boil again. Ladle hot sauce over vanilla ice cream.

BOYSENBERRY FLUFF TOPPING

2 cups fresh boysenberries
1 cup honey
1 unbeaten egg white

In large bowl of a mixer, combine whole berries, honey and unbeaten egg white. Beat, gradually using medium speed, until berries are crushed. Increase speed to high. Continue beating until mixture thickens and is light and fluffy. This requires approximately 10 minutes of beating. Boysenberry fluff keeps under refrigeration without separating for several days. To serve: Use as a topping for ice cream. Note: If frozen boysenberries are used, defrost only until berries can be separated or broken apart.

BUTTERSCOTCH SAUCE No. 1

1 cup dark corn syrup
1 cup sugar
¼ teaspoon salt
½ cup light cream
2 tablespoons margarine
1 teaspoon vanilla

Combine all ingredients except vanilla in saucepan. Cook over medium heat, stirring constantly, until mixture comes to a full rolling boil. Boil briskly 5 minutes, stirring occasionally. Remove from heat. Add vanilla. Serve hot. Sauce may be stored in refrigerator. To reheat, place in pan of hot, not boiling, water until sauce has thinned to pouring consistency.

BUTTERSCOTCH SAUCE No. 2

1 cup firmly packed brown sugar
¼ cup light corn syrup
½ cup water
¼ cup butter
½ cup half and half

Combine brown sugar, syrup, and water. Heat in a double boiler until dissolved. Add butter and stir until melted. Combine sugar mixture with half and half and whip until light and fluffy. Serve over vanilla ice cream.

CARAMALLOW SAUCE

⅔ cup light corn syrup
1½ cups brown sugar
⅓ cup water
4 tablespoons butter
⅔ cup cream
½ cup miniature marshmallows

Boil sugar, syrup, and water until it reaches the soft ball stage. Add butter. Beat in marshmallows and cream; cool. Serve over your favorite ice cream.

CHERRIES JUBILEE

1 1-pound can black pitted cherries
3 tablespoons sugar
1 tablespoon cornstarch
rind of ½ lemon
½ cup port
½ cup brandy

Drain cherries, reserving juice. Boil cherry juice until reduced to ½ cup. Mix sugar and cornstarch, stir into juice. Cook until the mixture is clear. Add cherries, lemon rind, and port. Bring to a boil. Warm the brandy and pour over the cherries. Ignite with a match. When the flames die down, ladle over vanilla ice cream.

CHERRY TOPPING

2 tablespoons cornstarch
¼ cup sugar
⅛ teaspoon salt
1 can (1 pound) red sour pitted cherries
¾ cup cherry juice
2 teaspoons lemon juice

In saucepan combine cornstarch, sugar and salt. Drain cherries and reserve ¾ cup juice; add juice to cornstarch mixture to make a smooth paste. Cook, stirring constantly until thickened; reduce heat and add cherries; cook an additional 2 minutes; add lemon juice. To serve, fill ring with 12 scoops of vanilla ice cream; spoon sauce over top.

CHOCOLATE SAUCE No. 1

½ cup sugar
⅓ cup cocoa
1 tablespoon cornstarch
¼ teaspoon salt
1¼ cups water
2 tablespoons margarine
1 teaspoon vanilla

Combine sugar, cocoa, cornstarch and salt in small saucepan. Gradually blend in water. Cook over medium heat, stirring constantly, until mixture thickens, comes to a boil, and boils 2 minutes. Remove from heat. Mix in margarine and vanilla. Chill.

CHOCOLATE SAUCE No. 2

1⅓ cups sweetened condensed milk
2 squares unsweetened chocolate
⅛ teaspoon salt
½ to 1 cup hot water
½ teaspoon vanilla extract

In top of double boiler put condensed milk, chocolate and salt. Cook over rapidly boiling water, stirring often, until thickened. Remove from heat. Slowly stir in hot water until sauce is of desired thickness. Stir in vanilla extract. Serve hot or chilled.

CHOCOLATE SAUCE No. 3

¼ cup butter
2 squares bitter chocolate
1½ cups sugar
⅛ teaspoon salt
¾ cup table cream
½ teaspoon vanilla

Melt butter and chocolate over very low heat. Add sugar gradually, blending well. Mixture will be thick and dry. Add salt; stir in cream, gradually. Cook 5 to 6 minutes to dissolve sugar. Remove from heat; add vanilla. Serve hot or cold.

CHOCOLATE SAUCE No. 4

2 eggs
½ cup sugar
½ cup butter
2 squares semisweet chocolate, melted

Mix eggs and sugar in top of double boiler and cook, stirring constantly until mixture is amber colored (about 10 minutes). Add butter and melted chocolate; continue heating, stirring constantly, until butter is melted. Cool.

CHOCOLATE ALMOND SAUCE

¼ cup butter
2 squares bitter chocolate
1½ cups sugar
⅛ teaspoon salt
¾ cup table cream
½ teaspoon vanilla
⅛ teaspoon pure almond extract
½ cup toasted, slivered almonds

Melt butter and chocolate over very low heat. Add sugar gradually, blending well. Mixture will be thick and dry. Add salt; stir in cream, gradually. Cook 5 to 6 minutes to dissolve sugar. Remove from heat; add vanilla. Stir in almond extract and toasted almonds. Serve hot or cold.

CHOCOLATE CHIP SAUCE

¼ pound semisweet chocolate chips
1 cup warm water
½ cup cream
1 tablespoon butter

Combine chocolate chips and water. Cook in a double boiler until dissolved, about 15 minutes. Add cream and butter. Serve hot.

CHOCOLATE MARSHMALLOW SAUCE

1 jar (7 ounces) marshmallow creme
¼ cup milk
½ cup semisweet chocolate bits

Combine marshmallow creme and milk in heavy saucepan. Warm over very low heat, stirring constantly, until blended. Remove from heat; add chocolate bits; stir until melted. Serve warm or cold over vanilla ice cream.

CHOCOLATE ORANGE SAUCE

¼ cup butter
2 squares bitter chocolate
1½ cups sugar
⅛ teaspoon salt
¾ cup table cream
½ teaspoon vanilla
2 teaspoons grated orange rind
2 tablespoons orange juice
½ teaspoon grated lemon rind

Melt butter and chocolate over very low heat. Add sugar gradually, blending well. Mixture will be thick and dry. Add salt; stir in cream, gradually. Cook 5 to 6 minutes to dissolve sugar. Remove from heat; add vanilla. Stir in orange rind, orange juice, and lemon rind. Serve hot or cold.

CHOCOLATE PEANUT BUTTER SUNDAE SAUCE

        1 8-ounce package semisweet chocolate bits
        ¼ cup peanut butter, creamy
            or chunk style
        ¼ cup light corn syrup
        2 tablespoons cream

Melt chocolate in double boiler. Add peanut butter and stir until
blended. Remove from heat and add corn syrup and cream. Serve
warm over vanilla ice cream. This sauce may be stored in the refrigerator and reheated at another time. If it becomes too thick,
add a small amount of cream.

CHOCOLATE PEPPERMINT SAUCE

        ¼ cup butter
        2 squares bitter chocolate
     1½ cups sugar
        ⅛ teaspoon salt
        ¾ cup table cream
        ½ teaspoon vanilla
        ½ cup heavy cream, whipped
        ½ cup crushed peppermint candy

Melt butter and chocolate over very low heat. Add sugar gradually,
blending well. Mixture will be thick and dry. Add salt; stir in
¾ cup table cream, gradually. Cook 5 to 6 minutes to dissolve
sugar. Remove from heat; add vanilla. Cool. Stir in ½ cup of
whipped cream and peppermint candy. Serve cold.

CREAMY CHOCOLATE SAUCE

        ¼ cup butter
        2 squares bitter chocolate
     1½ cups sugar
        ⅛ teaspoon salt
        ¾ cup table cream
        ½ teaspoon vanilla
        ½ cup heavy cream, whipped

Melt butter and chocolate over very low heat. Add sugar gradually, blending well. Mixture will be thick and dry. Add salt; stir in ¾ cup table cream, gradually. Cook 5 to 6 minutes to dissolve sugar. Remove from heat; add vanilla. Cool. Stir in ½ cup of whipped cream. Serve cold.

COFFEE CARAMEL SAUCE

½ pound vanilla caramels
2 tablespoons milk
2 teaspoons instant coffee

Combine caramels, milk and instant coffee. Cook in a double boiler until smooth and creamy. Serve hot.

COFFEE SAUCE

¼ cup sugar
1 tablespoon cornstarch
2 tablespoons instant coffee
⅛ teaspoon salt
1 cup hot water
½ cup evaporated milk

Mix sugar, cornstarch, instant coffee, and salt in a 1-quart sauce-pan. Stir in hot water and evaporated milk. Cook until thickened, stirring occasionally. Sauce will be ready in 12 to 15 minutes.

COFFEE SYRUP TOPPING

1 tablespoon water
3 tablespoons instant coffee powder
½ cup light corn syrup

Stir water into coffee powder in small saucepan, dissolving powder completely. Stir in corn syrup. Bring to boil, stirring frequently. Remove from heat. Let stand a few minutes, then skim off foam.

CRANBERRY SAUCE

    ½ cup sugar
    2 tablespoons cornstarch
    2 cups cranberry juice
    1 tablespoon lemon juice
      dash of salt
      rind of 1 lemon

Combine sugar and cornstarch, blend thoroughly. Add remaining ingredients and cook over medium heat until thick. Cool.

CREAMY FRUIT SAUCE

    ⅔ cup sweetened condensed milk
    3 tablespoons lemon juice
    1 cup fruit, use one of these fruits:
      drained crushed pineapple, sliced fresh
      strawberries, or banana cut into small cubes
      cold water

Blend together sweetened condensed milk and lemon juice until thickened. Fold in one of the fruits listed. Stir in water, a tablespoon at a time, until of desired consistency. Refrigerate.

CURRANT SAUCE No. 1

    2½ cups currant juice, unsweetened
    2 cups sugar
      dash of salt
    3 tablespoons cornstarch

Mix the sugar, salt, and cornstarch, blend thoroughly. Slowly add the currant juice. Cook in a double boiler until thickened. Cool. Serve over vanilla ice cream.

CURRANT SAUCE No. 2

    2 teaspoons cornstarch
    2 tablespoons lemon juice

1 cup (10-ounce jar) currant jelly,
stirred to break up

In a saucepan blend cornstarch and lemon juice; add jelly. Bring
to a boil over low heat, stirring constantly. Cool.

DARK SUNDAE SAUCE

½ cup sugar
1 tablespoon cornstarch
⅛ teaspoon cinnamon
⅔ cup dark corn syrup
⅔ cup heavy cream
¼ cup margarine

Combine sugar, cornstarch and cinnamon in saucepan. Mix in
other ingredients. Bring to boil stirring constantly. Simmer 3 to 4
minutes, stirring occasionally.

DATE SAUCE

½ cup chopped dates
½ cup corn syrup
¼ cup firmly packed brown sugar
¼ cup water
⅓ cup chopped pecans
½ teaspoon pure vanilla extract

Combine dates, syrup, brown sugar, and water. Cook until soft.
Stir in pecans and vanilla after the mixture has cooled. Serve
over your favorite ice cream.

DATE NUT SUNDAE SAUCE

½ cup chopped pitted dates
½ cup dark corn syrup
¼ cup firmly packed brown sugar
¼ cup water
¼ teaspoon salt
½ teaspoon vanilla
¼ cup chopped pecans

Combine dates, corn syrup, brown sugar, water, and salt in a saucepan. Bring to a boil and cook 2 minutes over medium heat, stirring constantly. Remove from heat and add vanilla and pecans. Cool and serve over vanilla ice cream.

DOUBLE FUDGE SAUCE

¾ cup sugar
⅓ cup cocoa
3 tablespoons water
2 tablespoons white corn syrup
½ cup evaporated milk
¾ teaspoon vanilla

Mix sugar, cocoa, water, and corn syrup in a saucepan. Boil until a few drops form a soft ball when dropped into cold water. Stir in evaporated milk and vanilla. Serve warm or cold on ice cream. Sauce can be stored in a covered jar in the refrigerator.

DOUBLE MOCHA SAUCE

4 squares unsweetened chocolate
2 cups sugar
1⅔ cups evaporated milk
2 tablespoons instant coffee
1 teaspoon vanilla extract

Combine chocolate, sugar, and evaporated milk. Heat in a double boiler until dissolved, stirring constantly. Add instant coffee and vanilla. Beat until smooth. Serve over ice cream.

FRESH FRUIT SUNDAE SAUCE

½ to ⅔ cup light corn syrup
1½ cups fresh crushed strawberries or
   raspberries, sieved or diced peaches or
   pitted, sliced sweet cherries

Combine ingredients. Chill. Serve over ice cream.

GALA CHERRY SAUCE

1 can (1 pound-1 ounce) pitted sweet red cherries
1 cup cherry liquid plus water or brandy
¼ cup honey
1½ tablespoons cornstarch

Drain cherries, reserving liquid. To cherry liquid, add water or brandy to make 1 cup. In a saucepan blend together cornstarch, cherry liquid and honey. Cook over low heat, stirring constantly, until sauce is thickened and smooth. Add cherries and stir gently. Spoon warm sauce over squares or scoops of ice cream. Note: For variety, fill baked meringue shells with scoops of ice cream and spoon sauce over top.

GOLDEN RAISIN CITRUS SAUCE

¾ cup seedless raisins
1½ cups water
1 cup brown sugar, packed
1½ tablespoons cornstarch
⅓ cup orange juice
1½ tablespoons lemon juice
3 tablespoons butter
⅛ teaspoon salt

Simmer raisins and water for 3 minutes. Add brown sugar that has been mixed with cornstarch and orange juice. Cook until mixture starts to simmer. Add lemon juice, butter, and salt. Continue cooking until the mixture thickens slightly.

GOLDEN RAISIN SAUCE FLAMBE

1 cup golden raisins
1 cup boiling water
¼ teaspoon grated lemon rind
1 tablespoon lemon juice
3 tablespoons brown sugar
¼ cup 100-proof brandy
¼ cup brandy

Cover raisins with boiling water. Let stand 5 minutes. Drain; add lemon rind, juice, brown sugar, and ¼ cup brandy. Cover; let stand 1 hour. Just before serving, add additional ¼ cup brandy and bring to boil in chafing dish. Ignite and spoon flaming raisins over hard ice cream.

GUAVA SAUCE

   1 cup sugar
   2 tablespoons cornstarch
  ⅛ teaspoon salt
   1 cup unsweetened guava juice
   1 cup water
   2 tablespoons butter

Combine sugar, salt and cornstarch, slowly add the guava juice. Stir in water and butter and cook until the sauce thickens. Serve over guava or vanilla ice cream.

HONEY CREME TOPPING

   1 package (3 ounces) cream cheese
  ¼ teaspoon salt
   2 tablespoons honey
  ¼ cup dairy sour cream
  ½ cup sliced strawberries

In small bowl, whip or mash cream cheese with salt, honey, sour cream, and berries. For smooth topping, whip with beater. If desired, you may fold sliced berries into topping instead of whipping. Serve over ice cream. Garnish with whole strawberries.

HONEY ORANGE SAUCE

   1 cup light flavored honey
   1 tablespoon fresh orange juice
  ¼ cup finely diced orange peel
  ⅛ teaspoon salt

Combine all ingredients. Heat, stirring about 5 minutes or until sauce is slightly thickened. Do not boil. Serve over vanilla ice cream.

HONEY CRISP TOPPING

1 cup honey
¼ cup butter
5 cups corn flakes
1 cup shredded coconut

In a skillet or saucepan, heat honey and butter stirring until it comes to a boil. In a large bowl mix cornflakes and coconut. Pour honey that has been heated over the cornflakes, tossing lightly to coat. Spread mixture out on a buttered baking sheet to cool and crisp. Serve over ice cream. Arrange pretzel sticks around sundae for garnish.

HOT CHERRY SAUCE

1 1-pound can dark sweet cherries in
  heavy syrup
1 tablespoon cornstarch
¼ cup light corn syrup
½ teaspoon almond extract
  vanilla ice cream

Drain syrup from cherries. Gradually stir into cornstarch in small saucepan. Add corn syrup. Cook over medium heat, stirring constantly, until mixture comes to boil and boils 1 minute. Add cherries. Cook 1 minute. Remove from heat. Stir in almond extract. Serve hot over vanilla ice cream.

HOT FUDGE SAUCE

⅔ cup sweetened condensed milk
½ cup water
⅛ teaspoon salt
¼ cup sugar
1½ squares unsweetened chocolate
½ teaspoon vanilla extract

In top of double boiler combine sweetened condensed milk, water, salt, and sugar. Add chocolate. Cook over rapidly boiling water, stirring often, until thickened. Remove from heat. Stir in vanilla extract. Serve hot.

IVORY POUR SAUCE

½ pint whipping cream
2 egg yolks
3 tablespoons honey
2 tablespoons lemon juice

Beat cream until slightly thick. Add egg yolks one at a time continue beating. Slowly drizzle in honey and lemon juice. Sauce will be thick and creamy. Serve over scoops of ice cream that have been topped with freshly sliced strawberries.

JAMAICAN MAGIC TOPPING

1 cup moist, shredded coconut
¼ cup brown sugar
1 tablespoon melted butter

Toss the coconut and brown sugar. Add melted butter. Brown in a moderately hot oven. Serve over ice cream.

JIFFY BUTTERSCOTCH SAUCE

1½ cups light brown sugar
⅔ cup corn syrup
⅔ cup evaporated milk

Put brown sugar and corn syrup into a heavy saucepan. Cook and stir until mixture comes to a full, all-over boil, about 5 minutes. Remove from heat and cool. Stir in evaporated milk. Serve warm or cold over ice cream.

JIFFY JUBILEE TOPPING

1 8-ounce jar currant jelly
2 1-pound cans drained,
   pitted bing cherries
1 tablespoon brandy flavoring

Beat the currant jelly until smooth. Add the bing cherries and brandy flavoring. Blend thoroughly. Serve cold over ice cream.

LEMON SAUCE

¼ cup sugar
2 teaspoons cornstarch
1 cup water
1 egg, beaten
2 tablespoons butter
2 tablespoons lemon juice
½ teaspoon grated lemon rind

In saucepan combine sugar, cornstarch and gradually add water. Cook until thickened. Blend a little into egg, return all to saucepan; heat and stir 2 minutes. Remove from heat; add butter, lemon juice and rind. Cool slightly and serve over ice cream.

MALLOWBERRY TOPPING

½ cup whole cranberry sauce
½ cup marshmallow creme

Fold the cranberry sauce into the marshmallow creme. Serve over vanilla ice cream.

MAPLE NUT SAUCE

¾ cup brown sugar
½ cup evaporated milk
½ teaspoon maple flavoring
2 tablespoons butter
¼ cup coarsely broken, unsalted nuts

Mix brown sugar and evaporated milk in a saucepan. Heat until steaming hot but do not boil. Remove from heat and add maple flavoring, butter, and nuts. Beat with a spoon until blended. Serve warm or cold.

MARASCHINO SAUCE

½ cup sugar
2 tablespoons cornstarch
dash of salt

    1 cup water
    ½ cup maraschino syrup
    ½ cup chopped maraschino cherries
    2 tablespoons butter

Mix sugar, cornstarch and salt; gradually add water and cherry syrup. Cook in top of double boiler until slightly thickened. Remove from heat and add cherries and butter. Cool. Serve over vanilla ice cream.

MARSHMALLOW SAUCE

    ¼ pound (16) marshmallows
    ⅓ cup evaporated milk
    ⅓ cup light corn syrup
       dash of salt

Put marshmallows, evaporated milk, corn syrup and salt into a saucepan. Cook and stir over medium heat until marshmallows are melted. Chill thoroughly. Makes an excellent topping for any flavor ice cream.

MINCEMEAT SAUCE

    1 9-ounce package condensed mincemeat
    ½ cup light corn syrup
    ½ cup water
    2 tablespoons rum

Break the condensed mincemeat into small pieces in medium saucepan. Add corn syrup, water, and rum. Stirring to break up pieces, bring to a boil over low heat and boil 1 minute. Serve warm or cool on ice cream. Makes a delicious sauce either way.

MINT PATTIE SAUCE

    28 to 30 small filled chocolate mint patties
       (10-ounce box)
    ¼ cup honey
    ½ cup heavy cream or undiluted
       evaporated milk

Melt chocolate mints with honey and cream over very low heat, stirring constantly. Serve warm over ice cream.

MOCHA SAUCE No. 1

      2 tablespoons cornstarch
      2/3 cup sugar
      1/2 teaspoon salt
      2 cups whole milk
      1/4 cup butter
      2 ounces unsweetened chocolate
      1 teaspoon instant coffee

Combine cornstarch, sugar, and salt in a 1-quart saucepan. Mix
well. Add milk slowly, stirring until smooth. Bring to a boil over
low heat, stirring constantly. Boil 1 minute. Add butter and chocolate. Boil, stirring constantly until thick and smooth, about 2 minutes. Stir in instant coffee. Cool. Serve over frozen dessert.

MOCHA SAUCE No. 2

      3/4 cup sugar
      1 tablespoon cornstarch
      1/4 cup cocoa
      2 tablespoons instant coffee
      1 cup boiling water
      1/2 cup evaporated milk

Mix together sugar, cornstarch, cocoa, and instant coffee in a 1-
quart saucepan. Gradually stir in boiling water and evaporated
milk. Cook and stir until mixture comes to a full, all-over boil and
is thick or about 5 minutes. Serve warm or cold.

NEAR EAST TOPPING

      1/2 cup chopped dates
      1/2 cup chopped pecans
      honey

Mix the chopped dates with the pecans. Moisten liberally with
honey. Serve over ice cream.

ORANGE SAUCE No. 1

      1/4 cup sugar
      1 tablespoon cornstarch

½ cup water
¾ cup (6-ounce can) frozen concentrated
orange juice, thawed

In a saucepan mix thoroughly sugar and cornstarch; gradually blend in water and orange juice. Bring to a boil. Cook, stirring constantly, until thick and clear. Cool.

ORANGE SAUCE No. 2

½ cup orange juice
1 tablespoon water
2 tablespoons sugar
1 teaspoon cornstarch
1 teaspoon grated orange rind

Combine orange juice, water, sugar and cornstarch in saucepan. Cook, stirring constantly, until thickened and clear. Stir in orange rind. Chill. Serve over ice cream.

ORANGE HONEY SAUCE

¾ cup honey
⅓ cup cornstarch
¼ teaspoon salt
1 cup fresh orange juice
1 cup boiling water
1 tablespoon grated orange rind
3 medium oranges, peeled,
seeded, and cut into
bite-size pieces

Combine honey and cornstarch with salt and orange juice. Add boiling water and cook over medium heat until thickened and clear, about 7 to 10 minutes. Add orange pieces. Serve warm or cold over frozen desserts. Store in refrigerator.

ORANGE BRANDY SAUCE

1 cup orange juice
rind of 1 lemon

rind of 1 orange
¾ cup sugar
3 tablespoons brandy

Boil orange juice and sugar for 5 minutes. Add rind and brandy.
Serve over vanilla ice cream.

PEACH MELBA SAUCE

1 package (12 ounces) frozen
    sliced peaches
1 package (10 ounces) frozen
    red raspberries
½ cup sugar
1 tablespoon cornstarch

Defrost fruit and drain syrup and combine with sugar and cornstarch; mix well. Cook over low heat, stirring constantly until
clear and thickened. Add fruits. Chill thoroughly before serving
over vanilla ice cream.

PEANUT BUTTER ICE CREAM TOPPING

⅓ cup peanut butter
⅔ cup light or dark corn syrup

Combine peanut butter and light or dark corn syrup. Stir until
well blended. Use as a topping for ice cream.

PEANUT BUTTER FUDGE SAUCE

1 cup semisweet chocolate chips
⅔ cup evaporated milk
¼ cup crunchy peanut butter

Combine all ingredients and cook in a double boiler until smooth.
Serve warm over ice cream. Garnish with peanuts.

PEANUT BUTTER SUNDAE SAUCE

1 cup brown sugar
1 cup maple syrup

Chocolate Sauce

Creamy Fruit Sauce

Mocha Sauce

Honey Sauces

Peanut Butter Sundae Sauce

Fruit Sundaes

¼ teaspoon salt
⅔ cup smooth or chunky peanut butter
1 cup whipping cream
1 teaspoon vanilla

Combine sugar, syrup and salt in saucepan. Cook to soft ball stage (234° to 240°) over low heat stirring frequently. Remove from heat; blend in peanut butter and cream. Stir in vanilla. Cool; spoon over a combination of vanilla and chocolate or vanilla and coffee ice cream.

PINEAPPLE MINT SAUCE

¾ cup light corn syrup
1 cup crushed pineapple
¼ teaspoon peppermint flavoring
few drops green food coloring

Combine all ingredients. Cover and chill thoroughly. Use as a sauce for ice cream.

PINE MINT SAUCE

1 Number 2 can crushed pineapple
green food coloring
1 cup sugar
½ teaspoon mint extract or
few drops oil of peppermint

Color crushed pineapple a delicate green with food coloring; add sugar. Cook 5 to 10 minutes, or until slightly thickened, stirring occasionally. Remove from heat; stir in extract. Cool. Serve over vanilla ice cream.

PLUM TOPPING

1 pound dark red or purple plums
1 tablespoon cornstarch
1 cup sugar
dash of salt
⅛ teaspoon cinnamon
dash of ground cloves
1 tablespoon lemon juice
rind of 1 lemon

Cut off all of the meat from the plums; removing pits. Mix cornstarch with sugar and add remaining ingredients. Simmer in a saucepan for 10 minutes. Cool. Layer with vanilla ice cream.

PRALINE SAUCE

1 cup firmly packed brown sugar
¼ cup light corn syrup
½ cup light cream
  dash of salt
2 tablespoons butter
1 teaspoon pure vanilla extract
1 cup chopped pecans

Combine brown sugar, corn syrup, cream, salt, and butter. Cook until thick and creamy. Cool. Stir in vanilla and nuts. Serve over vanilla ice cream.

PRUNE MARMALADE TOPPING

1 cup orange marmalade
½ cup plumped chopped prunes
2 tablespoons Curaçao liqueur

Warm the orange marmalade and rub through a coarse sieve. Add the plumped chopped prunes. Heat and stir in the Curaçao liqueur. Chill. Serve over vanilla ice cream.

RAISIN CARAMEL SAUCE

½ cup dark or golden raisins
3 tablespoons butter
1 cup brown sugar, packed
½ cup light cream
1 teaspoon vanilla

Rinse and drain raisins. Chop coarsely or leave whole. Melt butter in small saucepan, add brown sugar, and cook and stir over low heat until sugar is melted and lightly browned. Remove from heat, and very slowly stir in cream. Heat about 1 minute longer. Remove from heat and stir in raisins and vanilla. Serve warm or cold over ice cream.

RAISIN TOFFEE SUNDAE SAUCE

1 small can (⅔ cup) evaporated milk
¼ cup corn syrup
1 cup brown sugar, packed
1 cup sugar
⅛ teaspoon salt
1 teaspoon vinegar or lemon juice
2 tablespoons butter or margarine
2 teaspoons vanilla
½ cup dark or golden raisins

Blend evaporated milk with corn syrup, sugars and salt. Cook over very low heat, stirring frequently, 20 minutes, until thickened. Remove from heat; add remaining ingredients. Serve over ice cream.

RASPBERRY SAUCE

2 packages (10 ounces each) frozen raspberries
2 tablespoons cornstarch
½ teaspoon rum flavoring
1 teaspoon lemon juice

Drain raspberries and reserve juice. In saucepan combine cornstarch with juice. Cook, stirring constantly until thickened; reduce heat and cook 5 minutes. Add flavoring, lemon juice and berries; heat to serving temperature. Serve warm over frozen dessert.

RASPBERRY MELBA SAUCE

1½ teaspoons cornstarch
1 package (10 ounces) frozen raspberries, thawed
½ cup currant jelly

Blend cornstarch with 1 tablespoon juice from raspberries to make a smooth paste; set aside. In a 1-quart saucepan heat raspberries with jelly; stir in cornstarch mixture. Cook, stirring constantly, until thick and clear. Cool.

ROCKY ROAD FUDGE SAUCE

½ cup butter or margarine
1 cup half and half
1 cup sugar
⅓ cup cocoa
⅛ teaspoon salt
2 teaspoons vanilla
⅔ cup raisins
½ cup miniature marshmallows
¼ cup chopped walnuts

Melt butter; blend in half and half, sugar, cocoa and salt. Boil 2 minutes; cool. Add remaining ingredients. Excellent to serve over ice cream.

RUM SHERRIED SAUCE

1 pound dried prunes
½ cup sugar
½ teaspoon cinnamon
1 cup prune liquid
½ cup sherry
2 tablespoons rum
1 cup slivered toasted almonds

Place prunes in bowl; cover with cold water. Chill in refrigerator overnight. Halve prunes and pit. Combine sugar, cinnamon and prune liquid. Bring to boil and simmer 5 minutes. Add prunes, sherry, rum, and almonds. Chill. Serve on vanilla ice cream.

SHERRIED DATE SAUCE

2 cups pitted dates (about 12 ounces)
¾ cup honey
½ cup sherry
1 tablespoon chopped crystallized ginger
1 teaspoon grated orange peel

Cut or snip dates lengthwise into quarters. Combine with remaining ingredients; cover and refrigerate at least 2 hours. Serve over ice cream.

SOFT CUSTARD SAUCE

½ cup sweetened condensed milk
1 tablespoon flour
¼ teaspoon salt
1½ cups hot water
1 egg slightly beaten
½ teaspoon vanilla extract

In top of double boiler combine sweetened condensed milk, flour and salt. Slowly stir in hot water. Cook over boiling water, stirring constantly, until thickened. Remove from heat. Add a little milk mixture to egg while stirring rapidly; slowly return egg mixture to double boiler while stirring rapidly. Cook over hot water, stirring constantly, until mixture coats a metal spoon. Remove from heat at once and turn into bowl placed in cold water. Stir in vanilla extract. Remove bowl from water. Refrigerate.

SOUR CREAM SAUCE

¾ cup sour cream
¾ teaspoon cinnamon
¾ teaspoon nutmeg
1 tablespoon sugar

Mix sour cream, cinnamon, nutmeg, and sugar until thoroughly blended. Pour over your favorite frozen dessert.

STRAWBERRY SAUCE

1 cup strawberries
½ cup sugar
1 tablespoon cornstarch
½ cup water
½ cup lemon juice
2 tablespoons butter

Force strawberries through food mill or blend in electric blender. Strain to remove seeds. Mix sugar with cornstarch in medium saucepan. Gradually blend in ½ cup water. Stir over medium heat until sauce thickens and boils ½ minute. Stir in lemon juice, butter, and strawberry puree. Chill.

STRAWBERRIES FLORIDA TOPPING

1 cup drained, sliced strawberries
2 tablespoons orange juice
¼ teaspoon grated orange rind

Mix strawberries with orange juice and grated orange rind. Serve over ice cream, or layer with scoops of ice cream in parfait glasses.

SWEET CREAM SAUCE

2 eggs, separated
3 tablespoons sugar
½ teaspoon pure vanilla extract
½ cup heavy cream, whipped
dash of salt

Beat egg yolks with 2 tablespoons sugar and salt. Cook over low heat stirring constantly until thick, about 5 minutes. Chill. Beat egg whites until stiff, then beat in remaining sugar and vanilla. Fold this and whipped cream into chilled mixture. Serve over frozen dessert.

SWEET 'N TART APPLESAUCE TOPPING

¼ cup honey
1 cup gravenstein applesauce
1 tablespoon butter

Combine honey, applesauce and butter. Heat. Use as topping over ice cream. Or serve cool with spoons of ice cream in parfait glasses.

TANGY RAISIN SAUCE

2 tablespoons cornstarch
1 tablespoon sugar
1½ cups orange juice
⅔ cup seedless raisins

In saucepan combine cornstarch, sugar, orange juice, and raisins. Heat to boiling over medium heat, stirring constantly. Boil and stir 1 minute. Serve warm over ice cream.

VANILLA SAUCE

½ cup sugar
1 tablespoon cornstarch
dash of salt
1 cup boiling water
2 tablespoons butter
1 teaspoon pure vanilla extract

Combine sugar, cornstarch and salt. Stir in water; mix thoroughly. Cook in a double boiler until thickened. Stir in butter. Cool. Add vanilla. Serve over frozen dessert.

VANILLA SOUR CREAM SAUCE

1 cup sour cream
1 teaspoon vanilla extract
¼ cup powdered sugar

Combine sour cream with vanilla extract and powdered sugar. Blend thoroughly. Serve over frozen dessert.

WHIPPED CREAM TOPPING

1 cup heavy cream
1 tablespoon sugar
1 teaspoon pure vanilla extract

Whip cream until almost stiff. Add sugar and vanilla. Use as a topping or garnish for any frozen dessert.

WINE FRUIT COMPOTE TOPPING

2 cups dried apricots, cooked
2 cups dried prunes, cooked and pitted
1 cup brown sugar
rind of 1 lemon
2 tablespoons port wine

Drain cooked fruits and save liquid. Combine 2 cups liquid (add water if necessary to make 2 cups) with brown sugar and lemon rind. Boil until the mixture forms a thin syrup. Add fruit and wine. Serve warm or chilled over vanilla ice cream.

6.

LOW-CALORIE DESSERTS

A section on low-calorie desserts has been included in this book for people on reducing diets or for people who must restrict their intake of sugar. The methods used to prepare these frozen desserts are adaptable. The juices or fruits used can be substituted with juice or fruit of your preference. The calorie count in each recipe is approximate since the caloric value of a serving of frozen dessert varies with the composition of the mix.

There is one basic type of synthetic sweetener in use today. This sweetener has a base of saccharin. There are some saccharin-base sweeteners available that retain their natural-sugar tasting sweetness at both high cooking temperatures and freezing temperatures. On the other hand, some saccharin-base sweeteners may turn bitter or lose their sweetness when cooked. Be sure to read the manufacturer's directions before using any dietary sweetener for ingredients that have to be heated, cooked, or frozen.

There is no reason why you cannot experiment with other frozen dessert recipes in this book. Substitute the high-calorie ingredients for low-calorie ones, or decalorize your own favorite recipes. There are many noncaloric sweeteners available as replacements for table sugar. The taste, as well as the sweetening powers, of noncaloric sweeteners differs widely. If you are unfamiliar with their taste, shop around until you find one that suits your palate.

If you wish to experiment with other recipes in this book refer to the table of equivalents that is included with the liquid sweetener of your choice. The manufacturer's instructions will show you how to substitute either a noncaloric liquid sweetener, or a noncaloric granulated sugar substitute for table sugar.

When preparing frozen desserts and toppings it should be remembered that noncaloric sweeteners do not provide bulking, stabilizing, or the preservative properties of sugar. Therefore, if you do

152

not feel like experimenting, it is suggested that you use the tested recipes in this chapter.

Unless a particular sweetener is specified in the recipes use a liquid sweetener that has the following sweetening power. One-eighth of a teaspoon of noncaloric liquid sweetener is equivalent to 1 teaspoon of sugar and 1 tablespoon equals ½ cup sugar.

Note: Since the sweetening powers of the more recently developed artificial sweeteners vary it is recommended that you sweeten to suit your particular taste. You may want to use either less sweetener than is specified in the recipe. Or, you may want to add more sweetener.

Once the calorie-watcher has stabilized his weight there is no reason why ice cream or other frozen desserts cannot be a part of a slenderizing diet. A study of caloric values indicates that other desserts are far higher in calories than those found in this book. As an example, an ordinary serving of berry pie contains over 400 calories, whereas a large serving of ice cream contains only 200 calories.

APPLESAUCE SHERBET

1 cup applesauce, unsweetened
1 teaspoon lemon juice
½ teaspoon liquid sweetener
¼ cup cottage cheese
1 tablespoon nonfat milk
⅛ teaspoon pure almond extract
1 egg white, stiffly beaten
rind of 1 lemon

Combine all ingredients in the order given. Beat well after each addition. Freeze until mushy and whip. Refreeze mixture until firm. Makes 6 servings. *45 calories in each serving.*

APRICOT FREEZE

1 quart apricot puree, unsweetened
1 tablespoon orange juice
juice of 1 lemon
rind of 1 lemon
1 cup grapefruit juice
liquid sweetener,
sweeten to taste

Combine all ingredients and blend thoroughly. Freeze until firm. Makes 8 servings. *50 calories in each serving.*

APRICOT SHERBET

1 cup dietetic apricots
1 teaspoon gelatin
½ teaspoon lemon juice
rind of 1 lemon

Drain juice from apricots and heat. Soften gelatin in lemon juice and dissolve in hot apricot juice. Add lemon rind and freeze until mushy. Beat in a chilled bowl until fluffy. Add apricots and continue beating until smooth. Refreeze until firm. Serves 4. *30 calories in each serving.*

BANANA ICE CREAM DESSERT

2 teaspoons gelatin
1 cup cold water
¾ cup nonfat dry milk
1½ cups milk
3 tablespoons sugar
1 tablespoon liquid sweetener
2 teaspoons vanilla
2 tablespoons lemon juice
2 large bananas mashed

Soften the gelatin in ½ cup water. Mix ¼ cup dry milk with the milk and then scald. Dissolve the gelatin in it and stir in 2 tablespoons sugar, the liquid sweetener and vanilla. Chill until slightly thickened. (Place bowl in ice-cube compartment of refrigerator for about ½ hour, stirring occasionally.) Add the mashed bananas to the cooled gelatin mixture. Beat the remaining ½ cup dry milk with remaining ½ cup water until it begins to thicken. Add the lemon juice and beat until thick. Beat in the sugar and continue beating until the consistency of whipped cream. Fold in the chilled gelatin mixture. Freeze. Serves 8. *115 calories in each serving.*

CHOCOLATE ICE CREAM DESSERT

2 teaspoons gelatin
1 cup cold water
¾ cup nonfat dry milk
1½ cups milk
2 squares unsweetened chocolate

3 tablespoons sugar
1½ tablespoons liquid sweetener
2 teaspoons pure vanilla extract
2 tablespoons lemon juice

Soften the gelatin in ½ cup water. Mix ¼ cup dry milk with the milk and then scald. Melt the unsweetened chocolate when heating the milk. Dissolve the gelatin in it and stir in 2 tablespoons sugar, the liquid sweetener and vanilla. Chill until slightly thickened. (Place bowl in ice-cube compartment of refrigerator for about ½ hour, stirring occasionally.) Beat the remaining ½ cup dry milk with remaining ½ cup water until it begins to thicken. Add the lemon juice and beat until thick. Beat in the sugar and continue beating until the consistency of whipped cream. Fold in the chilled gelatin mixture. Freeze. Serves 8. *128 calories in each serving.*

COCOA ICE CREAM

1 cup light cream
1 cup milk
2 egg yolks
2 tablespoons sugar
1 tablespoon liquid sweetener
3 tablespoons unsweetened cocoa
1 teaspoon vanilla
2 egg whites
⅛ teaspoon salt

Scald the cream and milk. Beat the egg yolks, gradually adding the sugar, liquid sweetener and cocoa. Beat until smooth. Gradually add the scalded cream mixture, beating constantly to prevent curdling. Cook over low heat, mixing constantly, until mixture coats the spoon. Remove from the heat and stir in the vanilla. Beat with a rotary beater or electric mixer until frothy. Beat the egg whites and salt until stiff but not dry. Fold into the chocolate mixture and freeze. Serves 6. *161 calories in each serving.*

COFFEE FREEZE

½ cup lowfat dry milk
½ cup water
2 teaspoons liquid sweetener
2 teaspoons instant coffee
1 egg white

Combine all ingredients in the order given. Beat with an electric mixer after each addition. Freeze until firm. Makes 4 servings. *40 calories in each serving.*

COFFEE SHERBET

2 cups skim milk
½ cup evaporated milk
¼ cup instant coffee
1 tablespoon liquid sweetener

Combine all ingredients, mixing thoroughly. Freeze until mushy and whip with an electric mixer until creamy. Freeze until firm. Makes 5 servings. *45 calories in each serving.*

CRANBERRY SHERBET

1 cup dietetic cranberries
2 teaspoons lemon juice
rind of 1 lemon
2 egg whites, stiffly beaten

Combine all ingredients except egg whites. Freeze until firm. Place frozen sherbet in a cold bowl and whip until mushy. Fold in egg whites and freeze until firm. Makes 4 servings. *30 calories in each serving.*

CREAMY COCOA ICE CREAM

2 cups half and half, warmed
2 egg yolks
2 tablespoons sugar
dash of salt
1 tablespoon liquid sweetener
3 tablespoons cocoa
1 teaspoon pure vanilla extract
2 egg whites, stiffly beaten

Combine the egg yolks, sugar, salt, and liquid sweetener. Stir in cocoa. Beat until smooth. Add the cream, beating constantly. Cook in a double boiler until mixture coats a spoon. Cool. Fold in egg whites and vanilla extract. Freeze until firm. Makes 6 servings. *185 calories in each serving.*

FOUR FRUIT FROST

1 cup chilled orange juice
½ cup chilled lime juice
½ cup chilled lemon juice
1 cup chilled unsweetened pineapple juice
⅜ teaspoon liquid sweetener
    (⅛ teaspoon equals
    ¼ cup sugar)
1 pint sugar-free vanilla ice cream

Mix juices with sweetener; add ice cream; beat just until blended. Garnish each glass with thin slice orange, lemon, and lime, with slices touching. Makes 4 servings. *50 calories in each serving.*

FRESCA SHERBET

¾ cup evaporated milk
1½ teaspoons liquid sweetener
2 cups dietetic lemon-lime
    flavored carbonated beverage

Combine all ingredients and freeze until mushy. Beat until creamy and refreeze until firm. Makes 6 servings. *45 calories in each serving.*

GRAPE MOUSSE

1 cup nonfat dry milk
1 cup ice water
1 6-ounce can grape concentrate
1½ teaspoons liquid sweetener
    rind of 1 lemon

Beat dry milk and water with an electric mixer until stiff. Beat in grape concentrate, sweetener and lemon rind. Freeze until firm. Makes 6 servings. *75 calories in each serving.*

HAWAIIAN SHERBET

1 6-ounce can frozen orange-pineapple
    juice, unsweetened
¾ cup apple juice, unsweetened
¾ cup cold water
1½ teaspoons granulated sugar substitute
    (1 teaspoon equals ¼ cup sugar)
¼ cup nonfat dry milk solids

Combine liquids; add granulated sugar substitute, stirring until dissolved. Add dry milk; blend mixture well and pour into chilled refrigerator tray. (Moisten bottom of tray for faster freezing.) Place tray on bottom shelf of freezer compartment for 45 minutes to 1 hour, until sherbet has begun to freeze. Place a mixing bowl and rotary beater or wire whisk in refrigerator to chill. Turn sherbet into chilled bowl and beat until fluffy, but not melted; return to refrigerator tray at once and continue to freeze until almost set; then repeat beating procedure. Keep in freezer compartment until serving time. Makes 8 servings. *63 calories in each serving.*

ICE CREAM DESSERT

2 teaspoons gelatin
1 cup cold water
¾ cup nonfat dry milk
1½ cups milk
3 tablespoons sugar
1 tablespoon liquid sweetener
2 teaspoons vanilla
2 tablespoons lemon juice

Soften the gelatin in ½ cup water. Mix ¼ cup dry milk with the milk and then scald. Dissolve the gelatin in it and stir in 2 table-spoons sugar, the liquid sweetener and vanilla. Chill until slightly thickened. (Place bowl in ice cube compartment of refrigerator for about ½ hour, stirring occasionally.) Beat the remaining ½ cup dry milk with remaining ½ cup water until it begins to thicken. Add the lemon juice and beat until thick. Beat in the sugar and continue beating until the consistency of whipped cream. Fold in the chilled gelatin mixture. Freeze. Serves 8. *93 calories in each serving.*

KOOL-AID SHERBET

1 package sweetened soft drink
  mix (2 quart size), any flavor
3 cups nonfat milk

Dissolve drink mix in milk and freeze until mushy. Whip until smooth and freeze until firm. Makes 8 servings. *50 calories in each serving.*

LEMON ICE CREAM

1 tablespoon butter
1 tablespoon flour
⅛ teaspoon salt
3¼ cups milk
2 teaspoons liquid sweetener
½ cup lemon juice
2 teaspoons lemon rind

Melt the butter in a saucepan; stir in the flour and salt. Gradually add half the milk, stirring constantly to the boiling point. Cook over low heat 5 minutes. Remove from the heat and add the balance of the milk. Cool, turn into a bowl; add the liquid sweetener, lemon juice and rind. Freeze. Makes 5 servings. *158 calories per serving.*

LEMON de MENTHE SHERBET

1½ cups water
2 teaspoons liquid sweetener
½ cup lemon juice
½ cup orange juice
  rind of 1 lemon
⅓ cup powdered low fat milk
  white creme de menthe

Reserve the creme de menthe for garnish. Combine remaining ingredients and beat well. Yellow food coloring may be added to enhance the color of the sherbet. Freeze until mushy. Turn the mixture into a chilled bowl and whip until fluffy. Refreeze until firm. Top each serving with a teaspoon of creme de menthe. Makes 6 servings. *160 calories in each serving.*

MAPLE FREEZE

    2 tablespoons flour
        dash of salt
    1 cup nonfat milk
    2 teaspoons liquid sweetener
    2 egg yolks, beaten
    1 teaspoon maple flavoring
    2 egg whites, stiffly beaten

Combine flour, salt, milk, and sweetener. Cook in a double boiler until mixture coats a spoon. Add egg yolks and beat until smooth. Cook in a double boiler for 5 more minutes. Add flavoring and cool. Fold in egg whites. Freeze until firm. Makes 6 servings. *50 calories in each serving.*

PEACH SHERBET

    1 cup peaches, crushed
    1 cup skim milk
    3 teaspoons liquid sweetener
        juice of 1 lemon
        juice of 1 orange
        rind of 1 lemon
    2 egg whites, stiffly beaten

Combine all ingredients except egg whites. Blend thoroughly and freeze until firm. Turn mixture into a chilled bowl and whip until mushy. Fold in egg whites and refreeze until firm. Makes 6 servings. *25 calories in each serving.*

PERSIMMON ICE CREAM

    4 persimmons, pureed
    ½ teaspoon liquid sweetener, or more
    ¾ cup lemon juice
    ¼ cup orange juice
        rind of 1 lemon
    2 cups evaporated skim milk

Pour skim milk into refrigerator tray. Freeze until icy. Combine persimmons, liquid sweetener, lemon juice, orange juice, and rind.

Whip the evaporated milk until stiff and fold into the persimmon mixture. Freeze until firm. Makes 6 servings. *120 calories in each serving.*

PINEAPPLE CRUSH

1 quart buttermilk
1 cup sweetened crushed pineapple
1 tablespoon lemon juice
4 teaspoons liquid sweetener

Mix together and freeze. Makes 8 servings. *69 calories in each serving.*

PINEAPPLE SHERBET

1 quart buttermilk
¼ cup heavy cream
1 cup dietetic pineapple, crushed
1 tablespoon lemon juice
rind of 1 lemon
4 teaspoons liquid sweetener

Combine all ingredients. Mix thoroughly. Freeze until firm. Makes 8 servings. *80 calories in each serving.*

RASPBERRY SHERBET

2 cups raspberries, crushed
1 cup water
rind of 1 lemon
1½ teaspoons liquid sweetener

Combine all ingredients. Blend thoroughly. Freeze until mushy and beat until fluffy. Repeat this procedure once more. Refreeze until firm. Makes 6 servings. *35 calories in each serving.*

STRAWBERRY ICE CREAM DESSERT

2 teaspoons gelatin
1 cup cold water

¾ cup nonfat dry milk
1½ cups milk
3 tablespoons sugar
1½ tablespoons liquid sweetener
2 teaspoons pure vanilla extract
1½ cups mashed strawberries
2 tablespoons lemon juice

Soften the gelatin in ½ cup water. Mix ¼ cup dry milk with the milk and then scald. Dissolve the gelatin in it and stir in 2 tablespoons sugar, the liquid sweetener and vanilla. Chill until slightly thickened. (Place bowl in ice-cube compartment of refrigerator for about ½ hour, stirring occasionally.) Add the mashed strawberries to the cooled gelatin mixture. Beat the remaining ½ cup water and ½ cup dry milk until it begins to thicken. Add the lemon juice and beat until thick. Beat in the sugar and continue beating until the consistency of whipped cream. Fold in the chilled gelatin mixture. Freeze. Serves 8. *115 calories in each serving.*

STRAWBERRY ICE MILK

2 cups sugar
¼ cup cornstarch
¼ teaspoon salt
2 quarts skim milk
3 eggs, beaten
1 tablespoon unflavored gelatin
1½ tablespoons pure vanilla extract
2 cups strawberries, pureed
(other fruit may be substituted)

Mix sugar, cornstarch, and salt in the top of a double boiler. Blend in 4 cups skim milk gradually. Cook over hot water, stirring occasionally until thickened, 12 to 15 minutes. Stir a little of the hot cornstarch mixture into the beaten eggs; then stir the eggs into the remaining cornstarch mixture. Cook over hot water, stirring constantly 4 to 5 minutes longer, or until the mixture is about the consistency of soft custard. Soften gelatin in 1 cup skim milk. Stir into hot mixture. Chill thoroughly. This step is essential for a smooth ice milk. Stir in vanilla and remaining 3 cups skim milk. Pour into a 1 gallon ice-cream freezer canister; fill not more than two-thirds full. Freeze in a hand-cranked or electric ice-cream freezer. Makes 26 servings, ½ cup each. *120 calories in each serving.*

STRAWBERRY SHERBET

2 cups strawberries, crushed
1 cup ice water
1 teaspoon lemon juice
rind of 1 lemon
1½ teaspoons liquid sweetener

Combine all ingredients and blend thoroughly. Freeze until mushy. Beat until fluffy. Repeat this procedure once more. Refreeze until firm. Makes 6 servings. *35 calories in each serving.*

TEA ICE

1 quart orange spice tea
sweeten to taste

Freeze until flaky. Serve. Makes 8 servings. *No calories.*

VANILLA ICE CREAM No. 1

1 teaspoon gelatin
¼ cup cold water
1 cup milk
1 tablespoon flour
dash of salt
1 egg, well beaten
2 teaspoons pure vanilla extract
1½ cups evaporated skim milk
1 tablespoon liquid sweetener
plus 1 teaspoon

Pour evaporated milk into refrigerator tray and freeze until icy. Soften the gelatin in cold water. Combine flour, salt, egg, and liquid sweetener. Mix well and add milk slowly, stirring constantly. Cook in a double boiler until mixture coats spoon. Add gelatin and vanilla. Cool. Whip the evaporated milk until stiff. Fold into the custard mixture. Freeze in refrigerator tray. Whip 3 times at 30-minute intervals, and freeze until firm. Makes 6 servings. *65 calories in each serving.*

VANILLA ICE CREAM No. 2

    2 cups milk
    2 teaspoons cornstarch
      few grains salt
    2 eggs, separated
    ¼ teaspoon liquid sweetener
      (⅛ teaspoon equals
      ¼ cup sugar)
    1 cup heavy cream
    1½ teaspoons vanilla

Scald milk in top of double boiler. Mix cornstarch and salt. Add milk slowly, stirring constantly. Return to double boiler; cover; cook 20 minutes, stirring occasionally. Beat egg yolks; add hot milk mixture. Cook over hot water until slightly thickened, stirring constantly. Cool. Add sweetener. Whip cream; fold in. Beat egg whites stiff but not dry; fold in. Add vanilla. Pour into freezing tray of automatic refrigerator. When partly frozen, turn mixture into chilled bowl. Beat with rotary beater until fluffy. Return to tray and finish freezing, stirring once. Makes 6 to 8 servings. *120 calories in each serving.*

VANILLA ICE CREAM No. 3

    2 teaspoons gelatin
    1 cup water
    1 cup nonfat dry milk
    1½ cups milk
    3 tablespoons sugar
    1 tablespoon liquid sweetener
    2 teaspoons pure vanilla extract
    1½ tablespoons lemon juice
      rind of 1 lemon

Soften the gelatin in ½ cup cold water. Combine ½ cup dry milk, milk, sugar, and liquid sweetener. Heat in a double boiler and stir until dissolved. Add gelatin to the warm mixture. Chill. Beat ½ cup dry milk and ½ cup water until slightly thick. Add lemon juice and beat until thick. Combine all ingredients and freeze. Makes 8 servings. *95 calories in each serving.*

VANILLA ICE CREAM No. 4

    3 eggs, beaten
    3 cups milk

2 tablespoons liquid sweetener
3 cups half and half
1½ tablespoons gelatin
¼ cup cold water
2 tablespoons vanilla extract
½ teaspoon salt
rind of 1 lemon

Combine eggs, milk, and liquid sweetener. Cook in a double boiler until mixture coats a spoon. Dissolve gelatin in cold water and add to custard. Cool. Whip until smooth. Stir in remaining ingredients. Freeze in an ice cream freezer. Makes 12 servings. *120 calories in each serving.*

VANILLA CUSTARD ICE CREAM

1½ cups nonfat milk
¼ teaspoon salt
4 teaspoons cornstarch
2 egg yolks, beaten
2 teaspoons liquid sweetener
2 teaspoons pure vanilla extract
½ teaspoon nutmeg
½ cup evaporated milk
2 egg whites, stiffly beaten

Combine milk, salt, cornstarch, egg yolks, and sweetener. Beat well and cook in a double boiler until mixture coats a spoon. Combine all the remaining ingredients except egg whites. Cool. Fold in egg whites and freeze until mushy. Whip until creamy and refreeze until firm. Makes 6 servings. *75 calories in each serving.*

VANILLA ICE MILK

2 cups sugar
¼ cup cornstarch
¼ teaspoon salt
2 quarts skim milk
3 eggs, beaten
1 tablespoon unflavored gelatin
1½ tablespoons pure vanilla extract

Mix sugar, cornstarch, and salt in the top of a double boiler. Blend in 4 cups skim milk gradually. Cook over hot water, stirring occasionally until thickened, 12 to 15 minutes. Stir a little of the hot cornstarch mixture into the beaten eggs; then stir the eggs into the remaining cornstarch mixture. Cook over hot water, stirring constantly 4 to 5 minutes longer, or until the mixture is about the consistency of soft custard. Soften gelatin in 1 cup skim milk. Stir into hot mixture. Chill thoroughly. This step is essential for a smooth ice milk. Stir in vanilla and remaining 3 cups skim milk. Pour into a 1 gallon ice-cream freezer canister; fill not more than two-thirds full. Freeze in a hand-cranked or electric ice-cream freezer. Makes 26 servings, ½ cup each. *100 calories in each serving.*

DIABETIC VANILLA ICE CREAM

> 3 eggs
> 2¼ cups milk
> 6 saccharin tablets (½ grain) or
> 2 tablespoons liquid sweetener
> 3¾ cups half and half cream
> 1½ tablespoons plain gelatin
> 6 teaspoons pure vanilla extract
> ¾ teaspoon salt
> nutmeg to taste, if desired

Make cooked custard of eggs, milk and liquid sweetener. Soak gelatin in small amount of water and add enough hot custard to dissolve the gelatin. Add cream, vanilla, salt and gelatin to custard. Beat until smooth. Strain. Freeze. Makes 16 servings. *118 calories in each serving.*

WEIGHT WATCHER'S ICE CREAM

> 2 cups sugar
> ¼ cup cornstarch
> ¼ teaspoon salt
> 4 cups milk
> 4 eggs, beaten
> 2 tablespoons pure vanilla extract
> 4 cups chilled evaporated milk

Mix sugar, cornstarch, and salt in the top of a double boiler. Blend in milk gradually. Cook over hot water, stirring occasionally until thickened, 12 to 15 minutes. Stir a small amount of the hot cornstarch mixture into the beaten eggs; then stir the eggs into the remaining cornstarch mixture. Cook over hot water, stirring constantly 4 to 5 minutes longer, or until the mixture is about the consistency of pudding. Chill thoroughly. This step is essential for a smooth ice cream. Stir in vanilla and evaporated milk. Pour into a 1 gallon ice-cream freezer canister; fill not more than two-thirds full. Freeze in a hand-cranked or electric ice-cream freezer. Serves 28, ½ cup each. *140 calories per serving.*

CHOCOLATE SAUCE

4 squares unsweetened chocolate
1¼ cups hot water
¼ teaspoon salt
½ teaspoon liquid sweetener
(⅛ teaspoon equals
¼ cup sugar)
1 teaspoon vanilla

Cook chocolate with water and salt over low heat, stirring, until thick and well blended. Boil 2 minutes, stirring constantly. Remove from heat; add sweetener and vanilla. Cool; then refrigerate. Makes about 1½ cups. *(Calorie saving per recipe: approximately 864.)*

CRANBERRY SAUCE

4 cups cranberries
1½ cups water
1 teaspoon liquid sweetener
(⅛ teaspoon equals
¼ cup sugar)
2 teaspoons unflavored gelatin
½ cup cold water

Cook cranberries in 1½ cups water just until skins pop. Remove from heat; stir in sweetener. Soften gelatin in ½ cup cold water; add hot cranberry mixture; stir until gelatin dissolves. Chill. (This will not jell.) *(Calorie saving per recipe: approximately 1728.)*

CUSTARD SAUCE

1½ cups milk
¼ teaspoon salt

              4 egg yolks
             18 drops liquid sweetener
                (6 drops equal
                1 tablespoon sugar)
              ½ teaspoon vanilla

Scald milk; add salt. Beat egg yolks slightly; add milk mixture.
Cook over hot water, stirring constantly, until mixture coats spoon.
Add sweetener and vanilla. Serve warm. Makes 6 servings. *(Calorie
saving per recipe: approximately 162.)*

RAISIN ORANGE SAUCE

            1½ tablespoons flour
             1 cup water
             ½ cup orange juice
            4½ tablespoons lemon juice
             ¾ cup raisins
             ¼ teaspoon salt
            18 drops liquid sweetener
                (6 drops equal
                1 tablespoon sugar)
             2 tablespoons butter or margarine

Blend flour, water, orange juice, and lemon juice until smooth. Add
raisins and salt. Boil 5 minutes, stirring constantly, until thick;
then occasionally. Add sweetener and butter. Stir until butter melts.
Makes 6 servings. *(Calorie saving per recipe: approximately 162.)*

SPECIAL ORANGE SAUCE

             2 teaspoons cornstarch
               few grains salt
             1 cup orange juice
            12 drops liquid sweetener
                (6 drops equal
                1 tablespoon sugar)
             1 teaspoon lemon juice
             ⅛ teaspoon cinnamon
             ⅛ teaspoon nutmeg
            1½ cups orange sections

Mix cornstarch and salt. Add orange juice. Cook until thick, stirring constantly. Stir in sweetener, lemon juice, cinnamon, and nutmeg. Cool; add orange sections. Serve on ice cream. Makes 6 to 8 servings. *(Calorie saving per recipe: approximately 108.)*

WEIGHT WATCHER'S MOCHA SAUCE

2 tablespoons cornstarch
⅔ cup sugar
½ teaspoon salt
2 cups skim milk
1 tablespoon butter
⅓ cup cocoa
1 teaspoon instant coffee

Combine cornstarch, sugar, salt, and cocoa in a 1-quart saucepan. Mix well. Add milk slowly, stirring until smooth. Bring to a boil over low heat, stirring constantly. Boil 1 minute. Add butter. Boil, stirring constantly until thick and smooth, about 2 minutes. Stir in instant coffee. Cool. Serve over ice cream. *45 calories per tablespoon.*

7

BOMBES

Bombe, French for ball, is the name of a frozen dessert shaped into a spherical mold, hence its name. A bombe is made of two different frozen mixtures, one to line the mold, the other to fill it. Or, the mold can be filled by alternating two frozen mixtures in concentric layers. Mousse, sherbet, fruit ices, or ice cream are the most commonly used mixtures.

There is no other dessert that has as much beauty and mystery that can be molded and decorated to fit any menu and any occasion. It is a wise choice to top off any party dinner. The bombe is a dessert that speaks for itself in beauty and taste appeal.

TO LINE THE MOLD

Chill a 1- or 1½-quart mold or spring-form pan before preparing the dessert. Fill the mold with a slightly softened ice cream, sherbet, or ice, leaving a deep hole in the center. Use a spoon dipped in hot water to line the mold. Spread the frozen dessert evenly on the bottom and sides of the container ¾ to 1 inch thick. A second mixture is used to fill the center. Cover the mold with waxed paper or foil, and put a lid on it. The bombe should be placed in the freezing compartment for 24 hours.

TO UNMOLD THE BOMBE

Unmold by dipping the mold briefly into cool water. Never dip a mold into hot water. Run a spatula or knife around the edge to loosen. Invert onto a chilled plate. If you like, invert the mold onto a plate that has been covered with waxed paper. The ice cream may become slightly runny when the mold is dipped into water, and the paper will protect the plate from any melted dessert. The waxed paper can be peeled off before serving. After the dessert has been unmolded it should be set in the freezing compartment again to harden.

TO SERVE BOMBE

Slip the mold onto a plate that has been chilled. Decorate the base of the mold with fresh fruit, greenery, or flowers, and serve immediately. You may also garnish the bombe with whipped cream, nuts or cherries.

Combine any frozen dessert mixtures that appeal to you. There is no limit to what you can do with frozen creams and ices. Many delectable and glamorous combinations are possible. The following mixture combinations may be helpful:

Line the Mold with:	*Fill with:*
Praline ice cream	Champagne sherbet
Pistachio ice cream	Chocolate mousse
Almond ice cream	Strawberry mousse
Avocado ice cream	Avocado sherbet
French chocolate ice cream	Orange-chocolate mousse
Avocado ice cream	Raspberry sherbet
Honey ice cream	Champagne sherbet
Vanilla ice cream	Apricot-kirsch mousse
Vanilla ice cream	Strawberry mousse
Strawberry ice cream	Strawberry ice
Apricot ice	Apricot mousse
Pineapple ice	Pineapple mousse
Coffee ice cream	Chocolate mousse
Chocolate ice cream	Orange-chocolate mousse
Coconut ice cream	Orange-chocolate mousse
Peppermint ice cream	Chocolate mousse
Guava ice cream	Guava mousse
Chocolate chip ice cream	Chocolate mousse
Vanilla ice cream	Concord grape sherbet
Vanilla ice cream	Raspberry creme sherbet
Vanilla ice cream	Orange sherbet
Orange ice	Orange yogurt mousse
Raspberry ice	Raspberry yogurt mousse

ALMOND BOMBE

2 cups extra rich milk, warmed
3 egg yolks
1 cup sugar
¼ teaspoon salt
1¼ cups cream
1½ teaspoons pure vanilla extract
½ teaspoon pure almond extract
½ cup toasted, slivered almonds
strawberry mousse

Beat yolks and sugar together, slowly add the milk, stirring constantly. Cook this mixture in a double boiler for 5 minutes. Cool. Combine the remaining ingredients and the custard mixture. Freeze until firm. Line a chilled 1½ quart spring-form pan, or a mold of your choice, with slightly softened almond mixture. Leave a deep hole in center. Fill hole with strawberry mousse of your choice. Cover with foil and freeze overnight or several hours until firm. Unmold. Garnish with whipped cream and slivered almonds.

ALMOND SHERRY BOMBE

3 egg yolks, beaten
¼ cup water plus 2 tablespoons
¼ cup sugar
½ cup sweet sherry
1 cup cream
marshmallow mousse

Combine egg yolks, water, and sugar in the top of a double boiler. Cook until warm, stirring constantly. Add sherry, and cool. Stir occasionally while the mixture cools. Fold in cream, freeze until firm. Line a chilled 1 quart spring-form pan or a mold of your choice with slightly softened almond-sherry mixture. Leave a deep hole in center. Freeze until firm. Fill hole with marshmallow mousse. Cover with foil and freeze overnight or several hours until firm. Unmold. If desired, garnish with slivered almonds and whipped cream.

AVOCADO BOMBE

  2 avocados
  2 tablespoons lemon juice
  2 packages (3 ounces each) cream cheese
  ½ cup powdered sugar
  ⅛ teaspoon salt
  1 cup whipping cream
  1 tablespoon grated orange rind
  1 or 2 tablespoons chopped
    crystallized ginger
  1 pint lemon or orange sherbet

Chill 7 cup melon or other dome-shaped mold. Cut avocados lengthwise into halves; remove seeds and skin. Mash or sieve avocado
and beat together with lemon juice, cream cheese, powdered sugar
and salt. Whip cream; stir in orange rind and fold into avocado
mixture. Turn into chilled mold; line sides with avocado mixture,
using back of spoon to form a "well" in center. For easier handling,
place mold in freezer until slightly set (about 1 hour). Stir ginger
into slightly softened sherbet; spoon into "well," being careful
not to leave air spaces. Cover with waxed paper or plastic wrap.
Freeze until firm. About 30 minutes before serving remove mold
from freezer unit to refrigerator shelf. Just before serving, dip
quickly into lukewarm water, run a sharp knife around edges
and invert onto serving plate. Serve with thin orange wafers if
you wish.

AVOCADO 'N BERRY BOMBE

  2½ cups loganberries, sweetened
  1½ teaspoons lemon juice
     rind of 1 lemon
  ¼ cup water
  1 quart avocado ice cream

Line a chilled 1½ quart spring-form pan, or a mold of your choice,
with slightly softened avocado ice cream. Leave a deep hole in center. Freeze until firm. Puree the loganberries. Add lemon juice,
rind, and water. Blend well and freeze until very thick. Beat
by hand until smooth. Spoon the loganberry mixture into the avo-
cado-lined mold, being careful not to leave air spaces. Cover with
waxed paper or plastic wrap. Freeze until firm. About 30 minutes

before serving remove mold from freezer unit to refrigerator shelf. Just before serving, dip quickly into lukewarm water, run a sharp knife around edges and invert onto plate. Serve immediately.

CHERRY BOMBE

1 quart vanilla ice cream, softened
½ cup maraschino cherries, halved and drained
¼ cup coarsely chopped walnuts
1 8-inch-layer sponge cake, cut in ¾-inch strips
⅓ cup maraschino syrup
sherry extract to taste
1 pint cherry ice cream

Line a chilled 1½ quart spring-form pan or simple heart-shaped mold with slightly softened vanilla ice cream, leaving a deep hole in center. Place cherry halves and chopped walnuts on ice cream. Work quickly to avoid melting ice cream. Freeze until firm. Place cake strips over ice cream, pack firmly. Combine cherry syrup and sherry extract and pour over cake. Pack cherry ice cream layer into mold on top of cake; cover with foil and freeze overnight or several hours until firm. Unmold by placing hot towels around mold. Garnish with whipped cream and cherries.

CHOCOLATE MINT BOMBE

1½ teaspoons gelatin
1 cup water
1 cup half and half
1½ cups sugar
2 tablespoons cocoa
½ teaspoon vanilla
⅛ teaspoon mint flavoring
1 quart chocolate ice cream

Line a chilled 1½ quart spring-form pan, or a mold of your choice, with slightly softened chocolate ice cream. Leave a deep hole in center. Freeze until firm. Soften gelatin in water. Combine half and half, sugar, and cocoa in the top of a double boiler. Heat, stirring constantly until mixture is dissolved. Add gelatin and flavorings. Chill until thick. Spoon this mixture into the mold, being careful not to leave air spaces. Cover with waxed paper or plastic wrap. Freeze until firm. About 30 minutes before serving remove mold from freezer unit to refrigerator shelf. Just before serving, dip quickly into lukewarm water, run a sharp knife around edges and invert onto serving plate. If desired, garnish with whipped cream and shaved chocolate.

COCONUT RASPBERRY BOMBE

1/4 cup butter
2 tablespoon sugar
2 2/3 cups coconut macaroon crumbs
2 pints vanilla ice cream, softened
1/3 cup coarsely chopped walnuts
1 pint raspberry sherbet
1 1/2 teaspoons cornstarch
1 package (10 ounces) frozen raspberries, thawed
1/2 cup currant jelly

Cream butter until light and fluffy; gradually add sugar; then gradually add crumbs. Press onto bottom and sides of a 7-cup mold. Spread vanilla ice cream as evenly as possible with back of spoon or spatula about 1 inch thick over crumb shell. Press walnuts into bottom and sides of ice cream. Place in freezer to harden ice cream. Spoon raspberry sherbet into center to fill mold. Freeze. Unmold by dipping into warm water and turn out on chilled plate. Serve with raspberry sauce. To make sauce: Blend cornstarch with 1 tablespoon juice from raspberries to make a smooth paste; set aside. In a 1 quart-saucepan heat raspberries with jelly; stir in cornstarch mixture. Cook, stirring constantly, until thick and clear. Cool. Top bombe and individual servings with raspberry sauce.

CRUMB CRUST BOMBE

1 crumb crust, your preference
1 1/2 quarts ice cream, any flavor

Press crumb crust onto bottom and sides of a 5 cup mold. Chill for 1 hour, or bake in 350° oven for 8 to 10 minutes. A baked crust is

firmer. An unbaked crust must be thoroughly chilled or the filling
will immediately disintegrate the crust. Spoon softened ice cream
into center of mold. Freeze until firm. Unmold by dipping into
warm water and turn out on chilled plate. Serve with a sauce or
topping of your choice.

ICE CREAM BOMBE

1 quart orange sherbet
1 quart vanilla ice cream
1 8-inch cake layer
1 cup heavy cream, whipped
1 9-ounce package condensed mincemeat
½ cup light corn syrup
½ cup water
2 tablespoons rum

Chill a 6- to 8-cup mold in freezer at least 1 hour. With back of a
spoon, press sherbet around inside of mold to make a shell. Freeze
1 hour or until firm. Fill center with vanilla ice cream, pressing
firmly. Cover. Freeze 3 hours or until firm. To unmold: place cake
layer on sheet of foil. Wipe outside of mold with hot damp cloth.
Invert mold on cake. Gently shake mold to remove ice cream. Wrap
and place in freezer until serving time. Before serving, decorate
with whipped cream. Let stand 5 minutes for easier serving. Serve
with mincemeat sauce. To make sauce: break the condensed mincemeat into small pieces in medium saucepan. Add corn syrup, water,
and rum. Stirring to break up pieces, bring to a boil over low heat
and boil 1 minute. Serve warm or cool on ice cream. Makes a delicious sauce either way.

ICE CREAM 'N SHERBET BOMBE

1 crumb crust, your preference
1 quart ice cream, any flavor
½ cup coarsely chopped nuts
1 pint sherbet, any flavor

Press crumb crust onto bottom and sides of a 7-cup mold. Chill for
1 hour, or bake in 350° oven for 8 to 10 minutes. A baked crust is
firmer. An unbaked crust must be thoroughly chilled or the filling
will immediately disintegrate the crust. Spread ice cream as evenly
as possible with back of spoon or spatula about 1 inch thick over

crumb shell. Press nuts into bottom and sides of ice cream. Place in freezer to harden ice cream. Spoon softened sherbet into center to fill mold. Freeze until firm. Unmold by dipping into warm water and turn out on chilled plate. If desired, serve with dessert sauce or topping of your choice.

LEMON BOMBE

1½ teaspoons gelatin
¼ cup water
2 cups half and half
1½ cups sugar
2 egg yolks, beaten
juice of 1 lemon, unstrained
rind of 4 lemons
1 pint cream, whipped
2 egg whites, beaten
1 quart lemon sherbet

Line a chilled 2 quart spring-form pan, or a mold of your choice, with slightly softened lemon sherbet. Leave a deep hole in center. Freeze until firm. Soften gelatin in water. Combine sugar and lemon juice, stir in half and half. Heat in a double boiler; when warm stir in gelatin and cook until dissolved. Pour part of this mixture into the beaten egg yolks. Beat until blended and stir it into the remaining hot mixture. Cook in a double boiler until the custard coats a spoon. Add lemon rind. Cool. Fold in cream and egg whites. Spoon lemon mixture into bombe, being careful not to leave air spaces. Cover with waxed paper or plastic wrap. Freeze until firm. About 30 minutes before serving remove mold from freezer unit to refrigerator shelf. Just before serving, dip quickly into lukewarm water, run a sharp knife around edges and invert onto serving plate. Serve immediately.

ORANGE BOMBE

2 cups orange juice
½ cup sugar
rind of 2 oranges
1 teaspoon gelatin
¼ cup water
2 cups cream, whipped
1 tablespoon sugar

1½ teaspoons pure vanilla extract
1 quart vanilla ice cream

Line a chilled 1½ quart spring-form pan, or a mold of your choice, with slightly softened vanilla ice cream. Leave a deep hole in center. Work quickly to avoid melting ice cream. Freeze until firm. Heat until warm, 1 cup of the orange juice. Stir in sugar and gelatin that has been softened in ¼ cup water. When thoroughly dissolved add remaining orange juice. Freeze until mushy. Add vanilla and sugar to whipped cream. Fold into the icy orange mixture, blending well. Spoon orange mixture into bombe, being careful not to leave air spaces. Cover with waxed paper or plastic wrap. Freeze until firm. About 30 minutes before serving remove mold from freezer unit to refrigerator shelf. Just before serving, dip quickly into lukewarm water, run a sharp knife around edges and invert onto serving plate. Serve immediately.

PECAN BOMBE

2 teaspoons gelatin
¼ cup cold water
½ cup sugar
¼ cup hot water
2 egg whites, beaten stiff
1 cup pecans, chopped
1½ cups cream, whipped
½ teaspoon lemon juice
1 teaspoon pure vanilla extract
¼ teaspoon pure almond extract
1 quart vanilla ice cream

Line a chilled 1½ quart spring-form pan, or a mold of your choice, with slightly softened vanilla ice cream. Leave a deep hole in center. Work quickly to avoid melting ice cream. Freeze until firm. Soften gelatin in cold water. Combine sugar and hot water, cook until dissolved. Add the hot syrup to the egg whites, beating constantly. Heat softened gelatin over hot water until dissolved. Beat into egg white mixture. Add remaining ingredients, blending thoroughly. Spoon pecan mixture into bombe, being careful not to leave air spaces. Cover with waxed paper or plastic wrap. Freeze until firm. About 30 minutes before serving remove mold from freezer unit to refrigerator shelf. Just before serving, dip quickly into lukewarm water, run a sharp knife around edges and invert onto serving plate. Serve immediately.

SPUMONI BOMBE

      1 quart vanilla ice cream
    ½ teaspoon pure vanilla extract
    ¼ teaspoon pure almond extract
    ½ cup sugar
   1½ cups cream, whipped
    ½ cup chopped blanched almonds
    ⅓ cup chopped maraschino cherries
      3 tablespoons chopped candied orange peel
      1 teaspoon lemon juice
        rind of 1 lemon

Combine vanilla ice cream, vanilla extract, and almond flavoring. Line a chilled 1½ quart spring-form pan, or a mold of your choice, with slightly softened ice cream. Leave a deep hole in center. Work quickly to avoid melting ice cream. Freeze until firm. Combine remaining ingredients, blending thoroughly. Be sure the sugar is dissolved. Freeze until very thick. Remove from freezer and beat with a spoon until smooth. Spoon spumoni mixture into bombe, being careful not to leave air spaces. Cover with waxed paper or plastic wrap. Freeze until firm. About 30 minutes before serving remove mold from freezer unit to refrigerator shelf. Just before serving, dip quickly into lukewarm water, run a sharp knife around edges and invert onto serving plate. Serve immediately.

STRAWBERRY BOMBE

      1 quart strawberries, crushed
   1½ cups sugar
      2 teaspoons gelatin
      2 tablespoons water
    ¼ cup boiling water
      1 tablespoon lemon juice
      2 cups cream, whipped
      1 quart strawberry ice cream

Line a chilled 1½ quart spring-form pan, or a mold of your choice, with slightly softened strawberry ice cream. Leave a deep hole in center. Work quickly to avoid melting ice cream. Freeze until firm. Combine strawberries and sugar. Let stand ½ hour. Soften gelatin in 2 tablespoons water. Dissolve in boiling water and lemon juice. Cool. Stir gelatin into berries and cool until thick. Fold in whipped cream. Be sure the mixture is thoroughly blended. Spoon strawberry mixture into bombe, being careful not to leave air spaces. Cover with waxed paper or plastic wrap. Freeze until firm. About 30 minutes before serving remove mold from freezer unit to refrigerator shelf. Just before serving, dip quickly into lukewarm water, run a sharp knife around edges and invert onto serving plate. Serve immediately.

STRAWBERRY CREAM BOMBE

    2 pints strawberry ice cream
    2 egg yolks
  1/3 cup sugar
    1 tablespoon lemon rind
    2 tablespoons lemon juice
    1 tablespoon cold water
    1 egg white
    2 tablespoons sugar
    1 cup whipping cream, whipped

Chill a 7-cup mold in freezer. Quickly spread ice cream as evenly as possible with back of spoon or spatula on inside of mold to make a shell lining about 1/2 inch thick. Return to freezer to harden. Meanwhile, in top of double boiler beat egg yolks well. Beat in 1/3 cup sugar, lemon rind and juice and water. Cook, stirring constantly, over rapidly boiling water until thickened (about 10 minutes). Cool completely. In a small mixing bowl beat egg white until frothy. Gradually beat in 2 tablespoons sugar; beat until stiff peaks form. Fold in lemon mixture; then whipped cream. Pour into ice-cream-lined mold. Freeze. To unmold: Dip into warm water and turn out onto chilled plate. Garnish with fresh strawberries, if desired.

TUTTI FRUTTI BOMBE

    1 quart vanilla ice cream
  2/3 cup chopped maraschino cherries
    1 cup chopped pecans
    1 quart cranberry sherbet

Soften vanilla ice cream and stir in cherries and pecans. Line a chilled 1½ quart spring-form pan, or a mold of your choice, with slightly softened ice cream. Leave a deep hole in center. Work quickly to avoid melting ice cream. Freeze until firm. Soften cranberry sherbet and spoon into bombe, being careful not to leave air spaces. Cover with waxed paper or plastic wrap. Freeze until firm. About 30 minutes before serving remove mold from freezer unit to refrigerator shelf. Just before serving, dip quickly into lukewarm water, run a sharp knife around edges and invert onto serving plate. Serve immediately.

8.

MOUSSE

In French, the word *mousse* means foam. Mousse is a light, spongy dessert composed of a custard base and cream; egg whites are frequently folded in before freezing until firm. Mousse describes a number of dishes that can be served cold, iced, or even hot; however, the recipes that follow are only for iced mousse.

These frozen desserts are easy to make in any type of freezer or refrigerator. A mousse will usually freeze firm in 3 or 4 hours and does not require stirring or beating; so do not use a crank-type or electric freezer to agitate the mixture. If an automatic refrigerator is used, set the control for freezing. Pack the mousse in a freezing tray or other container and freeze until firm. Your container in the crank or electric freezer may also be used for this purpose. Fill the container with mousse and cover with Saran wrap or waxed paper, sealing tightly with tape. Pack the freezer as usual and skim off the salt water as it melts so it doesn't reach the top of the mold.

To freeze mousse in a bombe, line a mold with homemade or commercial ice cream or sherbet and fill the center with the unfrozen mixture. The mold should be filled until it overflows. Use a plate for a cover and press it down. You may cover the dessert with waxed paper before freezing. Remember mousse may be alternately layered with ice cream or sherbet. Each layer should be frozen before the next one is added.

APRICOT MOUSSE

1¼ cups evaporated milk
1 teaspoon lemon juice
1 cup apricot puree

1 teaspoon gelatin
2 tablespoons cold apricot juice
3 tablespoons hot apricot juice
¼ teaspoon salt
½ teaspoon pure vanilla extract

Put evaporated milk into refrigerator tray. Chill until ice crystals begin to form around edges. Put ice cold milk into a cold bowl. Whip with cold rotary beater by hand or with electric beater at high speed, until fluffy. Add lemon juice and whip until stiff. Soak the gelatin in cold juice and dissolve it in hot juice. Add gelatin to the puree and chill until thick. Stir in salt and vanilla and blend thoroughly. Combine all ingredients and mix thoroughly. Freeze until firm.

APRICOT 'N KIRSCH MOUSSE

1½ pounds very ripe apricots, pureed
2 cups powdered sugar, sifted
¼ cup kirsch
1½ cups cream, whipped
rind of 1 lemon

Combine all ingredients, blend thoroughly. Freeze until firm.

AVOCADO CRANBERRY MOUSSE

1 cup fresh cranberries
½ cup water
⅓ cup sugar
1 tablespoon fresh lime or lemon juice
dash of salt
½ cup diced avocado
½ pint whipping cream

Rinse cranberries, add water and boil about 5 minutes. Force through a sieve. Heat cranberry puree; add sugar and stir until sugar dissolves. Cool, and add lime juice and salt. To prepare avocado, cut into halves lengthwise, remove seed and skin, and cut fruit into small cubes. Whip cream until thick and gently fold in cranberry puree and avocado cubes. Pour into refrigerator tray, place in freezing compartment with control set at lowest temperature and freeze until firm. Reset temperature control to normal.

BANANA MOUSSE

¾ cup evaporated milk
2 teaspoons gelatin
3 tablespoons water
½ cup sugar
½ cup boiling water
2 bananas, mashed
dash of salt
¼ cup lemon juice
2 tablespoons orange juice

Put evaporated milk into refrigerator tray. Chill until ice crystals begin to form around edges. Put ice cold milk into a cold bowl. Whip with cold rotary beater by hand or with electric beater at high speed, until fluffy. Add 1 tablespoon lemon juice and whip until stiff. Combine sugar, boiling water, and salt. Dissolve gelatin in 3 tablespoons water and add to hot sugar and water mixture. Cool. Combine all ingredients and freeze. Stir the mixture once during the freezing process.

CHERRIES 'N KIRSCH MOUSSE

1½ pounds very ripe cherries, pureed
2 cups powdered sugar, sifted
¼ cup kirsch
1½ cups cream, whipped
rind of 1 lemon

Combine all ingredients, blend thoroughly. Freeze until firm.

CHOCOLATE MOUSSE

1½ teaspoons gelatin
2 tablespoons water
1 cup half and half
1½ squares unsweetened chocolate
¾ cup sugar
dash of salt
1 teaspoon pure vanilla extract
2 cups cream, whipped

Soften the gelatin in water. Heat the half and half and the chocolate in a double boiler. Add sugar, salt, vanilla, and gelatin, and stir until dissolved. Cool. Whip until smooth. Fold in the cream and freeze until firm.

CHOCOLATE MOUSSE SUPREME

3½ squares unsweetened chocolate
⅓ cup water
1 cup sugar
dash of salt
3 egg yolks, beaten
1 teaspoon vanilla
2 cups cream, whipped

Combine chocolate, water, sugar, and salt in a double boiler. Cook until creamy. Beat in yolks and cool. Fold in remaining ingredients and freeze until firm.

CHOCOLATE ALMOND MOUSSE

¼ cup light corn syrup
1 tablespoon water
1 6-ounce package semisweet chocolate chips
1 teaspoon pure vanilla extract
1½ cups cream
⅔ cup condensed milk
½ cup slivered almonds

Heat corn syrup and water. Add chocolate chips and vanilla; stir until smooth. Add the remaining ingredients to the semisweet chocolate mixture. Whip until fluffy and freeze.

CHOPPED PRUNE MOUSSE

1½ cups plumped chopped prunes
½ cup sugar
3 tablespoons grated lemon rind
¼ cup lemon juice
dash of salt
2 egg whites
1 cup heavy cream

Combine chopped prunes, ¼ cup sugar, lemon rind and juice and salt. Beat egg whites stiff; gradually add remaining ¼ cup sugar, beating constantly until stiff. Whip cream until soft peaks form. Combine prune mixture, egg white mixture and cream; mix thoroughly. Pour into freezing tray of refrigerator and freeze until firm.

COCONUT MOUSSE

2 egg whites, beaten stiff
2 cups cream, whipped
1 cup sugar
¼ teaspoon almond extract
½ teaspoon pure vanilla extract
2 cups toasted angel flake coconut

Combine egg whites and cream, gradually beating in sugar until blended. Combine remaining ingredients; blend thoroughly. Freeze until firm.

COFFEE MOUSSE

¾ cup sugar
1 cup strong coffee
dash of salt
1 teaspoon gelatin
2 cups cream, whipped

Cook coffee, sugar, salt, and gelatin until dissolved. Chill until thickened. Carefully fold in cream. Freeze until firm.

COFFEE COCONUT MOUSSE

1 cup strong coffee
¾ cup sugar
dash of salt
1 teaspoon gelatin
2 cups cream, whipped
1 cup toasted angel flake coconut

Cook coffee, sugar, salt, and gelatin over low heat until dissolved. Chill until thickened. Fold in cream and coconut. Freeze until firm.

CRANBERRY CHEESE MOUSSE

1 3-ounce package cream cheese
1 tablespoon fresh orange juice
  rind of 1 orange
2 tablespoons sour cream
½ cup cream, whipped
½ cup maraschino cherries, chopped
1 cup jellied cranberry sauce
1 cup sour cream
1½ tablespoons sugar

Beat cream cheese, orange juice, rind, and 2 tablespoons sour cream until creamy. Add whipped cream, blending thoroughly. Fold in cherries and cranberries. Freeze until firm. Serve with sweetened sour cream.

FRUIT MOUSSE

1 cup fruit puree, sweetened to taste
  dash of salt
½ cup water
¼ cup sugar
1 teaspoon gelatin
2 cups cream, whipped

Combine salt, water, sugar, and gelatin. Cook in the top of a double boiler until the gelatin is dissolved. Add fruit and chill until thickened. Beat with an electric mixer and fold in cream. Freeze until firm.

GOLDEN MALLOW MOUSSE

1 cup cream, whipped
¼ pound marshmallows
¼ cup half and half
2 teaspoons lemon juice
  rind of 1 lemon
½ cup peach jam
3 tablespoons orange marmalade

Put marshmallows and half and half in a double boiler. Cook until dissolved. Stir in lemon juice, rind, jam, and marmalade. Mix until well blended. Cool. Fold in cream and freeze until firm.

GREEN GAGE PLUM 'N KIRSCH MOUSSE

1½ pounds ripe green gage plums, pureed
2 cups powdered sugar, sifted
¼ cup kirsch
1½ cups cream, whipped
rind of 1 lemon

Combine all ingredients, blend thoroughly. Freeze until firm.

GUAVA MOUSSE

¾ cup sugar
1 tablespoon lemon juice
rind of 1 lemon
1 cup guava puree
1½ cups cream, whipped

Combine sugar, lemon juice, rind, and puree. Stir until dissolved. Fold the whipped cream into the guava mixture. Freeze until firm.

MAPLE MOUSSE

⅔ cup hot 100 percent maple syrup
6 egg yolks, beaten
2 cups cream, whipped
½ cup chopped pecans

Beat hot syrup into egg yolks and cook in a double boiler until thick. Cool. Fold in remaining ingredients and freeze until firm.

MARMALADE MOUSSE

1 cup sieved avocado
¼ cup lemon juice
dash of salt
1 cup orange marmalade
1 cup whipping cream, whipped

To prepare avocado, cut into halves lengthwise, and remove seed and skin. Force fruit through sieve. Blend in lemon juice and salt. Add cream and fold in marmalade and avocado. Pour into refrigerator tray and place in freezing compartment with control set at lowest temperature. Freeze without stirring. When firm, reset temperature control to normal.

MARSHMALLOW MOUSSE

24 large marshmallows
1 cup fruit juice
  (any juice except lemon)
2 tablespoons lemon juice
2 cups cream, beaten

Heat fruit juices and marshmallows in a double boiler until creamy. Cool. Thoroughly blend in whipped cream and freeze until firm.

ORANGE CHOCOLATE MOUSSE

$3/4$ cup instant cocoa
$1/4$ cup light corn syrup
$1/4$ cup water
2 tablespoons butter
$1\frac{3}{4}$ cups cream, whipped
$2/3$ cup sweetened condensed milk
$1/4$ teaspoon pure vanilla extract
  rind of 4 oranges

Combine cocoa, syrup and water. Stir until well blended. Add butter and cook in a double boiler until smooth. Cool for $1/2$ hour. Stir in whipped cream, condensed milk, and vanilla extract. Whip until thick and fluffy. Add orange rind and freeze until firm.

ORANGE COCONUT MOUSSE

2 egg whites, beaten stiff
2 cups cream, whipped
1 cup sugar
  rind of 2 oranges
1 teaspoon lemon juice
$1/2$ teaspoon vanilla
2 cups toasted angel flake coconut

Combine egg whites and whipped cream. Gradually beat in sugar until well blended. Stir in remaining ingredients. Freeze until firm.

ORANGE YOGURT MOUSSE

1 cup whipping cream, whipped
2 tablespoons sugar
1 egg white, beaten stiff
1 cup orange yogurt
¼ teaspoon pure vanilla extract
1 cup toasted coconut
rind of 1 orange

Add sugar to beaten egg white, blending thoroughly. Stir vanilla into whipped cream, and fold all ingredients together. Freeze until firm.

ORIENTAL MOUSSE

1 cup sieved avocado
3 tablespoons fresh lime or lemon juice
⅓ cup sugar
½ cup strawberry preserves
2 tablespoons finely chopped preserved ginger
dash of salt
1½ cups whipping cream

To prepare avocado, cut into halves, and remove seed and skin. Force fruit through sieve or puree in electric blender. Blend in lime juice, sugar, strawberry preserves, ginger and salt. Whip cream stiff; fold in avocado mixture. Pour into refrigerator tray, place in freezing compartment with control set at lowest temperature and freeze without stirring. When firm, reset temperature control to normal.

PEACH MOUSSE

2 cups peaches, crushed
(other fruit may be substituted)
⅛ teaspoon salt
1 cup sugar
1½ teaspoons gelatin
3 tablespoons water
3 tablespoons boiling water
2 tablespoons lemon juice
2 cups cream, whipped

Combine sugar, salt, and fruit. Soak gelatin in cold water and dissolve in hot water. Add lemon juice to the gelatin and stir into the fruit mixture. Chill. Fold in whipped cream. Freeze until firm.

PEACH 'N KIRSCH MOUSSE

1½ pounds very ripe peaches, pureed
2 cups powdered sugar, sifted
¼ cup kirsch
1½ cups cream, whipped
rind of 1 lemon

Combine all ingredients, blend thoroughly. Freeze until firm.

PINEAPPLE MOUSSE

2 teaspoons gelatin
¼ cup cold water
1 cup pineapple juice
dash of salt
3 tablespoons lemon juice
rind of 1 lemon
1¼ cups crushed pineapple
1 cup cream, whipped

Soften the gelatin in cold water. Heat the pineapple juice. Add the gelatin and salt and stir until dissolved. Cool. Stir in lemon juice and pineapple. Chill until thick. Fold in lemon rind and whipped cream. Be sure that all ingredients are well blended. Freeze until firm.

PRUNE MOUSSE

1 cup whipping cream
¼ cup sugar
1 teaspoon vanilla
1 large banana
1 cup prunes, pureed

Whip cream until stiff. Blend in sugar and vanilla. Crush banana thoroughly. Blend prunes and banana into cream mixture. Turn into refrigerator tray and place in freezing compartment with con-

trol set at lowest temperature. Freeze without stirring until firm.
When the mousse is firm reset the temperature control to normal.

PRUNE VELVET MOUSSE

3/4 cup evaporated milk
2 eggs, separated
8 tablespoons sugar
1/8 teaspoon salt
6 tablespoons lemon juice
2 teaspoons grated lemon rind
1 cup plumped, chopped prunes
1 teaspoon butter
1/2 cup graham cracker crumbs

Chill evaporated milk in ice cube tray until ice crystals form
around edge. While milk is chilling, beat egg yolks in top of double
boiler, add 6 tablespoons sugar, salt, lemon juice and rind. Cook
over hot water, stirring constantly, until thick. Cool; add prunes.
Whip egg whites stiff, gradually add remaining 2 tablespoons
sugar, beating constantly. Whip chilled evaporated milk until stiff.
Fold egg whites and evaporated milk into prune mixture. Butter
ice-cube tray; sprinkle bottom and sides with graham cracker
crumbs, reserving some for top. Pour in prune mixture; sprinkle
with remaining crumbs. Freeze until firm.

PRUNE YOGURT MOUSSE

1 cup whipping cream, whipped
3 tablespoons sugar
1 egg white
1 cup prune yogurt
dash of salt
1 teaspoon lemon juice
1/2 cup cooked prunes, chopped
1/2 cup sour cream
1 3/4 tablespoons sugar

Beat egg white until stiff, add sugar and cream. Mix until well
blended. Add yogurt, salt, lemon juice and prunes. Freeze until
firm. Serve with sour cream that has been sweetened with 1 3/4
tablespoons sugar.

RAMONA MOUSSE

½ cup sugar
½ cup water
½ teaspoon vanilla
2 medium-sized avocados
1 tablespoon lime or lemon juice
2 egg whites
dash of salt
1 cup whipping cream

Boil ¼ cup sugar with water 3 minutes. Cool. Add vanilla. Cut avocado into halves and remove seeds and skins. Sieve fruit to make about 1½ cups. Stir in lime juice and syrup. Beat egg whites with salt until stiff and gradually beat in remaining ¼ cup sugar. With same beater, whip cream until stiff. Fold in avocado mixture and egg white. Turn into freezing tray and place in freezing compartment with control set at lowest temperature. Freeze until firm. Reset temperature control to normal.

RASPBERRY YOGURT MOUSSE

1 cup whipping cream, whipped
2 tablespoons sugar
1 egg white, beaten stiff
1 cup raspberries, crushed
¼ cup sugar
½ teaspoon lemon rind
1 cup raspberry yogurt

Blend cream and sugar into stiffly beaten egg white. Add remaining sugar and lemon rind to raspberries. Stir in yogurt. Freeze until firm.

SALINAS SUMMER MOUSSE

¾ cup sieved avocado
½ cup sieved, cooked gooseberries
1½ cups whipping cream
¼ cup honey
dash of salt
¼ cup chopped maraschino cherries

To prepare avocado, cut fruit into halves and remove seed and skin. Puree in electric blender or force through sieve. To prepare gooseberries, cook until soft in small quantity of boiling water, removing lid to evaporate excess water during last few minutes of cooking. Puree in electric blender or force through sieve. Cool. Whip cream, combine avocado with gooseberries, honey, salt and cherries. Fold in whipped cream. Turn into refrigerator tray. Place in freezing compartment with control set at lowest temperature. Freeze until firm without stirring. Reset temperature control to normal.

SOUR CREAM PRUNE MOUSSE

1 cup cooked prunes, chopped
1 cup sour cream
1 can sweetened condensed milk
   rind of 1 lemon
½ teaspoon pure vanilla extract

Combine all ingredients, blending thoroughly. Freeze until firm.

STRAWBERRY MOUSSE No. 1

2 10-ounce packages frozen strawberries
⅔ cup corn syrup
⅓ cup sugar
⅓ cup water
3 egg whites
1½ teaspoons vanilla
3 egg yolks
2 cups heavy cream, whipped

Thaw strawberries. Combine corn syrup, sugar and water in a saucepan. Bring to a boil, and boil 2 minutes. Beat egg whites until stiff but not dry. Gradually beat in hot syrup, continuing until mixture is thick and creamy. Add vanilla. Beat egg yolks until thick; fold into egg whites. Fold in cream and strawberries. Pour into freezing trays lined with aluminum foil or into a 2-quart mold. Freeze without stirring. Turn out of trays; remove foil and cut into blocks. Or, to remove mousse from mold, cover outside of mold for a few seconds with a cloth wrung out of hot water.

STRAWBERRY MOUSSE No. 2

1½ cups cream, whipped
⅔ cup sweetened condensed milk

⅔ cup crushed strawberries, sweetened
   to taste
½ teaspoon lemon rind

Combine all ingredients, blending thoroughly. Freeze until firm.

STRAWBERRY YOGURT MOUSSE

1 cup whipping cream
2 tablespoons sugar
1 egg white
1 cup strawberry yogurt
1 cup crushed strawberries
2 tablespoons sugar

Beat egg white until stiff, add 2 tablespoons sugar and cream that
has been whipped. Mix until well blended. Stir in yogurt, strawberries, and remaining sugar. Freeze until firm.

TOASTED COCONUT MOUSSE

1½ cups dairy sour cream
½ cup sugar
1 teaspoon vanilla
1 egg white
1 cup coconut, toasted

Place sour cream in a small mixing bowl and chill with beaters at
least 30 minutes. Beat sour cream until very fluffy (about 5 minutes at high speed); fold in sugar and vanilla. Beat egg white until
stiff but not dry; blend into sour cream mixture along with coconut. Freeze until firm.

VANILLA MOUSSE

2 egg whites, beaten stiff
¼ cup powdered sugar
2 cups cream whipped
¼ cup powdered sugar
1 teaspoon pure vanilla extract

Gradually beat ¼ cup sugar into the egg whites. Beat remaining
powdered sugar and vanilla into the cream. Fold all ingredients
together and freeze.

9.

PARFAITS

A *parfait*, meaning "something perfect" in French, is a dessert that is less cold and more creamy than ice cream. Parfaits can be set in molds without lining them with an ice mixture, as is done in the case of bombes. This dessert has a flavored custard as a base and contains whipped cream and a syrup. It is frozen without stirring the same way as a mousse.

There is a second type of parfait that you are more familiar with. It is a rich sundae made of layers of ice cream, fruit, flavored sauces and whipped cream. Parfait makes an elegant party dessert. Alternate scoops of ice cream, or other frozen desserts, with spoonfuls of sauce, crushed fruit, marshmallows, cream, candied fruit, chopped nuts, crushed candy, marrons, or toasted coconut.

The parfait is a perfect dessert for birthday parties and special occasions. Let the children make their own. They can help themselves to sauces and toppings in separate bowls.

APRICOT PARFAIT

½ cup apricot syrup
  (other syrups may be substituted)
2 egg yolks, beaten
1 cup cream, whipped
2 egg whites, beaten stiff

Heat syrup. Slowly add the egg yolks, constantly stirring the syrup. Cook over a double boiler, stirring until thick, about 15 minutes. Cool. Add whipped cream and egg whites, folding in carefully. Freeze.

196

BERRY PARFAIT

1 quart of strawberries, or
  raspberries, crushed
1 cup sugar
¾ cup water
3 egg whites, beaten stiff
2 cups cream, whipped

Boil sugar and water until it forms a thread. Slowly beat the syrup into the egg whites. Fold in berries and cream. Freeze.

BUTTERSCOTCH PARFAIT

⅓ cup brown sugar
1½ tablespoons butter
¼ cup boiling water
2 egg yolks, beaten
2 cups cream, whipped
  dash of salt
1 teaspoon pure vanilla extract

Cook brown sugar and butter in a heavy skillet until melted, add water. Beat egg yolks in the top of a double boiler, slowly add the syrup and beat until fluffy. Chill. Fold in remaining ingredients and freeze.

COFFEE PARFAIT

½ cup sugar
¼ cup water
2 egg yolks, beaten
2 teaspoons instant coffee
1 cup cream, whipped
2 egg whites, beaten stiff

Boil sugar and water for 5 minutes. Slowly add the egg yolks, stirring constantly. Cook over a double boiler until the mixture thickens, about 15 minutes. Cool. Add instant coffee, whipped cream, and egg whites. Freeze.

CREAMY LEMON PARFAIT

1½ cups sugar
½ cup water
3 egg whites, beaten stiff
2 tablespoons lemon juice
rind of 2 lemons
3 cups cream, whipped

Boil sugar and water until it forms a thread. Slowly beat the syrup into the egg whites. When cool, add lemon juice and rind. Fold in cream and freeze.

CREME de MENTHE PARFAIT

1 cup sugar
1 cup water
3 egg whites, beaten stiff
¼ cup green creme de menthe
2 cups cream, whipped

Boil sugar and water for 5 minutes. Slowly pour the syrup into the egg whites, beating constantly. Add remaining ingredients and freeze.

LEMON PARFAIT

¾ cup sugar
⅓ cup water
2 egg yolks, beaten
rind of 2 lemons
2 tablespoons lemon juice
1 cup cream, whipped
2 egg whites, beaten stiff

Boil sugar and water for 5 minutes. Slowly add the egg yolks, constantly stirring the syrup. Cook over a double boiler, stirring until thick, about 15 minutes. Add lemon juice and rind, cool. Fold in whipped cream and egg whites. Freeze.

MACAROON PARFAIT

⅔ cup sugar
¼ cup water

6 egg yolks, beaten
1 tablespoon pure vanilla extract
2 cups cream, whipped
1 cup dry macaroon crumbs

Boil sugar and water for 5 minutes. Pour the syrup over the egg yolks and continue beating until cool. Fold in vanilla, macaroons, and cream. Freeze.

MAPLE PARFAIT

1 cup 100 percent pure maple syrup
4 egg yolks, beaten
4 egg whites, beaten stiff
⅛ teaspoon salt
2 cups cream, whipped

Heat the syrup and slowly pour over the egg yolks. Add salt and cook until thickened. Chill. Fold in stiffly beaten egg whites and whipped cream. Freeze until firm.

MARRON PARFAIT

⅔ cup sugar
¼ cup water
6 egg yolks, beaten
2 cups cream, whipped
1 cup preserved marrons, chopped
1 tablespoon pure vanilla extract

Boil sugar and water for 5 minutes. Pour the syrup over the egg yolks and continue beating until cool. Fold in marrons, vanilla, and cream. Freeze until firm.

ORANGE COINTREAU PARFAIT

1½ cups sugar
½ cup water
3 egg whites, beaten stiff
1 tablespoon Cointreau
rind of 1 orange
3 cups cream, whipped

Boil sugar and water until it forms a thread. Slowly beat the syrup into the egg whites. When cool, add Cointreau and orange rind. Fold in cream and freeze.

PARFAIT SUPREME

½ cup sugar
⅓ cup water
2 egg whites
⅛ teaspoon salt
1 cup sieved avocado
2 tablespoons lemon juice
1 cup whipping cream

Combine sugar and water in a small saucepan and cook and stir until sugar is dissolved. Continue cooking until syrup spins a thread. Beat egg whites with salt until stiff. Pour hot syrup slowly over beaten egg whites while continuing to beat. Beat until cool. To prepare avocado, cut into halves and remove seed and skin. Force fruit through a sieve and blend in lemon juice. Fold avocado and whipped cream into egg white mixture. Turn into refrigerator tray, place in freezing compartment with control set at lowest temperature and freeze to desired firmness. Reset temperature control to normal.

PEANUT BUTTER PARFAIT

1 quart sour cream
2 cups sugar
1 cup crunchy peanut butter

Combine all ingredients and blend thoroughly. Freeze until firm.

SPICED CHOCOLATE PARFAIT

1 square semisweet chocolate, grated
½ teaspoon cinnamon
⅔ cup sugar
¾ cup water
3 egg whites, beaten stiff
1 teaspoon pure vanilla extract
2 cups cream, whipped

Combine sugar and water and boil for 5 minutes. Beat syrup into egg whites until syrup cools. Add remaining ingredients. Freeze until firm.

STRAWBERRY PARFAIT No. 1

     1 quart strawberries, mashed
     1 cup sugar
     ½ cup water
     1 cup sugar
     3 egg whites, beaten stiff
     2 cups cream, whipped

Stir 1 cup of sugar into strawberries and let stand 2 hours. Strain.
Freeze strawberries until icy. Combine remaining sugar and water
and boil for 5 minutes. Beat syrup into the egg whites and continue
beating until the mixture is cool. Fold all ingredients together and
freeze until firm.

STRAWBERRY PARFAIT No. 2

     ½ cup sugar
     ¼ cup water
     1 tablespoon orange juice
     1 cup strawberries, crushed
     1 cup cream, whipped
     2 egg whites, beaten stiff

Boil sugar and water for 5 minutes. Add strawberries. Cook in a
double boiler, stirring until thick, about 15 minutes. Add orange
juice. Cool. Fold in whipped cream and egg whites. Freeze until
firm.

STRAWBERRY MALLOW PARFAIT

     1 cup strawberries, crushed
       (other fruit may be substituted)
     2 tablespoons lemon juice
     ½ pound cut-up marshmallows
     1 cup cream, whipped
     2 egg whites, beaten stiff
     2 tablespoons sugar

Heat strawberries, marshmallows, and lemon juice. Stir until
smooth and creamy. Cool. Add sugar to beaten egg whites. Beat
until thoroughly blended. Fold all ingredients together and freeze.

VANILLA PARFAIT

1 cup sugar
½ cup water
3 egg whites, beaten stiff
2 cups cream, whipped
2 teaspoons pure vanilla extract

Boil sugar and water for 5 minutes. Pour syrup into egg whites, beating constantly. Fold in remaining ingredients. Freeze until firm.

ICE CREAM PARFAITS

Ice cream
Ice cream sauces
Sweetened fruit
Whipped cream
Nuts

Alternate layers of ice cream and ice cream sauces or sweetened fruit in parfait glasses. If desired, use several flavors of ice cream. Top with sweetened whipped cream or nuts.

CHOCOLATE ICE CREAM PARFAIT

2 eggs
½ cup sugar
½ cup butter
2 squares semisweet chocolate, melted
½ cup whipping cream
2 tablespoons sugar
1 quart vanilla ice cream

Mix eggs and sugar in top of double boiler and cook, stirring constantly until mixture is amber colored (about 10 minutes). Add butter and melted chocolate; continue heating, stirring constantly, until butter is melted. Cool. Whip cream, blend in sugar. Alternate layers of ice cream and sauce in parfait glasses ending with ice cream. Top with whipped cream.

CURRANT ICE CREAM PARFAIT

2 teaspoons cornstarch
2 tablespoons lemon juice
1 **cup (10-ounce jar) currant** jelly,
    stirred to break up
½ cup whipping cream
2 tablespoons confectioner's sugar
1 quart vanilla ice cream

In a saucepan blend cornstarch and lemon juice; add jelly. Bring
to a boil over low heat, stirring constantly. Cool. Beat whipping
cream until cream begins to thicken; add sugar and continue beating until soft peaks form. Alternate layers of ice cream and sauce
in parfait glasses. Top each with spoonful of whipped cream.

ORANGE ICE CREAM PARFAIT

¼ cup sugar
1 tablespoon cornstarch
½ cup water
¾ cup (6-ounce can) **frozen concentrated**
    orange juice, thawed
3 pints vanilla ice cream
8 to 10 orange slices

In a saucepan mix thoroughly sugar and cornstarch; gradually
blend in water and orange juice. Bring to a boil. Cook, stirring constantly, until thick and clear. Cool. Alternate layers of ice cream
and sauce in parfait glasses. Garnish with orange slices.

10.

FROZEN PIES

If you've got ice cream in mind for that special dessert, make it ice cream with excitement—serve frozen pie.

The old expression "easy as pie" has now come true. The filling and crust can be prepared beforehand and put away in the freezer. Or, keep several unfilled crumb crusts in your freezer. When those unexpected guests come to call, fill quickly with ice cream before serving. Remember, when you store a pie in the freezer be sure to keep the pie well wrapped until you need it.

The desserts that follow are so easy to put together that they can be done the same day that you wish to serve them. Make pies with a "new look," lush with fruit, ice cream, sherbet, or other fillings. Step right up and take your choice of these melt-in-mouth frozen pies.

FLAKY BUTTER PIE CRUST

1½ cups sifted flour
1 teaspoon salt
¼ cup butter
¼ cup lard
¼ cup cold milk

Measure flour into mixing bowl and add salt. With pastry blender cut in half the shortening, until mixture looks like meal. Cut in remaining shortening coarsely until particles are the size of giant peas. Sprinkle mixture with milk, a tablespoon at a time, mixing in circular motion with knife until all the flour is moistened and dough gathers together. If necessary add more milk, a little at a time, until it is easy to handle. Press into a ball, then roll out. Line a 9-inch pie plate with the pastry, and prick with a fork. Bake at 425° F. for 15 to 18 minutes or until lightly browned.

CRUMB AND MERINGUE CRUSTS

Chocolate Crumb Crust

1½ cups chocolate wafer crumbs
⅓ to ½ cup melted butter

Combine all ingredients; blending well after each addition. Press firmly onto sides and bottom of a 9-inch pie plate. Chill for 1 hour, or bake in 350° oven from 8 to 10 minutes. A baked crust is firmer. An unbaked crust must be thoroughly chilled or the filling will immediately disintegrate the crust.

Coconut Chocolate Crumb Crust

3 squares unsweetened chocolate
3 tablespoons butter
¾ cup sifted powdered sugar
3 tablespoons milk
1 teaspoon pure vanilla extract
2¼ cups shredded coconut

Melt chocolate and butter in a double boiler. Mix powdered sugar and milk, and stir into the chocolate mixture. Add vanilla and coconut; mix well. Press the crumb mixture firmly onto sides and bottom of a 10-inch pie plate. Chill for 1 hour or until firm.

Dry Cereal Crust

1½ cups corn flakes, crisp rice cereal,
   or equivalent
⅓ cup sugar
⅓ to ½ cup melted butter

Combine all ingredients; blending well after each addition. Press firmly onto sides and bottom of a 9-inch pie plate. Chill for 1 hour, or bake in 350° oven for 8 to 10 minutes. A baked crust is firmer. An unbaked crust must be thoroughly chilled or the filling will immediately disintegrate the crust.

Filbert Crumb Crust

1 cup crushed graham cracker crumbs
1 cup ground filberts
⅓ cup sugar
⅓ to ½ cup melted butter

Combine all ingredients; blending well after each addition. Press firmly onto sides and bottom of a 9-inch pie plate. Chill for 1 hour, or bake in 350° oven for 8 to 10 minutes. A baked crust is firmer. An unbaked crust must be thoroughly chilled or the filling will immediately disintegrate the crust.

Gingersnap Crumb Crust

1½ cups gingersnap crumbs
⅓ to ½ cup melted butter

Combine all ingredients; blending well after each addition. Press firmly onto sides and bottom of a 9-inch pie plate. Chill until set. Do not bake Gingersnap Crumb Crust.

Graham Cracker Crumb Crust

1½ cups crushed graham cracker crumbs
⅓ cup sugar
⅓ to ½ cup melted butter.

Combine all ingredients; blending well after each addition. Press firmly onto sides and bottom of a 9-inch pie plate. Chill for 1 hour, or bake in 350° oven for 8 to 10 minutes. A baked crust is firmer. An unbaked crust must be thoroughly chilled or the filling will immediately disintegrate the crust.

Meringue Pie Crust

3 egg whites
¼ teaspoon salt
¼ teaspoon cream of tartar
¾ cup sugar

Preheat oven to 250° F. (very slow). Beat egg whites until foamy. Add salt and cream of tartar and beat until soft peaks form. Add sugar gradually, beating constantly, and continue beating until very stiff peaks form. Spoon the meringue mixture into a 9-inch pie plate, heaping it around the edge to form a shell. Bake 1 hour. Turn off heat and let meringue cool in the oven. Note: One teaspoon lemon juice may be used instead of cream of tartar. Add it after the sugar has been beaten into the egg whites.

Nut Crumb Crust

1¼ cups vanilla wafer crumbs
½ cup chopped nuts
⅓ to ½ cup melted butter

Combine all ingredients; blending well after each addition. Press firmly onto sides and bottom of a 9-inch pie plate. Chill for 1 hour, or bake in 350° oven for 8 to 10 minutes. A baked crust is firmer. An unbaked crust must be thoroughly chilled or the filling will immediately disintegrate the crust.

Vanilla Crumb Crust

1½ cups vanilla wafer crumbs
⅓ to ½ cup melted butter

Combine all ingredients; blending well after each addition. Press firmly onto sides and bottom of a 9-inch pie plate. Chill for 1 hour, or bake in 350° oven for 8 to 10 minutes. A baked crust is firmer. An unbaked crust must be thoroughly chilled or the filling will immediately disintegrate the crust.

Zwieback Crust

1½ cups zwieback crumbs
⅓ cup powdered sugar
½ teaspoon cinnamon
⅓ to ½ cup melted butter

Combine all ingredients; blending well after each addition. Press firmly onto sides and bottom of a 9-inch pie plate. Chill for 1 hour, or bake in 350° oven for 8 to 10 minutes. A baked crust is firmer. An unbaked crust must be thoroughly chilled or the filling will immediately disintegrate the crust.

BAKED ALASKA PIE

1 cup regular all purpose flour
3 tablespoons confectioner's sugar
½ cup butter, softened
⅓ cup finely chopped nuts

2 pints cherry ice cream, softened
1 pint vanilla ice cream, softened
2 egg whites
1/8 teaspoon cream of tartar
1/4 cup sugar

To prepare crust: In a small mixing bowl beat together flour, sugar and butter until well blended. Stir in nuts. Press on bottom and sides of a 9-inch pie plate building up edge; prick with fork. In a preheated 350° F. oven bake 15 to 18 minutes or until lightly browned. Cool on wire rack; chill. To fill pie: spoon 1 pint cherry ice cream into crust; pack down with back of spoon. Freeze. Repeat with vanilla ice cream and remaining 1 pint cherry ice cream. Cover and store in freezer. Just before serving prepare meringue.

To prepare meringue: In a small mixing bowl beat egg whites until frothy. Add cream of tartar and beat until soft peaks form. Add sugar, 1 tablespoon at a time and beat until stiff peaks form. Spread meringue over ice cream, making certain it is sealed to crust. Place pie plate on wooden board. Bake in a preheated 500° F. oven 1 to 3 minutes or until meringue is lightly browned. Serve immediately.

BLACK BOTTOM PIE

1 8-inch baked pie crust
1 cup semisweet chocolate pieces
1/2 cup milk
16 marshmallows
1 teaspoon vanilla
1 1/2 cups heavy cream, divided

Reserve 1 tablespoon of the semisweet chocolate pieces for garnish. Put remaining pieces of chocolate, milk, and marshmallows in top of double boiler. Place over boiling water, and cook, stirring occasionally, until mixture is melted and smooth. Remove from heat; stir in vanilla. Chill. Whip 1 cup of the heavy cream; fold in chilled chocolate mixture. If pie is to be frozen and stored use an aluminum foil plate or slip the pie shell into a paper pie plate. Turn chocolate mixture into pie shell. Whip remaining 1/2 cup cream; carefully spread over top of pie. Press point of remaining chocolate pieces into cream for polka dot effect. Freeze until firm. To store in freezer, cover with second pie plate and wrap in moisture proof plastic food wrap; return to freezer. Remove from freezer 30 minutes before serving. Pie may be served without freezing until firm, if desired.

Oriental Mousse

Rainbow Ice Cream Pie

Lincoln Ice Cream Log

Peach Tarts

Apricot Ice Cream Mold

Cantaloupe à la Mode—Two "Modes"

Confetti Ice Cream Cake

Ice Cream Blocks

BLACK BOTTOM ICE CREAM PIE

1 9-inch chocolate crumb crust
½ pint chocolate ice cream, softened
½ cup chocolate sauce
1 quart vanilla or coffee ice cream,
    softened

Spread chocolate ice cream in crust; spread ¼ cup chocolate sauce over ice cream. Spread ½ the vanilla or coffee ice cream over chocolate; repeat one more time and freeze. Top with shredded chocolate before serving.

CREAM BAKED ALASKA PIE

1 9-inch baked pastry shell, chilled
4 eggs
¼ cup sugar
1 cup corn syrup
1 teaspoon vanilla
1 cup heavy cream
3 egg whites
¼ teaspoon cream of tartar

Beat eggs until foamy. Gradually add sugar, then ½ cup of the corn syrup; beat until thick. Stir in vanilla. Fold in whipped cream. Turn into freezing tray. Freeze until almost firm. Turn into chilled bowl; beat until smooth. Turn into pastry shell and freeze until firm. Just before serving, beat egg whites until frothy; add cream of tartar, beat until stiff peaks form. Gradually beat in remaining ½ cup corn syrup; beat until very stiff. Cover pie with meringue; seal edges. Place on several thicknesses of wrapping paper on a wet board. Bake in a very hot oven 500° F. about 5 minutes. Serve immediately.

DATE ICE CREAM PIE

1 9-inch vanilla crumb crust
1 envelope gelatin
1 cup water
1½ cups dates, cut up
½ cup sugar
⅓ cup chopped pecans

    1 teaspoon lemon juice
    rind of one lemon
    2 pints vanilla ice cream

Soften gelatin in ½ cup water. Cook sugar, dates, and remaining water until soft; add gelatin. Mix thoroughly, and add pecans, lemon juice and rind; cool. Fill crust with 1 pint of ice cream; add date mixture. Spread remaining ice cream over dates; freeze.

DOUBLE DECKER PUMPKIN PIE

    1 9-inch pie crust
    1 pint vanilla ice cream
  1¾ cups canned pumpkin
    ½ teaspoon salt
    ½ teaspoon nutmeg
    ½ teaspoon ginger
    1 teaspoon cinnamon
    1 cup honey
    1 tablespoon unflavored gelatin
    1 cup heavy cream, whipped
    ¼ cup toasted blanched slivered
       almonds (optional)

Slowly heat pumpkin, salt, spices, honey and gelatin in a saucepan; stirring until gelatin is dissolved (about 5 minutes). Cool until slightly thickened. Whip cream until stiff, combine cooled pumpkin and whipped cream. Spread vanilla ice cream over cold baked pastry shell. Top ice cream with pumpkin pie mixture, arrange toasted slivered almonds over top. Place pie unwrapped in freezer. When solidly frozen (about 2 hours) wrap and return to freezer. Remove from freezer about 5 minutes before serving.

FROSTY PUMPKIN PIE

    ⅓ cup butter
    2 tablespoons sugar
    ⅛ teaspoon nutmeg
  1¼ cups graham crackers, crushed
    1 cup pumpkin, canned or cooked, mashed

⅓ cup brown sugar, packed
¼ teaspoon salt
½ teaspoon cinnamon
¼ teaspoon ginger
½ teaspoon nutmeg
1 quart vanilla ice cream, softened
½ cup cream, whipped (if desired)
6–8 candied ginger slivers (if desired)

Stir butter, sugar, and ⅛ teaspoon nutmeg together in a saucepan over low heat until butter is melted. Blend in cracker crumbs. Press evenly into an 8-inch pie pan. Chill. Combine pumpkin, brown sugar, salt, cinnamon, ginger, and ½ teaspoon nutmeg; mix well. Stir ice cream just until smooth. Stir pumpkin mixture into ice cream, mixing just enough to blend. Or, for a swirl effect, fold mixture gently into ice cream, allowing streaks to remain. Pour into graham cracker crust. Freeze until firm. Garnish with whipped cream and slivers of candied ginger, if desired.

FRUIT COCKTAIL PIE

1 can (8¾ ounce) fruit cocktail
3 eggs
¾ cup sugar
¼ teaspoon salt
¼ cup lime or lemon juice
12 graham crackers
3 tablespoons butter or margarine
1 cup whipping cream
1–2 drops green food coloring

Drain fruit cocktail. Separate 2 eggs; beat 1 whole egg and 2 yolks together. Add ½ cup sugar, salt and lime juice. Cook in double boiler until thickened, stirring frequently. Cool. Crush graham crackers and blend with butter. Beat remaining egg whites stiff; beat in ¼ cup sugar. Whip cream. Fold together egg whites, cream and cooked mixture. Stir in food coloring and fold in drained fruit cocktail, reserving a few pieces of fruit for garnish. Press ¾ths of cracker crumbs into bottom of refrigerator tray. Spoon in fruit cocktail mixture and sprinkle remainder of crumbs on top. Garnish with reserved fruit cocktail. Chill in freezing compartment at least 2 hours. Cut into triangles to serve.

GHOST OR GOBLIN PIE

1 9-inch chocolate crumb crust
1 tablespoon unflavored gelatin
¾ cup orange juice
1 tablespoon grated orange rind
2 tablespoons lemon juice
3 egg yolks
3 egg whites
¼ teaspoon salt
⅔ cup honey
1 cup heavy cream, whipped

Dissolve gelatin in ¼ cup orange juice. Combine balance of orange juice, rind, and lemon juice with slightly beaten egg yolks. Cook over low heat, stirring until thick. Remove from heat, add dissolved gelatin. Cool. Beat egg whites and salt until they hold their shape. Continue beating and drizzle in half of the honey. When whites are stiff, fold into gelatin mixture. Using same beater and bowl, whip cream, sweeten with balance of honey. Combine with pie filling. For a deeper orange color add 6 drops yellow and 2 drops red food coloring to the cream. Turn into prepared chocolate crumb shell. Freeze until firm. Pie may be served while frosty cold.

GREEN GAGE PLUM ICE CREAM PIE

1 9-inch graham cracker crust
3½ cups cooked green gage plums, pitted
    (preferably fresh)
1½ tablespoons sugar
⅓ teaspoon cinnamon
    dash of salt
1 quart vanilla ice cream, softened

Combine sugar, salt, cinnamon, and plums, blending thoroughly. Fold plums into ice cream and spread into pie crust and freeze. Garnish with fresh strawberries and serve.

ICE CREAM PIE

½ cup light or dark corn syrup
½ cup creamy or chunk style peanut butter
3 cups crisp rice cereal
2 pints desired flavor ice cream

Combine all of the ingredients except the ice cream; blend well. Press the peanut crunch mixture into 9-inch pie plate, covering bottom and sides. Chill until firm. Fill with 2 pints of ice cream. Serve at once or wrap and freeze until needed.

ICE CREAM LEMON PIE

1 9-inch graham cracker crumb crust
2 cups lemon-pie filling
2 cups vanilla ice cream
  whipped cream

Freeze lemon-pie filling until icy. Beat the ice cream into the pie filling. Pour into the chilled graham cracker crust. Freeze overnight. Before serving top with sweetened whipped cream.

ICE CREAM SUNDAE PIE

1 egg white
¼ teaspoon salt
¼ cup granulated sugar
1½ cups chopped walnuts
  butter or margarine
1 pint coffee ice cream
1 pint vanilla ice cream
½ cup dark or golden raisins
3 tablespoons butter or margarine
1 cup brown sugar, packed
½ cup light cream
1 teaspoon vanilla

Beat egg white with salt until stiff but not dry; gradually beat in sugar. Fold in walnuts. Turn into very well buttered 9-inch pie plate. Spread evenly on bottom and sides, but not on rim. Mixture will be sticky, and it can best be pushed into place with a spoon. Prick well. Bake in hot oven 400° F. 10 to 12 minutes. Cool, then chill. Fill with layers of coffee and vanilla ice cream. Serve with Raisin Caramel Sauce (pie shell may be filled with ice cream and stored in freezer until serving time). Rinse and drain raisins. Chop coarsely or leave whole. Melt butter (or margarine) in small saucepan, add brown sugar, and cook and stir over low heat until sugar is melted and lightly browned. Remove from heat, and very slowly stir in cream. Heat about 1 minute longer. Remove from heat, and stir in raisins and vanilla. Serve warm or cold over ice cream pie.

KRISPIE BLACK AND WHITE PIE

¾ cup semisweet chocolate chips
3 tablespoons butter
2 cups crisp rice cereal
½ cup toasted flake coconut
2 cups vanilla ice cream, softened
2 cups chocolate ice cream, softened
whipped cream

Melt chocolate and butter in a heavy saucepan. Add cereal and coconut and mix well. Press into a 9-inch buttered pie plate. Chill until firm. Spread the vanilla ice cream in the pie crust. Spread the chocolate ice cream on top of this. Freeze until firm. When ready to serve top with whipped cream and grated chocolate.

KRISPIE PEPPERMINT PIE

1 cup light brown sugar
½ cup butter
1 cup coconut
½ cup chopped walnuts
2½ cups crisp rice cereal, crushed
½ gallon peppermint ice cream
whipped cream
sliced cherries

Combine sugar and butter and melt in a double boiler. Add walnuts, rice cereal and coconut. Mix well and spread half the mixture in a 10-by-12-inch cake pan. Spoon softened ice cream over the coconut mixture and top with the remaining mixture. Freeze until firm. Before serving top with whipped cream and sliced cherries.

LEMON PIE

1¼ cups chocolate cookie crumbs
2 tablespoons butter
1 cup whipping cream
or ⅔ cup evaporated milk

3 eggs
⅔ cup sugar
⅛ teaspoon salt
¼ cup lemon juice
1 tablespoon lemon rind, grated

Mix 1 cup cookie crumbs with butter; spread in an 8-inch pie plate or a refrigerator tray. Chill. Chill whipping cream or put evaporated milk in bowl in freezer compartment until ice crystals form around edges. Beat eggs. Add sugar, salt, and lemon juice. Cook over hot water until thick, stirring constantly. Cool. Add lemon rind. Whip the cream or evaporated milk. Fold whipped cream or milk into egg mixture. Pour egg mixture over crumb crust. Top with remaining crumbs. Freeze. Cut into wedges to serve.

MINCEMEAT ICE CREAM PIE

1 9-inch graham cracker crumb crust
1 quart vanilla ice cream, softened
1 cup well-drained mincemeat
½ teaspoon rum extract

Combine ice cream, mincemeat, and extract. Spoon into crust; freeze. If desired, garnish with whipped cream.

PEACHES 'N CREAM ICE CREAM PIE

1 9-inch graham cracker crumb crust
1 cup chopped peaches, sweetened to taste
1 quart vanilla ice cream, softened
½ cup firmly packed brown sugar
1 tablespoon water
¼ cup butter
¾ cup chopped pecans

Combine ½ cup peaches and 1 pint of ice cream. Spread in crust; freeze. Combine brown sugar, water, and butter. Cook until thick; stir in ¼ cup of pecans. Cool. Add this to the pie and freeze. Mix remaining ice cream and peaches and add to pie. Top with remaining pecans and freeze.

RAINBOW ICE CREAM PIE

1 9-inch pie crust, baked
1 pint lime sherbet
1 pint vanilla ice cream
1 pint lemon sherbet
1 pint strawberry ice cream
¼ cup sugar
2 teaspoons cornstarch
1 cup water
1 egg, beaten
2 tablespoons butter
2 tablespoons lemon juice
½ teaspoon grated lemon rind

Line pie shell with lime sherbet; freeze. In mixing bowl blend vanilla ice cream and lemon sherbet; spread on lime layer and freeze. Scoop strawberry ice cream on top layer and freeze.

To prepare sauce: In saucepan combine sugar, cornstarch and gradually add water. Cook until thickened. Blend a little into egg, return all to saucepan; heat and stir 2 minutes. Remove from heat; add butter, lemon juice and rind. Cool slightly and serve over Rainbow Ice Cream Pie.

Note: For best results, prepare Rainbow Ice Cream Pie at least one day prior to serving. Remove from freezer to refrigerator about 15 to 20 minutes before slicing. The lemon sauce may be made ahead and reheated just before serving.

RAISIN-TOP PIE

1 9-inch pie crust, baked
1½ quarts vanilla ice cream, softened
2 tablespoons cornstarch
1 tablespoon sugar
1½ cups orange juice
⅔ cup seedless raisins

Prepare pie shell as directed and fill with slightly softened vanilla ice cream; freeze. Let pie stand at room temperature a few minutes before serving. To prepare sauce: In a saucepan combine cornstarch, sugar, orange juice, and raisins. Heat to boiling over medium heat, stirring constantly. Boil and stir 1 minute. Spoon warm tangy raisin sauce over pie or serve sauce in separate bowl. Serve immediately.

ICE CREAM STRAWBERRY PIE

1 9-inch crumb crust
2 cups strawberries, crushed and sweetened
 to taste
1 quart strawberry ice cream
½ cup whipping cream

Spoon ice cream into pie crust, overlapping scoops to make a firm, full filling. Pour the crushed berries over the ice cream and top with whole berries. Whip the cream and sweeten to taste. Decorate the edge of the pie with whipped cream. Serve immediately.

ICE CREAM 'N STRAWBERRY PIE

1 9-inch vanilla crumb crust
1½ cups fresh sliced strawberries
¼ cup sugar
1 quart vanilla ice cream, softened
 whipped cream

Combine sugar and strawberries; stir until dissolved. Spread half the strawberries over the pie crust. Spread ice cream over strawberries then cover with remaining berries; freeze. Before serving top with whipped cream.

STRAWBERRY BAKED ALASKA PIE

1 9-inch pie plate lined with lady fingers,
 sponge cake, or pound cake
1½ cups strawberries, sweetened
 to taste
1 quart vanilla ice cream, softened
3 egg whites, beaten until frothy
6 tablespoons sugar

Spread berries on cake, add ice cream. Repeat this procedure once more; freeze until hard. Beat sugar into egg whites, one tablespoon at a time. Spread meringue over pie and bake in 500° oven for 1 to 3 minutes or until meringue is golden brown. Serve immediately.

STRAWBERRY SOUR CREAM PIE

1 9-inch vanilla crumb crust
1½ cups sliced strawberries
1 cup sugar
1 egg white
1 cup sour cream

Combine strawberries, sugar, and egg white; whip until creamy with an electric mixer. Fold in sour cream; freeze. Garnish with strawberries before serving.

TAFFY PIE

1 3½-ounce can flaked coconut
2 tablespoons margarine, melted
1 envelope unflavored gelatin
1½ cups milk
1 cup dark corn syrup
1 cup heavy cream, whipped
½ teaspoon vanilla

Toss coconut and margarine with fork until well mixed. Press on bottom and sides of a 9-inch pie pan. Bake in 350° F. oven 12 to 15 minutes or until lightly browned. Chill. Sprinkle gelatin over ¼ cup milk in large bowl. Bring remaining 1¼ cups milk just to boil. Pour over gelatin; stir until gelatin is completely dissolved. Cool 10 minutes. Stir in dark corn syrup. Chill until mixture mounds slightly when dropped from spoon. Fold in whipped cream and vanilla. Turn into coconut shell. Freeze until firm. Let stand at room temperature ½ hour before serving.

TOASTED COCONUT MOUSSE PIE

1½ cups dairy sour cream
½ cup sugar
1 teaspoon vanilla
1 egg white
1 cup coconut, toasted
2 cups graham cracker crumbs
½ cup butter, melted
1 1-pound package frozen strawberries,
   slightly thawed

1 12-ounce package frozen peaches,
slightly thawed

Place sour cream in a small mixing bowl and chill with beaters at
least 30 minutes. Beat sour cream until very fluffy (about 5 minutes at high speed); fold in sugar and vanilla. Beat egg white until
stiff but not dry; blend into sour cream mixture along with coconut. Turn into refrigerator tray and freeze. For crust, blend
crumbs and butter thoroughly; press firmly on bottom and sides
of pan. Chill. When ready to serve, spoon mousse into crust and
arrange slightly thawed fruits over top.

TROPICAL ICE CREAM PIE

⅓ cup coconut bar cookie crumbs
2 tablespoons melted butter
15 to 16 coconut bar cookies
½ cup broken pecans
½ cup caramel or butterscotch
   ice cream topping
½ cup drained crushed pineapple
3 pints vanilla ice cream

Combine cookie crumbs and butter. Press mixture evenly over
bottom of buttered 9-inch pie plate. Stand whole cookies upright
around edge. (Cookies may have to be trimmed if too long). Chill.
Combine pecans and ice cream topping. Chill. Spoon 1 pint ice
cream into cookie shell. Top with ½ ice cream sauce, then ½
crushed pineapple. Add additional 1 pint ice cream, then remaining sauce and pineapple. Top with remaining ice cream. Freeze
until serving time.

VANILLA CREME PIE

1 9-inch chocolate crumb crust
½ cup sugar
½ cup water
   dash of salt
2 egg whites, stiffly beaten
1 cup cream, whipped
1 teaspoon pure vanilla extract

Boil sugar and water until it spins a thread. Add salt to the egg
whites and beat in the sugar syrup. Add vanilla to the whipped
cream and fold into the egg white mixture. Pour into crust and
freeze.

YOUR CHOICE BAKED ALASKA PIE

> 1 9-inch crumb crust
> 1 quart of ice cream, any flavor
> 3 egg whites, beaten until frothy
> 6 tablespoons sugar

Spread ice cream onto crust; freeze. Beat sugar into egg whites, one tablespoon at a time. Spread meringue over pie and bake in 500° oven for 1 to 3 minutes or until meringue is golden brown. Serve immediately.

11.

SPECIAL OCCASION FROZEN DESSERTS

If it's a party you have in mind, plan on serving a spectacular frozen dessert. Try your ingenuity on cake filled with ice cream, or pack your favorite ice-cream flavors into a mold. It's amazing how many different frozen dessert ideas there are and how much they can do to glamorize a dinner or a party.

Planning a party for the youngsters? Of course you'll serve ice cream; but why not give it a brand-new look? There are many enchanting new ways to give a party look to your table with ice cream desserts. For the younger children serve Party Pop Corn Sundaes, Ice Cream Blocks, Birthday Funny Faces, Peppy the Clown Cone, or a Cherry Circus Ring.

For a slightly older group of children you might serve a Confetti Ice Cream Cake, Flower Pots, or Igloos. Whatever the occasion, you will find brand-new desserts here for the children's party fun.

Having guests tonight? Whenever you're entertaining . . . after the theater, an evening dessert party, or whatever the occasion you'll be proud to serve these colorfully elegant "Special Occasion" desserts.

LINCOLN ICE CREAM LOG

1 cup sifted cake flour
1 teaspoon baking powder
½ teaspoon salt
2 eggs
1 cup sugar

221

    1 teaspoon vanilla
    ½ teaspoon rum extract, optional
    ½ cup milk
    1 tablespoon butter
    2 pints vanilla ice cream
    1 cup whipping cream
    ½ cup sifted confectioner's sugar
    ⅓ cup cocoa
    1 teaspoon vanilla
    maraschino cherries, cut in half

For sponge roll, sift together flour, baking powder and salt. Beat eggs until foamy; add sugar, 2 tablespoons at a time, beating until fluffy and light-colored. Blend in vanilla and rum extract. Add dry ingredients; blend well. Heat milk with butter just to boiling; stir into batter quickly, blending well. Pour into buttered and waxed paper-lined 15 x 10 x 1-inch jelly-roll pan. Bake in moderate oven, 350°, until done, 15 to 18 minutes. Turn out on towel sprinkled with confectioner's sugar. Remove paper. Starting at narrow end, roll up jelly-roll fashion over towel. Cool. Unroll and spread with softened ice cream. Reroll and freeze. For frosting, combine whipping cream, confectioner's sugar and cocoa in well-chilled beater bowl. Beat until mixture holds peaks. Fold in vanilla. Spread on top and sides of roll; garnish with candied or maraschino cherries. Freeze.

RAISIN HOLLY YULE LOG

    ¾ cup seedless raisins
    1 square semisweet chocolate
    1 (3¾ ounce) package vanilla whipped dessert mix
    ½ cup vanilla wafer crumbs
    1 tablespoon chopped maraschino cherries
    1 teaspoon brandy extract
    2 squares semisweet chocolate
    1 tablespoon butter
    2 teaspoons light corn syrup

Chop raisins. Shave chocolate with vegetable peeler. Reserve the remaining 2 squares of chocolate for chocolate glaze. Prepare whipped dessert mix as package directs. Fold in raisins, chocolate shavings, cookie crumbs, cherries, and brandy extract. Remove top and bottom of a 3-cup can. Flatten can slightly to make oval. Fasten double thickness of foil over one end with rubber band.

Spoon raisin mixture into can. Cover with foil. Freeze until firm. Unmold and spread with chocolate glaze. Serve at once or return to freezer until serving time. To make chocolate glaze, melt 2 squares of semisweet chocolate with 1 tablespoon butter over hot water. Remove from heat. Stir in light corn syrup. Cool slightly before spreading.

RAINBOW JELLY ROLL

        4 egg yolks
        ¾ cup sugar
        1 teaspoon vanilla
        ¾ cup sifted cake flour
        ¾ teaspoon baking powder
        ¼ teaspoon salt
        4 egg whites
        1 quart mint or pistachio ice cream
        ½ pint whipping cream, whipped
          few drops red food coloring
          tinted coconut

Beat egg yolks until light and lemon colored. Add sugar and beat until thick. Add vanilla, then sifted dry ingredients, tint pink with a few drops of red food coloring. Fold in egg whites which have been beaten until stiff but not dry. Line bottom of a 10 x 15-inch jelly-roll pan with waxed paper and butter top of paper. Pour batter into pan, spreading out evenly. Bake in 375° oven for 13 to 15 minutes. Turn out onto clean towel which has been sprinkled evenly with confectioner's sugar. Remove waxed paper from bottom of cake immediately. If edges are brown and crisp, trim them off. Roll cake up in towel, let stand until cool. When cool unroll and spread with softened ice cream. Roll up and wrap in moisture-vapor proof material, place in freezer. When ready to serve, frost with sweetened whipped cream, garnish with tinted coconut. (To tint coconut, place in a covered jar with a few drops of green food coloring and shake until evenly colored.) Cut into slices and serve plain or with chocolate sauce.

MELBA CREAM CAKE ROLL

        4 egg yolks
        ¼ cup sugar
        ½ teaspoon vanilla

    4 egg whites, room temperature
   ½ cup sugar
   ¾ cup sifted cake flour
   1 teaspoon baking powder
   ¼ teaspoon salt
     confectioner's sugar
 2½ pints peach ice cream
   2 packages (10 ounces each) frozen raspberries
   2 tablespoons cornstarch
   ½ teaspoon rum flavoring
   1 teaspoon lemon juice

Line bottom of jelly roll pan with waxed paper; butter and dust with flour; set aside. In large mixing bowl beat egg yolks and sugar until well blended and foamy; add vanilla. In small bowl beat egg whites until foamy; gradually add ½ cup sugar and beat until soft peaks form. Fold yolks into whites (transfer mixture into large bowl when volume becomes too great for small bowl). Sift together flour, baking powder and salt; sprinkle mixture, tablespoon at a time, into egg mixture and gently fold. Turn batter into pan; cut through batter with knife to release air bubbles. Bake in a preheated 375° F. oven 12 to 15 minutes or until done. Loosen cake from sides of pan; invert onto towel sprinkled with confectioner's sugar. Peel off paper; cool cake 2 minutes; roll from short side in towel and cool completely. Unroll; cover ¾ of cake with softened ice cream and reroll. Wrap tightly in foil or plastic wrap and freeze. To prepare sauce: Drain raspberries and reserve juice. In saucepan combine cornstarch with juice. Cook, stirring constantly until thickened; reduce heat and cook 5 minutes. Add flavoring, lemon juice and berries; heat to serving temperature. Serve warm over cut slice of cake roll.

CHOCOLATE CRUMB ROLL

   4 dozen chocolate wafer cookies, crushed
   1 quart vanilla ice cream, softened
     (other flavors may be substituted)

Pour softened ice cream into a 1 quart round container; refreeze until firm. Place crushed cookies on waxed paper and roll the unmolded ice cream in the crumbs, coating thoroughly. Refreeze until serving time. Serve with sauce or topping of your choice.

ICE CREAM LAYER CAKE

1 angel food loaf cake
1 pint raspberry ice cream, softened
1 pint pistachio ice cream, softened
    (or flavors of your choice)
1 cup cream, whipped

Cut angel food loaf lengthwise into 4 layers. Spread raspberry ice cream on 2 layers and pistachio ice cream on 2 layers. Stack layers alternating flavors; freeze. Before serving frost sides of cake with sweetened whipped cream.

PEACHES AND CREAM CAKE

1 can (1 pound 13 ounces) cling peach slices
2 packages (3¾ ounces each) strawberry-
    flavored whipped dessert mix
1 cup whipping cream, whipped
7 or 8 slices pound cake

Drain peaches. Combine the two packages of dessert mix and mix according to package directions. Let stand 10 minutes. Fold in whipped cream and all but 8 slices drained peaches. Place 7 or 8 slices of pound cake in spoke fashion from the center outward in an 8-inch spring-form pan. Pour dessert mix over cake to fill pan. Freeze. Thaw in refrigerator 1 hour before serving. Garnish with peach slices.

STRAWBERRY ANGEL LOAF

1 angel food cake loaf
1 quart strawberry ice cream
2 cups cream, whipped
1 cup miniature marshmallows
½ cup chopped walnuts
⅔ cup crushed pineapple, well drained
2 cups fresh strawberries, sliced and
    sweetened to taste

Slice the cake in half lengthwise. Spread the ice cream between the cake slices, sandwich style. Combine all of the remaining ingredients and frost the loaf. Store in freezer until ready to serve.

SUNSHINE CROWN CAKE

2 pints vanilla ice cream
2 pints lemon sherbet
2 packages (3½ ounces each) lady fingers
2 teaspoons cornstarch
¼ cup sugar
⅛ teaspoon salt
¼ cup water
1 cup blueberries
1 teaspoon lemon juice

In mixing bowl blend ice cream and sherbet; freeze. Line bottom of pan with 8 split lady fingers, cutting where necessary to fit. Line sides of pan with 16 lady fingers placing on slight diagonal to form crown. Spoon ice-cream and sherbet mixture into pan; freeze. In saucepan combine cornstarch, sugar and salt; gradually add water; cook stirring constantly until mixture comes to a boil. Reduce heat; add blueberries and cook 5 minutes; add lemon juice and chill. Spoon blueberry sauce on top of crown just before serving. Note: For best results, prepare Sunshine Crown Cake at least 1 day prior to serving. Remove from freezer to refrigerator 15 to 20 minutes before slicing.

BAKED ALASKA SUPREME

½ recipe of your favorite sponge cake, baked in
   a 10-inch circular pan
½ teaspoon cream of tartar
6 egg whites
1 cup sugar
2 quarts fresh strawberry ice cream, softened

Place cake on a small bread board. Whip egg whites and cream of tartar until stiff. Gradually beat in sugar 1 tablespoon at a time, and continue beating until meringue is stiff and glossy. Pile ice cream on top of cake; refreeze. Completely cover ice cream and sides of cake with meringue. Place in 500° oven for 3 to 5 minutes, or until lightly browned. Slip dessert onto serving platter and serve at once.

ICE CREAM 'N MERINGUE SHELLS

3 egg whites
¼ teaspoon salt
¼ teaspoon cream of tartar
¾ cup sugar
1 quart ice cream, any flavor
1 cup dessert sauce, your choice
(see chapter on Sauces and Toppings)

Preheat oven to 250° F. (very slow). Beat egg whites until foamy. Add salt and cream of tartar. Beat until soft peaks form. Add sugar gradually, beating constantly, and continue beating until very stiff peaks form. Shape meringue into six mounds on heavy brown paper on a baking sheet. Using the back of a spoon, form a hollow in the center of each mound. Bake 1 hour. Turn off heat and let meringues cool in oven. Fill each shell with a big scoop of ice cream and top with dessert sauce. Truly a dish fit for a king!

Note: Individual meringues can be made in the shape of four-leaf clovers, hearts, or any other shape for a particular occasion. They can be tinted pretty colors, too.

IGLOOS

6 egg whites
½ teaspoon cream of tartar
1 cup sugar
1 quart ice cream, any flavor
1 round 8 or 9-inch layer of plain cake or
8 individual cake rounds (3 inches diameter and
1 to 1½ inches thick)

First make meringue: beat egg whites with cream of tartar until soft peaks are formed. Beat in sugar a little at a time until meringue will stand in stiff glossy peaks, but is not dry. To make one large Igloo: use the one 8 or 9-inch layer of cake. Place cake on a heavy bread board. Pack large scoops of ice cream on top of cake, to within ½ inch of edge. Quickly spread the meringue over ice cream and cake, completely covering both, and sealing to board at edges. Place in a very hot oven (450°) for 4 to 5 minutes, until meringue is lightly browned. Remove from oven. Slip Igloo from board onto serving platter (garnish edges with flaked coconut if desired) and serve at once. To serve, slice into wedges. To make individual Igloos, place one scoop of ice cream on each of the individual cake rounds, cover with meringue, and proceed as described.

PRUNE WHIP ALASKA

>   ¾ to 1 cup cooked prunes
>   4 egg whites
>   ⅛ teaspoon salt
>   ½ cup sugar
>   1½ teaspoons lemon juice
>   1 quart firm ice cream (vanilla,
>   chocolate, peppermint or strawberry)
>   plain or sponge cake

Heat oven very hot, 450 to 500° F. Cut cake about 1-inch thick in square or circle about 1-inch larger on all sides than the block of ice cream. Prepare prune whip. Place cake on board covered with aluminum foil. Center ice cream on cake. Cover cake and ice cream thickly with prune whip. To make prune whip, sieve prunes (should be ½ to ¾ cup prune pulp). Beat egg whites with salt to fine foam stage. Add sugar gradually and beat until very stiff. Fold in sieved prunes and lemon juice. Bake in very hot oven 3 to 5 minutes, until lightly browned. Remove to serving plate with broad spatula, and serve at once.

PEACH TARTS

>   6 sponge cake shells
>   your favorite preserves
>   3 cups freestone peach slices
>   1 quart vanilla ice cream
>   whipping cream, sweetened to taste

Coat the inside of sponge cake shells with your favorite preserves and fill with freestone peach slices. Top with scoops of vanilla ice cream. Garnish with whipped cream, if desired.

ORANGE BUTTER CREAM CHEESE ICE CREAM TARTS

>   1⅔ cups sifted all-purpose flour
>   ½ teaspoon salt
>   1 3-ounce package cream cheese

⅔ cup butter
1 tablespoon grated orange rind
1 tablespoon orange juice
1 quart vanilla ice cream
½ cup orange juice
1 tablespoon water
2 tablespoons sugar
1 teaspoon cornstarch
1 teaspoon grated orange rind

Sift together flour and salt into mixing bowl. Blend cream cheese and butter until smooth; stir in 1 tablespoon grated orange rind. Chill. Blend cream cheese-butter mixture into dry ingredients. Add 1 tablespoon orange juice a few drops at a time and mix gently. Shape dough into a ball. Wrap and chill until firm. Divide into 8 equal portions. Roll out each portion on a lightly floured board or canvas into a circle, 5½ inches in diameter and ⅛ inch thick. Fit over outside of tart shell pans, 4 inches in diameter and 1½ inches deep. Trim off top edge of crust. Prick crust with fork. Place pans on baking sheet, crust side up. Bake in a hot oven, 425°, until lightly browned, about 10 minutes. Cool. Fill cooled tart shells with vanilla ice cream. Top with orange sauce, if desired. To make orange sauce: Combine ½ cup orange juice, water, sugar, and cornstarch in saucepan. Cook, stirring constantly, until thickened and clear. Stir in orange rind. Chill. Serve over ice cream tarts.

PEACH ICE CREAM MERINGUE

½ cup butter
½ cup sugar
4 egg yolks
⅔ cup cake flour
1 teaspoon baking powder
¼ teaspoon salt
¼ cup milk
4 egg whites
¼ teaspoon cream of tartar
1 teaspoon vanilla
¾ cup sugar
⅓ cup sliced almonds
1 pint peach ice cream

Butter 2 round 9 inch cake pans; line with waxed paper; set aside. In a mixing bowl cream butter; gradually add sugar and beat until light and fluffy. Add egg yolks one at a time, beating well after each addition. Sift together flour, baking powder, and salt. Add to creamed mixture alternately with milk beginning and ending with dry ingredients. Pour into pans. In a small mixing bowl sprinkle cream of tartar over egg whites. Beat until stiff. Add vanilla. Gradually beat in sugar, beating constantly until dissolved. Divide onto top of cake batter. Sprinkle nuts over meringue in one pan. Bake in preheated 350° F. oven 30 to 40 minutes. Cool in pans 5 minutes. Turn out of pans onto wire racks. Place cake side down on racks. To serve: Place layer without nuts on serving plate, cake side down. Slice ice cream over layer. Top with remaining cake layer, meringue side up.

APRICOT ICE CREAM MOLD

½ cup apricot preserves
½ cup sliced toasted almonds
2 pints vanilla ice cream, softened

Chill 4-cup mold in freezer. In a small bowl combine preserves and almonds. Press into bottom and part-way up the sides of mold. Freeze until firm. Press ice cream into mold. Return to freezer to harden. To unmold, dip into warm water and turn out onto chilled plate. Return to freezer to harden. Variation: One-half cup pineapple preserves may be substituted for the apricot preserves; 2 pints strawberry ice cream may be substituted for the vanilla ice cream. Continue with the above directions.

PRALINE PECAN CRUNCH RING

½ cup butter
1 cup firmly packed brown sugar
½ cup pecans, coarsely chopped
2¼ cups corn flakes
1 quart cherry vanilla ice cream
maraschino cherries

Place ring mold, 8 inches in diameter, in refrigerator so it will be well chilled. Place butter and sugar in a saucepan, slowly bring to a boil for 2 minutes. Add corn flakes and nuts. Remove from heat and lightly press hot corn flake mixture into chilled mold. Chill about 10 minutes. Unmold on serving dish. When ready to serve, spoon ice cream rounded sides up into ring. Garnish with maraschino cherries arranged in clusters.

FLOWER POTS

8 to 10 colorfully glazed flowerpots that will
    hold about 1 cup of boysenberry ice cream
1 jar boysenberry preserves for garnish
    clear straws
    flowers
1 large can evaporated milk
1 tablespoon grated lemon peel
⅓ cup lemon juice
½ cup boysenberry preserves

Pour milk into ice-cube tray to chill in freezing section of your refrigerator until crystals form around edges. Pour chilled milk into
bowl and whip until stiff. Carefully fold in lemon peel, juice and
preserves. Use only ½ cup boysenberry preserves. Spoon boysenberry ice cream mixture into flower pots to within one inch of tops.
Insert a half length of clear straw into center of each flower pot.
Place in freezer section to freeze firm. When ready to serve, slip
artificial flowers or fresh flowers from your garden, into the
straws. Wide stems of flowers may be trimmed to fit. Spread 2 to 3
tablespoons of boysenberry preserves over top of ice cream and
serve at once on your prettiest plates.

APRICOT DESSERT

1⅓ cups sweetened condensed milk
¼ cup lemon juice
2 eggs, separated
¼ teaspoon cream of tartar
42 vanilla wafers
1½ cups chopped apricots

Line bottom of a loaf pan with waxed paper. In large mixing bowl
combine sweetened condensed milk, lemon juice and egg yolks.
Blend well. Add chopped apricots, mixing thoroughly. Add cream
of tartar to egg whites and beat until stiff peaks form. Gently fold
into apricot mixture. Cover bottom of prepared pan with mixture,
to ½-inch depth. Arrange 14 wafers on top of apricot layer. Repeat layers until there is a total of 3 layers each of apricot mixture
and of wafers, ending with wafers on top. Place in freezer 4 hours,
or until firm. To serve, turn out on platter and carefully remove
waxed paper. If mixture sticks to pan in removing, first loosen
sides with a knife. Cut into slices for individual servings after
removing from pan. If desired, dessert may be garnished with
extra apricot halves and sweetened whipped cream.

FROSTY CITRUS DESSERT

1 cup chocolate nut cookies, crushed
3 tablespoons butter, melted
1 package (3 ounces) lime dessert gelatin
1 cup boiling water
1¼ cups sugar
2 teaspoons lemon rind, grated
1 teaspoon orange rind, grated
¼ cup lemon juice
¼ cup orange juice
2 cups milk, whole
1 cup cream
9 orange sections

Combine crushed cookies and melted butter. Press firmly in the bottom of a 9 x 9 x 2-inch baking pan. Chill while preparing citrus layer. Dissolve gelatin in boiling water. Cool. Combine remaining ingredients except orange sections. Stir until sugar dissolves. Add gelatin mixture and blend well. Chill until thick but not set. Pour over chilled crumb layer. Freeze 5 hours without stirring. Remove from freezer 5 to 10 minutes before serving. Garnish with orange sections.

HAWAIIAN PAPAYA AND ICE CREAM DESSERT

2 fresh papayas
1 pint strawberry ice cream,
   or lemon sherbet
   sprig of mint and
   cherries for garnish

Peel papaya, cut in half and remove seeds. Slice. Dish up two scoops of ice cream or sherbet, and one half papaya cut in slices for each serving. Garnish with mint and cherries if desired. Serves 4.

MOUNT EVEREST DESSERT

1 15-ounce can sweetened condensed milk
⅓ cup lemon juice
1 tablespoon grated lemon rind
1 pint sour cream
1 3½-ounce can coconut
½ pint heavy cream, whipped

In a large bowl, blend sweetened condensed milk, lemon juice and rind. Fold in sour cream and coconut. Spoon into individual parfait glasses or dessert dishes. Freeze until firm. Garnish with whipped cream after removing from freezer.

ORANGE DIVINITY FROZEN DESSERT

1 cup light corn syrup
2 eggs, separated
1 6-ounce can frozen orange juice concentrate, partially thawed
1 cup well-chilled undiluted evaporated milk
1 cup ginger-snap crumbs

Pour evaporated milk into freezing tray. Chill in freezing unit until ice crystals begin to form around edges. Bring corn syrup to boiling point. Meanwhile, beat egg whites until soft peaks form when beater is raised. Beating constantly, pour continuous fine stream of hot syrup over beaten egg whites. Continue beating until mixture holds stiff peaks. Beat egg yolks well. Fold into egg white mixture. Fold in orange juice concentrate. Whip chilled evaporated milk until thick and fluffy. Lightly fold into egg mixture. Sprinkle 9-inch-square pan with ½ cup crumbs. Pour in orange mixture. Sprinkle with remaining crumbs. Freeze until firm.

PRINCESS FROZEN DESSERT

1½ cups fresh milk
½ cup sugar
¼ cup light corn syrup
⅛ teaspoon salt
2 eggs
1 cup evaporated milk
1½ teaspoons vanilla
1½ teaspoons grated orange rind
½ cup ground unblanched almonds
¾ cup sieved avocado

Combine fresh milk, sugar, syrup, and salt, and heat to just below boiling. Stir mixture into beaten eggs. Add evaporated milk, vanilla, orange rind and almonds. To prepare avocado, cut into halves and remove seed and skin. Force fruit through a sieve or puree in electric blender. Stir into milk mixture. Beat until well blended. Pour into refrigerator tray, place in freezing compartment with control set at lowest temperature and freeze to desired consistency. Stir once during freezing process. Reset temperature control to normal when firm.

SPECIAL OCCASION RAISIN DESSERT

    ¾ cup seedless raisins
    1 square semisweet chocolate
    1 (3¾ ounce) package vanilla
        whipped dessert mix
    ½ cup vanilla wafer crumbs
    1 tablespoon chopped maraschino cherries
    1 teaspoon brandy extract
    2 squares semisweet chocolate
    1 tablespoon butter
    2 teaspoons light corn syrup

Chop raisins. Shave 1 square of semisweet chocolate with a vegetable peeler. Prepare whipped dessert mix as package directs. Fold in raisins, chocolate, cooky crumbs, cherries and brandy extract. Spoon into 3-cup fancy mold; cover with foil. Freeze until firm. Unmold and spread with chocolate glaze. Serve at once or return to freezer until serving time. To make chocolate glaze, melt 2 squares of chocolate with 1 tablespoon butter over hot water. Remove from heat. Stir in corn syrup. Cool slightly before spreading.

FIG NAPOLI

    1 cup whipping cream
    1 6-ounce can frozen concentrated orange juice
    ¼ cup slivered almonds
    ½ cup dried figs, chopped
        to about ¼-inch pieces
    1 fig cut in eighths
    8 paper muffin baking cups

Defrost frozen orange juice; do not dilute. Whip cream until stiff. Fold orange juice concentrate into whipped cream. Mix in chopped figs. Put 8 paper muffin baking cups in a muffin tin, so paper will hold shape. Divide slivered almonds among paper cups. Pour orange-fig-cream mixture over nuts in cups. Top each with one fig eighth. Place in freezer compartment until firm, or until ready to serve. Remove from freezer about 10 minutes before serving. Serve in paper cup. Variations: Instead of nuts try chopped maraschino cherries, crumbled coconut cookies or grated fresh coconut. You may wish to turn the frozen dessert upside down, remove the paper and serve garnished side up.

BRANTONI

¾ cup crushed dry macaroons
½ cup light cream
¼ cup sugar
3 tablespoons brandy
dash of salt
1 envelope whipped topping mix
¼ cup crushed dry macaroons

Combine ¾ cup macaroons, light cream, sugar, brandy, and salt; blend well. Prepare whipped topping mix as directed on package. Gradually add the macaroon mixture, beating until fluffy peaks form. Spoon into paper souffle cups and sprinkle with remaining ¼ cup macaroons. Freeze about 4 hours.

CHESTNUT SUPREME

½ pound glazed chestnuts
½ cup brandy
1 quart vanilla ice cream
1 cup cream, whipped

Marinate chestnuts in brandy for ½ hour. Drain off the brandy and reserve. Chop chestnuts coarsely. Line the bottom of the serving dish with half the chestnuts. Scoop ice cream on top and sprinkle the remaining chestnuts on ice cream. Freeze. To serve: pour brandy on ice cream and top with whipped cream.

FAVORITE FROZEN CUSTARD

1 cup milk
⅓ cup sugar
¼ teaspoon salt
1 egg

    1 teaspoon plain gelatin
    1 tablespoon cold water
    1 avocado
    1 tablespoon fresh lime or lemon juice
  ¾ cup whipping cream

Scald milk with sugar and salt. Stir into lightly beaten egg. Place over hot water, and cook and stir until mixture coats spoon. Soften gelatin in cold water and dissolve in hot custard. Cool. Cut avocado in half lengthwise and remove seed and skin. Force fruit through a sieve or puree in electric blender, adding part of custard so mixture blends easily. Combine with remaining custard and lime juice. Fold in whipped cream. Turn into refrigerator tray and place in freezing compartment with control set at lowest temperature. Freeze until barely firm. Stir thoroughly with a fork. Freeze to desired consistency. Reset temperature control to normal. Makes about 1 quart.

MAPLE PERFECT

  ½ cup maple-blended syrup
    2 eggs, beaten
    1 envelope whipped topping mix
  ¼ teaspoon almond extract

Heat syrup. Stir a small amount of the hot syrup into the eggs, mixing well. Return to remaining syrup. Continue cooking until mixture thickens and coats a metal spoon. Cool. Prepare whipped topping mix as directed on package, adding ¼ teaspoon almond extract before whipping. Blend prepared whipped topping into custard. Pour into 8-inch-square pan; freeze until firm, about 3 hours. Garnish with finely chopped nuts, if desired.

AVOCADO MALLOW

  16 marshmallows (1 4-ounce package)
    1 cup milk
  ⅔ cup sieved avocado
    1 cup light cream
       dash of salt
    1 tablespoon fresh lime or lemon juice
  ¼ teaspoon grated lime or lemon rind

Cut marshmallows into pieces, add milk and heat slowly, stirring until marshmallows are melted. Cool and force through a sieve. Blend avocado, cream, salt, lime juice and rind into cooled marshmallow mixture. Turn into refrigerator tray and place in freezing compartment with control set at lowest temperature. Freeze until firm, stirring occasionally with a fork. Reset temperature control to normal.

CHERRY MALLOW

> ½ pound fresh marshmallows
> 2½ cups fresh cherries and juice,
> pitted and sweetened
> dash of salt
> ½ teaspoon almond extract
> 1 cup cream, whipped
> 2 teaspoons lemon juice
> rind of one lemon

Combine the marshmallows and cherry juice. Cook in a double boiler until the mixture is fluffy. Cool. Combine the remaining ingredients; stirring well after each addition. Freeze until firm.

FUDGE MALLOW

> ½ cup semisweet chocolate pieces
> 8 marshmallows, quartered
> ½ cup evaporated milk
> ¼ cup water
> ⅔ cup evaporated milk

Combine chocolate pieces, marshmallows, ½ cup evaporated milk and water into a 2-quart saucepan. Cook and stir over low heat until chocolate and marshmallows are melted. Remove from heat. Chill thoroughly. Meanwhile, put ⅔ cup of evaporated milk into an ice tray and chill until ice crystals begin to form around edges. Put ice cold milk into a cold quart bowl. Whip with cold rotary beater by hand or with electric beater at high speed, until fluffy. Mix whipped milk gently into cooled chocolate mixture. Put into 1-quart ice tray and freeze without stirring at coldest temperature until firm. Sprinkle nuts over the top if desired.

PRUNE MALLOW

1 cup sweetened prune juice
¼ pound marshmallows
¼ cup prune puree
2 tablespoons lemon juice
    rind of one lemon
1 cup whipping cream, whipped

Combine the prune juice and the marshmallows. Heat in a double boiler until fluffy. Cool. Add the lemon rind, lemon juice, and puree. Beat well and freeze until mushy. Beat again, fold in the cream and freeze until firm. Stir occasionally during the freezing process.

RHUBARB MALLOW

3 cups diced rhubarb
2 tablespoons water
¾ cup sugar
    dash of salt
¼ pound marshmallows
2 tablespoons lemon juice
    rind of one lemon
1 cup cream, whipped

Heat the rhubarb and water; then add the sugar. Cook until tender. Add the salt, marshmallows, lemon juice and rind. Cool. Red coloring may be added to enhance the appearance of the dessert. Beat until fluffy, add cream, and freeze until firm.

AVOCADO CREAM FREEZE

1 cup light cream
1 cup milk
⅓ cup sugar
¼ teaspoon salt
1 teaspoon plain gelatin
2 teaspoons cold water
2 eggs

1 cup sieved avocado
1 tablespoon fresh lime or lemon juice

Combine cream, milk, sugar, and salt, and heat to just below boiling. Soften gelatin in cold water and dissolve in hot liquid. Beat eggs and stir in hot mixture. Chill. To prepare avocado, cut into halves, remove seed and skin, and force through sieve or puree in electric blender. Blend avocado and lime juice into gelatin mixture. Pour into refrigerator tray, placing in freezing compartment with control set at lowest temperature and freeze. Stir 2 or 3 times during freezing process. Reset temperature to normal. (May also be frozen in ice-cream freezer.)

BLACK AND WHITE FREEZE

1½ cups cold milk
½ cup cold light or heavy cream
1 package (3¾ ounces) vanilla
   instant pudding
1 square unsweetened chocolate, melted

Pour milk and cream into a bowl. Add pudding mix. Slowly beat with rotary beater (or at a low speed of electric mixer) until well blended—1 to 2 minutes. Fold in melted chocolate. Pour into an 8- x 4-inch loaf pan. Freeze until firm. Unmold and serve in slices.

CHERRY CREAM FREEZE

1⅓ cups sweetened condensed milk
¼ cup lemon juice, reconstituted
2½ cups cherry pie filling
¾ cup crushed pineapple, well drained
¼ teaspoon almond extract
2 cups heavy cream, whipped

In large size mixing bowl combine sweetened condensed milk, lemon juice, pie filling, crushed pineapple, and almond extract; mix well. Gently fold in whipped cream until evenly blended. Turn mixture into a 9 x 5 x 3-inch loaf pan. Cover tightly with aluminum foil. Freeze for 24 hours or until thoroughly firm. Unmold onto serving tray. If desired, additional whipped cream may be piped through decorators' tube to garnish top and base.

GALLON FREEZE

6 cups of fruit puree
2 cups sugar
2 tablespoons lemon juice
dash of salt
2 tablespoons gelatin
1/4 cup cold water
1/4 cup hot water

Soften the gelatin in 1/4 cup of cold water. Combine the sugar, lemon juice, salt, and puree. Add the gelatin to hot water, stirring until dissolved. Add to the fruit mixture and freeze. Makes 1 gallon.

GELATIN DESSERT FREEZE

1 package (3 ounces) dessert gelatin, any flavor
3/4 cup sugar
1/8 teaspoon salt
1 cup boiling water
2 cups half and half
1 cup cream, whipped

Dissolve gelatin, sugar, and salt in boiling water. Chill until slightly thickened. Blend in half and half with a beater. Chill until mixture is frozen at edges of tray. Beat mixture until fluffy and fold in cream. Freeze again for approximately one half hour, and beat until smooth. Refreeze until firm.

HOLIDAY FREEZE

1/2 cup mixed candied fruit
1/2 cup raisins, chopped
1/2 cup pecans, chopped
3 tablespoons sherry
1 cup sugar
1 cup boiling water
4 egg whites
1/8 teaspoon salt
2 teaspoons pure vanilla extract
2 cups cream, whipped

Combine fruit, raisins, pecans, and sherry. Let stand for 1½ hours. Cook sugar and water until it forms a soft ball. Beat egg whites and salt until stiff. Gradually add the syrup, beating constantly. Combine remaining ingredients. Freeze.

LEMON CREAM FREEZE

1⅔ cups evaporated milk
½ cup lemon juice
¾ cup sugar
dash of salt
rind of two lemons

Put evaporated milk into refrigerator tray. Chill until ice crystals begin to form around edges. Put the ice cold milk into a bowl and whip with a cold rotary beater by hand or with an electric beater at high speed, until fluffy. Add remaining ingredients and freeze until mushy. Remove to a cold bowl and beat once more. Return to refrigerator tray and freeze until firm.

PEANUT BUTTER FREEZE

1 quart sour cream
2 cups granulated sugar
1 cup peanut butter

Thoroughly blend all ingredients and freeze until firm. Do not stir during the freezing process.

PECAN FREEZE

¼ cup finely chopped pecans
1 tablespoon sugar
1½ teaspoons butter
1½ cups cold milk
½ cup cold light or heavy cream
1 package (4 ounces) butterscotch instant pudding

Combine pecans, sugar, and butter in a saucepan. Cook over medium heat, stirring constantly, until golden brown. Drain on absorbent paper. Cool. Break into small pieces. Pour milk and cream into a bowl. Add pudding mix. Slowly beat with rotary beater (or at a low speed of electric mixer) until well blended, 1 to 2 minutes. Fold in nut mixture. Pour into an 8 by 4-inch loaf pan. Freeze until firm, about 6 hours. Unmold. Serve in slices.

PINEAPPLE FREEZE

⅔ cup evaporated milk
¼ cup sugar
2 tablespoons lemon juice
dash of salt
6 2½ inch graham crackers
1 cup crushed, undrained pineapple

Put evaporated milk into refrigerator tray and chill until ice crystals begin to form around edges. Meanwhile, mix until dissolved, sugar, lemon juice, and salt. Break graham crackers into large pieces. Put ice cold milk into cold 1 or 2-quart bowl. Whip with cold rotary beater, or electric beater at high speed, until fluffy. Beat in sugar mixture at low speed. Stir in pineapple. Fold in crackers and put into 1 quart ice tray. Freeze without stirring at coldest temperature until firm.

PRUNE FREEZE

1½ cups plumped prunes
½ cup powdered sugar
2 teaspoons lemon juice
dash of salt
1 cup whipping cream
¼ cup chopped walnuts

Pit prunes; save ½ cup for garnish. Puree remainder in blender. Add sugar, lemon and salt. Beat cream until thick. Fold in half of prune puree mixture and nuts. Pour into refrigerator tray or 1 quart mold. Dollop remaining prune puree on top of cream mixture. With a spatula swirl puree through cream mixture to have a marble effect. Freeze until firm. Unmold, slice and garnish with reserved plumped prunes.

RASPBERRY FREEZE

1 cup evaporated milk
1 tablespoon lemon juice
rind of one lemon
dash of salt
¾ cup of seedless raspberry jam

Put evaporated milk into refrigerator tray and chill until ice crystals begin to form around edges. Put the ice cold milk into a cold bowl. Whip with cold rotary beater by hand, or electric beater at high speed, until fluffy. Add lemon juice and whip until stiff. Combine remaining ingredients; freeze until mushy. Remove to a cold bowl and beat. Return to refrigerator tray and freeze until firm.

TANGY ORANGE FREEZE

1 tablespoon gelatin
½ cup orange juice
rind of 3 large oranges
1 tablespoon lemon juice
⅔ cup sugar
1 cup buttermilk
1 cup cream, whipped

Soften gelatin in orange juice and heat until dissolved. Combine the gelatin with the remaining ingredients, except cream. Freeze until firm, and whip until smooth. Fold in whipped cream and re-freeze.

EGGNOG PUDDING

1 can fruit cocktail (No. 2½)
½ cup maraschino cherries
2 3-ounce packages cream cheese
⅛ teaspoon salt
1 teaspoon vanilla
1 cup commercial eggnog
1 cup whipping cream
2 cups miniature marshmallows (or about 24 cut in small pieces)
red vegetable coloring

Drain fruit cocktail. Drain and cut cherries in quarters. Blend softened cream cheese with salt, vanilla and eggnog until smooth.

Fold in stiffly beaten cream, marshmallows and drained fruit. Tint a delicate pink with red coloring, if desired. Turn into ring mold, small angel food pan or any container which will fit into freezing unit of refrigerator, or freezer. Freeze until firm, at least 8 hours or overnight. Unmold on cold platter and decorate as desired. Serve at once.

HOLIDAY PUDDING

1 quart vanilla ice cream, softened
1 cup mixed candied fruit
1 cup cream, whipped
¼ teaspoon cardamom
¼ teaspoon ginger
¼ teaspoon mace

Stir candied fruit into ice cream, blending well. Stir spices into the whipped cream and combine with the fruit mixture. Red or green food coloring will give an added touch of holiday cheer. Freeze until firm. When ready to serve, unmold and frost with additional whipped cream.

PRUNE PUDDING

1 package vanilla or butterscotch
   pudding powder
2 cups milk
½ cup powdered sugar
¼ cup chopped walnuts
1 cup chopped cooked prunes
2 tablespoons lemon juice
1 cup whipping cream

Mix pudding with cold milk and cook according to directions on the package. Add sugar and let cool. Add nuts, prunes, and lemon juice, then fold in cream which has been whipped to consistency of soft custard. Freeze without stirring.

APPLE CREME

2 cups applesauce
¼ teaspoon cinnamon
¼ teaspoon nutmeg

1 tablespoon melted butter
1 tablespoon lemon juice
rind of 1 lemon
1 quart cream, whipped

Combine all ingredients and mix until well blended. Freeze until firm.

CURACAO CREME

1 6-ounce can orange juice, thawed
¼ cup water
1 tablespoon gelatin
1¼ cups ice water
¾ cup sugar
dash of salt
½ cup Curaçao
2 cups cream, whipped

Soften gelatin in ¼ cup water. Beat orange juice and ice water until blended. Heat ¼ cup of this mixture and dissolve gelatin in it. Combine remaining ingredients. Freeze in refrigerator trays.

SPICED BANANA CREAM

2 cups mashed bananas
¼ cup sugar
1 cup cream, whipped
⅓ cup orange juice
juice of one lemon
dash of salt
1 teaspoon ground ginger
2 tablespoons rum

Thoroughly blend all ingredients and freeze. When mushy whip until fluffy and refreeze. Let stand at room temperature before serving.

FROSTY PRUNE DELIGHT

1 cup plumped prunes
½ cup heavy cream, whipped
2 eggs

3 tablespoons powdered sugar
1 cup crushed pineapple (No. 211 can)
1 teaspoon vanilla
dash of salt

Cut prunes from pits into small pieces. Whip cream until stiff. Beat eggs until very light; beat in sugar. Combine all ingredients, blending well. Pour into refrigerator tray and place in freezer. Freeze until firm.

FRUIT SURPRISE

⅓ cup evaporated milk
½ cup canned peaches, cut
   in small pieces
½ cup drained, crushed pineapple
½ cup thinly sliced bananas
¼ cup sliced maraschino cherries,
   well drained
6 marshmallows, quartered
1 3-ounce package softened white cream cheese
2 tablespoons mayonnaise, if desired
2 tablespoons sugar
2 teaspoons lemon juice

Put evaporated milk into ice tray of refrigerator. Chill milk until ice crystals begin to form around edges. Combine all the fruit and marshmallows in a 1-quart bowl. Put cream cheese into another quart bowl and stir in mayonnaise and sugar, mixing until smooth. Fold fruit mixture into cream cheese mixture. Put ice cold milk into a cold 1-quart bowl. Whip with cold rotary beater by hand, or electric beater at high speed, until fluffy. Add 2 teaspoons of lemon juice and whip until stiff. Fold in fruit and cheese mixture. Put into a 1-quart refrigerator tray and freeze, without stirring, at coldest temperature until firm. Use for party salad and dessert.

CANTALOUPE à la MODE—TWO "MODES"

Ice Cream Melon Boats

2 medium cantaloupe
1 pint strawberry ice cream
   strawberries, optional

Halve cantaloupe in "scalloped" fashion, remove seeds. Scoop out melon balls. Fill each half with a large scoop of ice cream; garnish with melon balls and strawberries, if desired.

Ice Cream Melon Rings

1 cup blueberries
¼ cup sugar
¼ teaspoon grated lemon rind
2 tablespoons lemon juice
⅛ teaspoon cinnamon
1 large cantaloupe
1 pint vanilla ice cream

Make blueberry sauce by heating together blueberries, sugar, lemon rind and lemon juice, just until sugar is thoroughly dissolved and sauce begins to thicken. Remove from heat, stir in cinnamon and chill. Meanwhile, peel cantaloupe and cut into crosswise slices, about 1½ inches thick. Remove seeds and chill until ready to serve. Then, fill each cantaloupe ring with scoop of ice cream and top with blueberry sauce.

SUMMER FRUIT SALAD WITH SHERBET

Assorted fresh fruits such as melon,
   pineapple, oranges, strawberries
   and red grapes
lettuce cups
1½ pints lemon or pineapple sherbet
2 tablespoons honey
2 tablespoons orange juice
1 cup dairy sour cream
grated orange rind

Prepare fruits; keep chilled until serving time. Line salad plates with lettuce; arrange fruit in small groups on lettuce. Top each with large scoop of sherbet; serve immediately. If desired garnish with orange dressing. To make dressing: Blend honey and orange juice; gently fold in sour cream and top with orange rind. Use for party salad and dessert.

AMBROSIA

1 package (3 ounces) orange dessert gelatin
1 cup boiling water
3 tablespoons sugar
¼ teaspoon salt

  1 small can mandarin oranges
  1 cup cream, whipped
 1⅓ cups angel flake coconut
   rind of 1 orange
   rind of 1 lemon
  2 tablespoons mayonnaise, if desired

Dissolve gelatin in boiling water; add salt and sugar. Drain juice from mandarin oranges and combine with water to make one cup. Add to gelatin and chill until thick. Add remaining ingredients and freeze until firm. Use for party salad and dessert.

FRUIT LOAF

  1 package (3 ounces) lemon dessert gelatin
  ¼ teaspoon salt
  1 cup boiling water
  ¾ cup sugar
  1 cup of pineapple tidbits, and juice
  4 tablespoons lemon juice
  ¼ cup mayonnaise, if desired
  1 cup sour cream
  1 cup cream, whipped
  1 small can of mandarin oranges, drained
  ¼ cup diced maraschino cherries

Dissolve gelatin dessert, salt, and sugar in boiling water. Chill. Add the remaining ingredients in the order given; mixing thoroughly after each addition. Freeze until firm. Use for party salad and dessert.

PARTY FUN

Ice Cream Sandwiches

Cut ice cream into squares and put between plain cookies or graham crackers; wrap and freeze. They make deliciously different ice cream sandwiches. For something special use leftover or frozen waffles to make the sandwich.

Doughnut Sundae

Serve a scoop of your favorite ice cream on a hot doughnut; top with sauce.

Ice Cream Cake

Hollow out an angel food cake, fill with ice cream, frost with whipped cream and freeze.

Easy Ice Cream Pie

To make an easy ice-cream pie, line a refrigerator tray with graham cracker or cookie crumbs. Freeze ice cream in tray. At serving time cut diagonally into pie-shaped wedges.

Devil's Food 'n Ice Cream Cake

Slice a devil's food cake (or any family favorite) lengthwise into 3 or 4 slices. Alternate a layer of cake with softened ice cream. Wrap and freeze. Slice and serve.

Ice Cream Shells

Make ice cream shells of melted chocolate pieces and coconut or cornflakes. Shape shells in greased muffin tin or paper cups. Fill each shell with a big scoop of ice cream and top with chocolate sauce.

Birthday O'Lanterns

Place scoops of ice cream on a shallow pan and place in freezer until hard. On one side of scoop use chocolate bits and slices of cherry to make a face. Do this just before serving time. Top with a tiny birthday candle and serve lighted.

Quickie Sundaes

Make individual sundaes by putting ice cream in paper cups and topping with syrup. Cover with small squares of aluminum foil and freeze. These sundaes are wonderful for those last minute parties or for friends who drop in for coffee.

Coconut Balls

Roll scoops of ice cream in toasted coconut and top with your favorite sauce.

Ice Cream Puffs

Fill cream puffs with ice cream. Serve with your favorite sauce.

CONFETTI ICE CREAM CAKE

 1 package (1 pound 3½ ounces)
  white cake mix
½ cup multicolored shot
 1 pint lime sherbet
 1 pint strawberry ice cream
 1 cup sweetened whipped cream

Generously butter bottoms of two 8-inch-square pans and dust with flour; set aside. Prepare cake according to package directions. Stir in colored shot. Spread into pans; bake in preheated 450° oven according to package directions. Cool in pans on wire racks 10 minutes. Remove from pans onto wire racks to cool completely. To serve: Invert one layer onto serving plate. Spread lime sherbet over top of layer. (If necessary place in freezer to harden before adding next layer.) Place top layer of cake over sherbet; spread strawberry ice cream over top. Frost sides of cake with whipped cream that has been tinted with red food coloring. Return to freezer to harden before slicing if necessary. Note: Cake layers may be placed in freezer to "firm up" before putting cake together.

CHERRY CIRCUS RING

 3 cups marshmallow topping
  red food coloring
 2 teaspoons almond extract
 4 cups rice cereal, ready to eat
 1 quart vanilla ice cream
 2 tablespoons cornstarch
¼ cup sugar
⅛ teaspoon salt
 1 can (1 pound) red sour pitted cherries
¾ cup cherry juice
 2 teaspoons lemon juice

In heavy saucepan combine marshmallow topping and food coloring; stir until well blended and topping has been heated (about 5 minutes); add extract. In large bowl combine rice cereal and topping mixture; mix well to coat cereal. Press into buttered ring mold, 4½ cups; chill 20 minutes to set. Unmold on platter and cover until ready to serve. To prepare sauce: In saucepan combine cornstarch, sugar and salt. Drain cherries and reserve ¾ cup juice; add juice to cornstarch mixture to make a smooth paste. Cook, stirring constantly until thickened; reduce heat and add cherries; cook an additional 2 minutes; add lemon juice. To serve, fill ring with 12 scoops of vanilla ice cream; spoon sauce over top.

"PEPPY" THE CLOWN CONE

1 scoop of ice cream
1 cone with a pointed base
  pecans
  chocolate chips
  raisins
  coconut
  (or decorations of your choice)

Here is a delightful idea for a children's party. "Peppy" is equally attractive and delicious in a variety of flavor combinations. For a starter, we suggest using one scoop vanilla ice cream for his head, pecans for eyes, and chocolate bits for a nose and mouth. Use coconut for a collar or hair, whichever you prefer, and give him a cookie cone hat. Or how about orange sherbet with cherries, marshmallows, and candy gum drops for decorations? Make up your own favorite combinations. Use 1 scoop of ice cream, top with a cone hat, and give "Peppy" a face with various fruits, nuts and candies. It's as easy as that and fun, too!

BIRTHDAY FUNNY FACES

1 quart of ice cream, any flavor
  chocolate chips
  raisins
  sliced cherries
  gumdrops
  (or decorations of your choice)

Scoop 8 ice-cream balls (one ball should take approximately ¼ pint ice cream). Place balls on shallow pan in freezer until hard. Make faces on scoops of ice cream and refreeze. When ready to serve stick a candle into each scoop. Children love funny faces! You can even place them on squares of cake.

ICE CREAM BLOCKS

1 pint chocolate ice cream
1 pint vanilla ice cream
butter icing, tinted

Cut ice cream in blocks and freeze hard in freezer compartment of refrigerator. Later, decorate with white and colored butter icing. Do one block at a time and return quickly to freezer. Serve the blocks on a large platter with an appropriate center decoration. Your young guests will be delighted with these decorated ice cream blocks.

PEANUT CRUNCH LAYER CAKE

½ cup light or dark corn syrup
½ cup creamy or chunk style peanut butter
3 cups crisp rice cereal
2 pints desired flavor brick ice cream

Blend corn syrup and peanut butter. Add cereal and stir until well coated. Crisscross 2 5-inch strips of waxed paper in each of 3 8-inch layer-cake pans, with ends of paper extending beyond sides of pans. Press half of the peanut crunch mixture into each of two prepared pans. Press 1 pint of ice cream into third pan. Chill until firm. Unmold 1 crunch layer onto serving plate; top with ice cream layer and then second crunch layer. Decorate as desired. Serve immediately or wrap and freeze until needed.

PEANUT CRUNCH ICE CREAM BARS

½ cup light or dark corn syrup
½ cup creamy or chunk style peanut butter
3 cups crisp rice cereal
2 pints desired flavor brick ice cream

Blend corn syrup and peanut butter. Add cereal and stir until well coated. Cut piece of waxed paper 12 inches wide, and place in 13 x 9½-inch pan with ends extending beyond sides of pan. Press mixture into pan, covering bottom. Chill until firm. Lift out using waxed paper. Cut into 12 3-inch squares. Cut each ice cream brick into 3 slices and place each slice between two crunch squares. Cut each square into two bars. Serve immediately or wrap and freeze until needed. Makes 12 ice-cream bars.

PEANUT CRUNCH TARTS

½ cup light or dark corn syrup
½ cup creamy or chunk-style peanut butter
3 cups crisp rice cereal
2 pints desired flavor ice cream

Combine all of the ingredients except the ice cream. Press the peanut crunch mixture into 8 medium tart pans, covering bottom and sides. Chill until firm. Fill with the ice cream. Serve at once or wrap and freeze until needed.

PARTY PUFFS

6 medium-sized cream puffs
1 quart of ice cream, any flavor
1 cup of dessert sauce, your choice
(see chapter on Sauces and Toppings)

Fill the cream puffs with softened ice cream. Place cream puffs on a shallow pan and place in freezer until hard. Spoon 2 tablespoons of your favorite dessert sauce over each cream puff; serve immediately. Note: You may heat the dessert sauce.

CREAM PUFFS WITH RASPBERRY SAUCE

6 cream puffs
1 quart vanilla ice cream, softened
1 pint raspberries, crushed and sweetened

Make the cream puffs if you like, or buy them at the bakery. Fill the puffs with vanilla ice cream and store in the freezer until serving time. Top with crushed raspberries.

COOKIE CRUMB CRUNCH BALLS

2 pints ice cream, any flavor
1½ cups cookie crumbs
1 cup dessert sauce, your choice
(see chapter on Sauces and Toppings)

Scoop 8 ice-cream balls (one ball should take approximately ¼ pint ice cream). Place balls on shallow pan in freezer until hard.

Roll each ice cream ball in cookie crumbs; return immediately to freezer to harden. Reserve remaining cookie crumbs. Spoon 2 tablespoons of your favorite dessert sauce over each ice cream ball; sprinkle additional crumbs over top; return to freezer until hard. Note: Do not heat the dessert sauce.

ICE CREAM CRUNCH BALLS

2 pints vanilla ice cream
1 can (6¾ ounces) salted peanuts, crushed
1 can (3 ounces) chow mein noodles, crushed
¼ cup light corn syrup
3 tablespoons water
2 tablespoons butter
1 package (6 ounces) semisweet chocolate pieces

Scoop 8 ice cream balls (one ball should take approximately ¼ pint ice cream). Place balls on shallow pan in freezer until hard. Combine peanuts and chow mein noodles; place on pan and toast in preheated 350° oven 5 minutes. Cool. Roll each ice cream ball in peanut-noodle mixture; return immediately to freezer to harden. Reserve remaining peanut-noodle mixture.

To prepare glaze: In a saucepan combine corn syrup, water and butter; bring to boiling. Remove from heat and stir in chocolate pieces. Cool to lukewarm. Spoon 2 tablespoons of glaze over each ice cream ball; sprinkle additional peanut-noodle mixture over top; return to freezer until hard.

MARSHMALLOW-COCONUT CRUNCH BALLS

2 pints strawberry ice cream
1 can (3½ ounces) flaked coconut
1 7-ounce jar marshmallow creme
2 tablespoons butter

Scoop 8 ice-cream balls (one ball should take approximately ¼ pint ice cream). Place balls on shallow pan in freezer until hard. Roll each ice cream ball in flaked coconut; return immediately to freezer to harden. Reserve remaining flaked coconut. To prepare marshmallow sauce: Heat together in a small saucepan the jar of marshmallow creme and butter. Heat only until the marshmallow sauce becomes thinner. Cool to lukewarm. Spoon 2 tablespoons marshmallow sauce over each ice cream ball; sprinkle additional coconut over top; return to freezer until hard.

NUT-BUTTERSCOTCH CRUNCH BALLS

2 pints butter pecan ice cream
1½ cups coarsely chopped nuts
1 cup butterscotch topping

Scoop 8 ice-cream balls (one ball should take approximately ¼ pint ice cream). Place balls on shallow pan in freezer until hard. Roll each ice cream ball in chopped nuts; return immediately to freezer to harden. Reserve remaining nuts. Spoon 2 tablespoons of butterscotch sauce over each ice cream ball; sprinkle additional nuts over top; return to freezer until hard. Note: Do not heat butterscotch topping.

PEANUT BUTTER ICE CREAM BALLS

1 cup graham cracker crumbs
¼ cup creamy or chunk style peanut butter
2 tablespoons sugar
¼ teaspoon cinnamon
1 quart vanilla ice cream
chocolate-flavored syrup

Blend graham cracker crumbs, peanut butter, sugar and cinnamon. Scoop ice cream into large balls and roll in crumb mixture until well coated. Freeze until serving time. Serve with chocolate syrup.

12.
SODA FOUNTAIN TREATS

Ice cream, sherbet, and ices may be served in many ways, in a large assortment of soda-fountain specialties. Some frequent combinations include the banana split, the parfait, fruit sundaes, ice cream with fruit, sodas, milk shakes, and malts. The procedure for making these desserts is as follows:

BANANA SPLIT

1 medium ripe banana
3 scoops of ice cream, assorted flavors
1 tablespoon each of three toppings
  whipped cream
  nuts
2 cherries

Slit the banana in half lengthwise. Place one half of the banana on each side of the dish. Place three scoops of ice cream on the banana halves. Vanilla ice cream should be placed in the center and the other flavors should be placed on each side. Cover each scoop of ice cream with a different topping. Garnish the top and between each scoop with whipped cream. Additional slices of banana or fruit may be added. Top the center scoop of ice cream with nuts and place a cherry on each side.

PARFAIT

4 tablespoons crushed fruit, or a
  specially prepared parfait mixture

3 scoops of ice cream
nuts
whipped cream
cherry

Place one tablespoon of crushed fruit in a parfait glass. Add one
scoop of ice cream. Cover with one tablespoon of crushed fruit.
Cover with nuts and top with whipped cream and a cherry.

FRUIT SUNDAES

3 tablespoons crushed fruit
2 scoops of ice cream
nuts
whipped cream
cherry

Place one tablespoon of crushed fruit into a dish. Add two scoops
of ice cream. Surround the ice cream with two tablespoons of
crushed fruit. Place the nuts on top of the crushed fruit. Top with
whipped cream and a cherry. Sliced fruit may be substituted for
crushed fruit.

ICE CREAM WITH FRUIT

¼ cup of sliced or crushed fruit
2 scoops of ice cream

Place the ice cream in a dish and surround with fresh sliced fruit,
or crushed fruit.

SODA

3 tablespoons of syrup or fruit in syrup
1 tablespoon thick cream
¾ cup carbonated water
2 scoops of ice cream
¼ cup carbonated water
whipped cream

Use a 14-ounce glass to make this soda. Place the syrup or fruit
in the bottom of the glass. Stir the cream into the syrup. Fill the
glass with ¾ cup of carbonated water, and gently mix in two

scoops of ice cream. Add the remaining carbonated water and garnish with whipped cream.

MILK SHAKE

¾ cup of cold milk
2 scoops of ice cream
3 tablespoons of syrup

Place the ice cream into a chilled container. Add the syrup and milk. Mix thoroughly and rapidly. Pour into a serving glass. A blender may be used instead of mixing by hand.

MALTED MILK

½ cup of cold milk
3 tablespoons of syrup, chocolate
   syrup or preference
1 tablespoon of malted milk powder
4 scoops of vanilla ice cream

Combine all ingredients and blend. A blender may be used instead of mixing by hand.

PAPAYA PARADISE SUNDAE

1 tablespoon cornstarch
¼ cup water
¼ cup honey
2 tablespoons butter or margarine
2 tablespoons lime juice
⅛ teaspoon salt
6 marshmallows (or ¼ cup miniature)
2 medium-sized papayas
   ice cream or sherbet

Blend cornstarch into water; add honey and butter. Bring to a boil and simmer 5 minutes. Add lime juice, salt and quartered marshmallows. Cool. Cut papayas lengthwise into halves. Scoop out seeds and membranes with tip of teaspoon. Top each half with ball of ice cream. Serve with sauce and a sprinkling of fresh coconut, if desired. *Makes 4 servings.*

PARTY POPCORN SUNDAES

2 quarts popped popcorn
1 package (14 ounces) caramels
6 tablespoons milk
1 cup chopped salted peanuts
¼ teaspoon salt
2 pints vanilla ice cream

Place popcorn in large bowl; set aside. In top of double boiler melt caramels in milk, stirring frequently until smooth and creamy. Remove from heat; add peanuts and salt. Pour over popcorn. Toss until all corn is coated with caramel mixture. On foil, divide mixture into 8 mounds. Shape each mound into a shell about 4 inches in diameter. (Butter fingers well to prevent caramel mixture from sticking.) Place in refrigerator to harden. To serve: Fill center of shells with 1 to 2 scoops of ice cream.

PEACH de MENTHE

1 (No. 2½) can cling peach halves
1 quart vanilla ice cream
   fresh or canned flaked coconut
   green creme de menthe

Chill and drain peaches. Place one half in each serving dish. Roll balls of ice cream in coconut and place on peach half. Drizzle with creme de menthe and serve.

TOWERING SUNDAE

Ice cream
Ice cream sauces
Fresh or frozen fruit
Chopped nutmeats
Sugar wafers
Bananas, sliced
Sweetened whipped cream

Use a large bowl or glass. Choose your favorite flavors of ice cream, ice-cream sauces and fruits. Arrange in bowl alternating ice cream, sauces and fruits. Garnish with sugar wafers and banana slices. Top with sweetened whipped cream. *Makes 1 serving.*

CHOCOLATE PEPPERMINT STICK SHAKE

1 pint vanilla ice cream
⅓ cup chocolate syrup
¼ teaspoon peppermint extract
3 cups cold milk
1 pint peppermint-stick ice cream

Combine vanilla ice cream, chocolate syrup, peppermint extract, and milk. Blend thoroughly. Pour into chilled glasses and top with scoops of peppermint-stick ice cream. *Makes 4 generous servings.*

DOUBLE CHOCOLATE MILK SHAKE

1 quart chocolate milk or
  chocolate dairy drink
1 pint softened chocolate ice cream
1 or 2 pints peppermint, strawberry,
  cherry, maple, or coffee ice cream

Beat chocolate milk and chocolate ice cream together until smooth. Pour into 5 or 6 chilled tall glasses. Top each glass with 1 or 2 scoops of peppermint, strawberry, cherry, maple or coffee ice cream as desired. *Makes 5 to 6 tall shakes.*

MOCHA MILK SHAKE

2 tablespoons instant coffee
¼ cup warm water
1 cup instant nonfat dry milk
4½ cups cold milk
1 quart chocolate ice cream, slightly softened

Dissolve the instant coffee in warm water. Add to mixture of nonfat milk and cold milk. Blend thoroughly. Add softened ice cream and beat or shake just enough to blend ingredients. Pour into tall glasses and serve immediately. *Makes 6 servings.*

PINEAPPLE AVOCADO SHAKE

1 quart milk
1 small avocado
1 cup crushed pineapple

½ cup sugar
1 tablespoon fresh lime or lemon juice
dash of salt

Pour milk into refrigerator tray and freeze until frozen around sides and bottom of tray. Cut avocado in half; remove seed and skin. Mash avocado (should be about ½ cup). Combine all ingredients in electric blender (or chilled bowl). Beat at high speed until smooth and thick. *Makes 5 or 6 servings.*

STRAWBERRY MILK SHAKE

1 10-ounce package frozen strawberries
1 cup instant nonfat dry milk
4½ cups cold milk
1 quart softened strawberry ice cream

Thaw strawberries until soft but still very cold; crush. Add nonfat dry milk and whole milk to strawberries and blend thoroughly. Add softened ice cream and beat or shake just enough to blend ingredients. Pour into tall glasses and serve immediately. *Makes 6 servings.*

STRAWBERRY SMOOTHIE

1 cup milk
½ pint vanilla ice cream
1 cup fresh strawberries
¼ cup honey

Whip all ingredients together by using a chilled blender or electric mixer. Shakes will be a beautiful pink color filled with fresh fruit flavor and natural nutrition. Delicious with pretzel sticks. Note: If using electric mixer, slice or mash berries. *Makes 2 shakes.*

CHERRY CHOCOLATE SODA

1 quart cherry soda
1½ quarts chocolate ice cream

Pour ⅓ cup cherry soda into 6 8-ounce glasses. Add 1 scoop chocolate ice cream. Stir until well blended. Fill glasses ⅔ full with cherry soda; add 2 scoops ice cream. Fill to top with soda.

CRANBERRY SODA

2 cups cranberry juice cocktail
1 quart strawberry ice cream
3 7-ounce bottles carbonated water

Pour ⅓ cup cranberry cocktail into 6 8-ounce glasses. Add 1 scoop of ice cream to each glass. Stir until well blended. Fill each glass ⅔ full with carbonated water and add 2 scoops ice cream. Fill to top with carbonated water.

PEACH CREAM SODA

¼ cup crushed, sweetened ripe,
   frozen or canned peaches
¼ cup light cream or
1 tablespoon ice cream
1 scoop vanilla ice cream
   carbonated water (4–6 ounces)

Combine all ingredients. Stir gently and serve. *Makes 1 soda.*

PINEAPPLE ROYAL SODA

1 tablespoon canned, crushed
   pineapple
2 tablespoons ice cream or
   light cream
   carbonated water
1 or 2 scoops vanilla ice cream

Pour fruit syrup, then light cream or ice cream into a glass and stir to mix. Fill glass ¾ full with chilled carbonated water, add ice cream, then more carbonated water to fill to the top. *Makes 1 soda.*

RASPBERRY SODA

2 tablespoons frozen raspberries
2 tablespoons ice cream or
   light cream

carbonated drink, plain
  or fruit flavored
1 or 2 scoops raspberry ice cream

Pour fruit syrup, then ice cream or light cream into a glass and stir to mix. Fill glass ¾ full with chilled carbonated drink, add ice cream, then more carbonated drink to fill to the top. *Makes 1 soda.*

STRAWBERRY SODAS

2 pints fresh strawberries
1 cup milk
¼ cup sugar
1 pint vanilla ice cream, softened
1 quart crushed ice
  club soda

Force strawberries through food mill or blend in electric blender. Strain to remove seeds. Stir milk into strawberry puree. Add sugar and ice cream. Beat or blend in electric blender. Pour over part of the ice into soda glasses. Fill up with soda. Add remaining ice. Serve at once. *Makes 6 sodas.*

If desired, serve sodas with a plate of glazed strawberries. To make glazed strawberries: Dip whole dry berries into a mixture of heated cornstarch and water. Or you may use currant jelly heated and thinned with water. Use a wooden pick or skewer for dipping.

BROWN COW

1 6-ounce bottle cola
2 heaping teaspoons chocolate syrup
2 scoops vanilla ice cream

Empty the cola-flavored carbonated beverage into tall glass. Add 2 heaping teaspoons chocolate flavored syrup and stir gently to dissolve. Add 2 scoops vanilla ice cream. Stir quickly till foamy. Serve at once with straw and spoon. *Makes 1 brown cow.*

FROSTY MOCHA

¼ cup boiling water
2 teaspoons instant coffee

2 teaspoons sugar
2½ cups cold milk
2 teaspoons pure vanilla extract
1 cup chocolate ice cream

Dissolve instant coffee and sugar in boiling water. Chill. Add milk and vanilla. Mix well. Serve with ice cream in tall glasses.

ORANGE APRICOT FROST

1½ cups (12-ounce can) apricot nectar
1 quart vanilla ice cream
1 quart orange soda

Pour ¼ cup apricot nectar into 6 8-ounce glasses and add 1 scoop vanilla ice cream. Stir until well blended. Fill glass ⅔ full with orange soda and add 2 scoops ice cream. Fill to top with orange soda.

PINEAPPLE LEMON MIST

¾ cup (6-ounce can) frozen pineapple
    juice concentrate
1 cup water
1 quart vanilla ice cream
1 pint lemon soda

Allow pineapple juice concentrate to thaw and dilute with water. Pour ⅓ cup juice into 6 8-ounce glasses. Add 1 scoop vanilla ice cream and stir until well blended. Fill each glass ⅔ full with lemon soda.

FRUIT COMBO FLOAT

1 can (12 ounces) apricot nectar
1 cup milk
¼ cup honey
¼ cup lemon juice
1 pint orange sherbet

Combine apricot nectar, milk, honey, lemon juice and half of orange sherbet. Blend, covered at high speed ½ minute or until smooth. Pour into 4 chilled glasses and top with balance of orange sherbet. Note: This can be made in an electric mixer.

MAPLE FLOAT

¾ cup 100 percent pure maple syrup
1 teaspoon vanilla extract
6 cups cold milk
⅛ teaspoon salt
1 quart vanilla ice cream
whipped cream

Combine syrup, vanilla extract, milk, and salt; beat 1 minute. Pour into 6 glasses. Serve with scoops of ice cream and garnish with whipped cream.

ORANGE BUTTERMILK FLOAT

1½ cups buttermilk, chilled
1½ cups orange juice, chilled
⅓ cup sugar
2 teaspoons lemon juice
1 pint orange sherbet

Combine buttermilk, orange juice, sugar, and lemon juice. Stir until dissolved. Pour into chilled glasses and top with scoops of orange sherbet. *Makes 4 generous servings.*

PRUNE GINGER FLOAT

1 quart chilled prune juice
1 quart chilled ginger ale
2 tablespoons lemon juice
vanilla ice cream

Combine prune juice with chilled ginger ale and 2 tablespoons lemon juice. Pour into tall glasses. Top each with a large scoop of vanilla ice cream. *Makes 4 servings.*

SHERBET FLOAT

1 pint sherbet
1 quart cold milk
¼ teaspoon pure vanilla extract
4 scoops sherbet

Blend 1 pint sherbet and milk until thoroughly mixed. Stir in vanilla. Serve in chilled glasses and top with a scoop of sherbet. *Makes 4 generous servings.*

TROPICAL FRUIT FLOAT

1 medium pineapple, cut into chunks
1 papaya, skinned, and cut into chunks
1 mango, skinned, seeded and cut into chunks
1½ cups orange juice
1 fresh coconut shredded

Prepare pineapple, papaya, and mango chunks. Combine fruits and orange juice in a bowl. Chill. Grate fresh coconut and spread in shallow pan. Place grated coconut in 350° F. oven for 5 to 7 minutes; shake to toast evenly. Scoop mound of firm vanilla ice cream in center of fruit. Use a ladle to serve. Pass the toasted coconut. *Makes 6 to 8 servings.*

HACIENDA COCKTAIL

1 cup canned pineapple juice
1 cup diced papaya
mint leaves

Pour pineapple juice into freezing tray of refrigerator and freeze until mushy. To prepare papaya, cut into halves lengthwise and scoop out seeds and membrane. Cut off rind and dice papaya. Divide among 3 or 4 small cocktail glasses. Top with partially frozen pineapple juice. Add a mint sprig and serve immediately. *Serves 3 to 4.*

BANANA POPS

5 to 6 firm medium bananas
1 6-ounce package butterscotch or
    chocolate chips
½ cup creamy peanut butter
10 to 12 popsicle sticks
    chopped nuts

Cut peeled bananas in half crosswise. Insert sticks in cut ends. Place in pan and freeze until firm. Meanwhile melt butterscotch or chocolate chips in double boiler top over boiling water. Blend in peanut butter. Remove from boiling water. Coat bananas completely with peanut butter mixture, smoothing mixture and removing excess with spatula. Sprinkle with chopped nuts. Peanut butter mixture will firm up quickly. Pops can be eaten immediately or returned to freezer for later use. Remove from freezer 10 to 15 minutes before serving. *Makes 10 to 12 pops.*

"COCO" COCONUT ICE CREAM BARS

1 quart ice cream, any flavor
flaked coconut
chocolate chips
raisins
marshmallows
cherries
ice cream bar sticks

Cut the top off a 1-quart milk carton; fill with softened ice cream and refreeze. Unmold ice cream and slice into 8 pieces. Insert a stick in each for a handle. Roll in coconut or make comic faces and refreeze until serving time.

FRUIT COCKTAIL FREEZIES

1 can fruit cocktail (No. 2½)

Spoon canned fruit cocktail and syrup into 6 or 8 small paper cups. Set a wooden spoon into each one—it serves as the handle. Set in freezer or freezing compartment of refrigerator until firm. Tear off paper cups when ready to serve.

LEMON POPSICLES

3 7-ounce bottles lemon-lime flavored
carbonated beverage
⅓ cup light corn syrup
1 tablespoon lemon juice

Blend carbonated beverage, corn syrup and lemon juice. Pour into popsicle molds; insert sticks and covers. Freeze until firm. Makes about 9⅓ cup popsicles. To prepare in ice cube trays: Pour mixture into trays with ice cube divider in place. Freeze until firm, inserting sticks or wooden spoon into each when partially set. A deep ice cube tray is best.

TANGY PINEAPPLE POPS

2½ cups crushed pineapple
¾ cup sugar
2 cups buttermilk
½ teaspoon pure vanilla extract
2 egg whites, stiffly beaten

Heat pineapple until warm; add sugar and stir until dissolved. Cool. Add remaining ingredients and fold in carefully. Pour into small paper cups or other containers; freeze. When partly frozen place a wooden stick in the center of each tangy pop.

TANGY STRAWBERRY POPS

1 10-ounce package thawed sliced
    strawberries
¾ cup sugar
2 cups buttermilk
½ teaspoon vanilla
2 egg whites, stiffly beaten

Heat strawberries until warm; add sugar and stir until dissolved. Cool. Add remaining ingredients and fold in carefully. Pour into small paper cups or other containers; freeze. When partly set place a wooden stick in the center of each pop.

INDEX

269